INSTRUCTION GIVING IN ONLINE LANGUAGE LESSONS

This concise volume calls attention to the instruction-giving practices of language teachers in online environments, in particular videoconferencing, employing a Multimodal (Inter)action Analysis approach to explore the challenges, affordances, and pedagogical implications of teaching in these settings.

The book examines the unique competences necessary for language teachers in multimodal synchronous online environments, which require mediating a mix of modes, including spoken language gaze, gesture, posture, and textual elements. Satar and Wigham's innovative approach draws on Sigrid Norris's work on Multimodal (Inter)action Analysis to examine variance in practices, combining in-depth micro-analytic analysis of mediation with a consideration of the modal density and complexity in the act of giving instructions. The volume shows how studying instruction giving can offer a better understanding of how online teachers mediate learning multimodally in electronic environments, but also research-informed guidance for practical implementation in the classroom.

This book is a valuable resource for scholars in applied linguistics, language education, and language learning and teaching as well as practicing online language teachers.

Müge Satar is Reader in Applied Linguistics at Newcastle University, UK. She is interested in communicative and pedagogical aspects of multimodal interaction for online language learning and teaching, focusing on social presence and meaning-making. She is the co-editor of the *Journal of Virtual Exchange* and General Council member of UNICollaboration.

Ciara R. Wigham is Senior Lecturer in English Language Teaching at *Université Clermont Auvergne*. Her research interests include multimodal pedagogical communication in online language learning, teacher education in computer-assisted language learning, and methodologies for multimodal CMC corpora. She is a member of the the *Activité, Connaissance, Transmission, éducation* research laboratory.

Routledge Focus on Applied Linguistics

Mobile Assisted Language Learning Across Educational Contexts
Edited by Valentina Morgana and Agnes Kukulska-Hulme

Complicity in Discourse and Practice
Jef Verschueren

Moving Beyond the Grammatical Syllabus
Practical Strategies for Content-Based Curriculum Design
Jason Martel

Contesting Grand Narratives of the Intercultural
Adrian Holliday

Sustainability of Blended Language Learning Programs
Technology Integration in English for Academic Purposes
Cynthia Nicholas Palikat and Paul Gruba

Discourses of Borders and the Nation
A Discourse-Historical Analysis
Massimiliano Demata

Health Disparities and the Applied Linguist
Maricel G. Santos, Rachel Showstack, Glenn Martínez, Drew Colcher, Dalia Magaña

Instruction Giving in Online Language Lessons
A Multimodal (Inter)action Analysis
Müge Satar and Ciara R. Wigham

For more information about this series, please visit: www.routledge.com/Routledge-Focus-on-Applied-Linguistics/book-series/RFAL

Instruction Giving in Online Language Lessons
A Multimodal (Inter)action Analysis

Müge Satar and Ciara R. Wigham

NEW YORK AND LONDON

First published 2023
by Routledge
605 Third Avenue, New York, NY 10158

and by Routledge
4 Park Square, Milton Park, Abingdon, Oxon, OX14 4RN

Routledge is an imprint of the Taylor & Francis Group, an informa business

© 2023 Müge Satar and Ciara R. Wigham

The right of Müge Satar and Ciara R. Wigham to be identified as authors of this work has been asserted in accordance with sections 77 and 78 of the Copyright, Designs and Patents Act 1988.

With the exception of Chapter 6, no part of this book may be reprinted or reproduced or utilised in any form or by any electronic, mechanical, or other means, now known or hereafter invented, including photocopying and recording, or in any information storage or retrieval system, without permission in writing from the publishers.

Chapter 6 of this book is available for free in PDF format as Open Access from the individual product page at www.routledge.com. It has been made available under a Creative Commons Attribution-Non Commercial-No Derivatives 4.0 license.

Trademark notice: Product or corporate names may be trademarks or registered trademarks, and are used only for identification and explanation without intent to infringe.

Library of Congress Cataloging-in-Publication Data
Names: Satar, Müge, author. | Wigham, Ciara R., author.
Title: Instruction giving in online language lessons : a multimodal (inter)action analysis / Dr Müge Satar, Newcastle University, United Kingdom ; Dr Ciara R. Wigham, Activité, Connaissance, Transmission, éducation (ACTé), Université Clermont Auvergne, France.
Description: New York, NY : Routledge, 2023. | Series: Routledge focus on applied linguistics | Includes bibliographical references and index.
Identifiers: LCCN 2022056081 (print) | LCCN 2022056082 (ebook) | ISBN 9781032227948 (Hardback) | ISBN 9781003274216 (eBook)
Subjects: LCSH: Language and languages—Computer-assisted instruction. | Language and languages—Study and teaching. | Web-based instruction. | Teaching—Methodology.
Classification: LCC P53.28 .S28 2023 (print) | LCC P53.28 (ebook) | DDC 418.0078/5--dc23/eng/20230125
LC record available at https://lccn.loc.gov/2022056081
LC ebook record available at https://lccn.loc.gov/2022056082

ISBN: 978-1-032-22794-8 (hbk)
ISBN: 978-1-032-22795-5 (pbk)
ISBN: 978-1-003-27421-6 (ebk)

DOI: 10.4324/9781003274216

Typeset in Times New Roman
by Apex CoVantage,.LLC

The Open Access version of chapter 6 was funded by Newcastle University & Laboratoire ACTé, Université Clermont Auvergne.

To Drina and Sonia

Contents

Acknowledgements   *xi*
Preface and introduction   *xii*

1 Online language teaching and giving task instructions   1

  1.1 Online language teaching as a semio-pedagogical activity 1
  1.2 What are instructions and why are they important in task-based multimodal online language teaching? 4
  1.3 Previous studies that set the ground work 6
  1.4 Research gap 8
  1.5 Chapter summary 9

2 Methods   13

  2.1 Context 13
    2.1.1 Participants 13
    2.1.2 Pedagogical organisation 14
    2.1.3 Data collection procedures 15
  2.2 Methodological framework 17
    2.2.1 Grounded Theory 17
    2.2.2 Multimodal (Inter)action Analysis (MIA) 17
      2.2.2.1 Mediated actions and communication modes 18
      2.2.2.2 Site of engagement 18
      2.2.2.3 Modal configuration, modal density, and attention/awareness continuum 18
    2.2.3 Operationalising Multimodal (Inter)action Analysis (MIA) 20
  2.3 Chapter summary 22

3 Task repetition: do teachers' instructions change when they repeat the same lesson with different learners?   25

    3.1 Task repetition: higher-level actions in task instructions-as-process   26
    3.2 Task repetition: lower-level actions in task instructions-as-process   32
        3.2.1 Sustained and central hand gestures following learners' lack of understanding   34
        3.2.2 Same gestures or same type of gestures in both iterations   40
            3.2.2.1 Communicating key task information: there is student A and B   40
            3.2.2.2 Communicating key task information: different information   42
        3.2.3 Alignment of the teacher's spoken language, gesture, gaze, and posture with the layout mode   44
        3.2.4. Signalling removal from interaction in the proxemics/posture mode   48
        3.2.5 Bimodal instruction giving in the modes of spoken language and print   49
        3.2.6 Site of engagement and semiotic misalignment: layout, webcam framing, gaze patterns   51
    3.3 Modal configuration and modal density   54
    3.4 Semiotic misalignment *and* modal density misalignment   57
    3.5 Chapter summary   58

4 Number of learners: do teachers' instructions change when they repeat the same lesson with only one learner?   61

    4.1 Number of learners: site of engagement   62
    4.2 Number of learners: higher-level actions in task instructions-as-process   64
    4.3 Number of learners: lower-level actions in task instructions-as-process   68
        4.3.1 Multimodal composition of similar higher-level actions prior to launching the task with different number of learners   69

Contents ix

    4.3.2 Multimodal composition of managing resources with different number of learners 74
  4.4 Modal configuration and modal density misalignment: managing resources 88
  4.5 Chapter summary 97

5 **Task type: do teachers' instructions change when they give instructions for a different type of task?**   99

  5.1 Divergent task micro-tasks: task-as-workplan versus task-as-process 100
  5.2 Teacher perspectives on the impact of task type on their instruction-giving behaviour 103
  5.3 Comparison of higher-level actions used in convergent and divergent tasks 104
  5.4 Multimodal configuration of higher-level actions and lower-level actions in different task types 116
    5.4.1 Sarah's multimodal composition of higher-level actions and lower-level actions 116
    5.4.2 Karen's multimodal composition of higher-level actions and lower-level actions 122
    5.4.3 Craig's multimodal composition of higher-level actions and lower-level actions 124
    5.4.4 Modes, modal configurations, and modal density 127
  5.5 New higher-level actions observed in the divergent task for managing resources 135
  5.6 Chapter summary 140

6 **Contributions, pedagogical reflections, and future perspectives**   141

  6.1 Contributions to methodology and knowledge 142
  6.2 Instruction giving and task repetition 145
  6.3 Instruction giving and number of learners 147
  6.4 Instruction giving and task type 149
  6.5 A heuristic framework of higher-level actions in task instructions-as-process 151
  6.6 Pedagogical reflections for language teachers 153
    6.6.1 Managing electronic resources 153
    6.6.2 Managing semiotic resources 154

  6.6.3 *Instructions-as-workplan in light of our findings* 155
 6.7 *Limitations and future research* 158
 6.8 *Final thoughts* 159

Appendices   *165*
 Appendix 1: Information-gap task 167
 Appendix 2: Opinion-exchange task 169
 Appendix 3: Semi-structured interview guide 170
Index   *171*

Acknowledgements

We thank Newcastle University (Faculty of Humanities and Social Sciences Research Fund, 2018 Spring call) and Université Clermont Auvergne (Foreign researchers – short research visit, 2018 call) for funding towards the project titled "An Examination of Experienced Online Language Teachers' Multimodal Instruction-Giving Practices."

We are grateful to the learners and teachers who participated in this project, colleagues and anonymous reviewers for their constructive comments, and the Routledge editorial team.

Full-size Figures, Extracts and Tables are available in colour at https://doi.org/10.25405/data.ncl.20315142.

Preface and introduction

Described as a semio-pedagogical activity, synchronous online language learning requires socio-affective, pedagogical, semiotic, and technological competencies (Guichon, 2009) to ensure that teachers can (1) establish and maintain relationships with their learners, (2) design and deliver effective learning scenarios, (3) employ appropriate semiotic resources to optimise learning potential, and (4) choose and use technologies and tools appropriate to the learning scenarios and communication needs. Multimodal synchronous online teaching via videoconferencing requires teachers to have "a high level of consciousness regarding all the information they are conveying when they interact with their learners" (Guichon & Wigham, 2016, p. 67). In other words, they need to develop *critical semiotic awareness* (Guichon, 2013; Kern, 2015) to capitalise on the affordances of the modes of spoken language, gaze, gesture, head movement, posture and proxemics, and print.

One element of online language teachers' pedagogical competencies is the ability to provide "clear and concise instructions" (Guichon, 2009, p. 169). In classroom contexts, instructions determine learners' success in the designed learning scenarios: it is crucial for learners to understand what is required for successful task completion (Watson Todd, Chaiyasuk, & Tantisawatrat, 2008). Yet, complex multimodal affordances of videoconferencing require effective use of the semiotic resources to ensure that task instructions are clearly understood and can be followed by all learners.

In previous work, we investigated multimodal instruction-giving practices of trainee-teachers (Satar & Wigham, 2017) as well as experienced online language teachers (Satar & Wigham, 2020; Wigham & Satar, 2021). Drawing on this body of work, this book investigates small group and one-to-one multimodal synchronous online language teaching mediated via videoconferencing technologies. It aims to enrich our understanding of teachers' instructions delivered multimodally; more specifically, the hierarchical organisation and multimodal composition of (foreign) language teachers' (inter)actions when explaining to learners what to do in a task or activity. As such, we perceive instructions as directives: procedural information for "setting up tasks and making them followable" (St. John & Cromdal, 2016, p. 253).

Preface and introduction xiii

Six chapters compose this book. Chapter 1 provides an overview of research on teachers' instruction-giving practices in physical and online classrooms, including our own previous contributions to this research area. We demonstrate that our understanding of the components, organisation, and multimodal composition of language teachers' task instructions is limited. Moreover, research exploring variety in teachers' instruction-giving practices is almost non-existent. For instance, very few emerging studies demonstrate that teachers' instructions become shorter as they are repeated within the same lesson (Kunitz, 2021). However, no research to date has explored change in (language) teachers' instructions for the same task or activity as they are repeated across different lessons with different (number of) learners. To the best of our knowledge, potential differences in teachers' instructions for different task types have also not yet been investigated.

While previous research in the area has employed conversation analysis to elucidate the sequential organisation of talk in teachers' task instructions at a micro-level, we suggest a methodology that can address the hierarchical organisation of macro-, meso-, and micro-levels of teachers' (inter)actions is needed to fully understand the complexity of *mediated* multimodal (inter)actions in online platforms. To this end, we have found Multimodal (Inter)action Analysis (Norris, 2004, 2019, 2020) an apt tool to explore both the macro and meso higher-level actions (i.e. various actions that make up instructions), and the micro lower-level actions (i.e. the modal shifts that compose each higher-level action). This method enables a deeper understanding of the multimodal construction of *mediated* actions. Within this perspective, multimodal discourse is explored through a focus on action; whereby "all action is always also interaction" and "all interaction is action" which is expressed "by using the term (inter)action" (Norris, 2020, p. xv). Thus, employing the concept of (inter)action, it is possible to discover how a single individual, or two or more individuals together (inter)act with their environment and objects. Chapter 2 explains the analytical procedures of Multimodal (Inter)action Analysis, as well as our context and data collection procedures.

We present a Multimodal (Inter)action Analysis of screen-recorded lessons to understand variance in teachers' instruction-giving (inter)actions as a result of task repetition (Chapter 3), number of learners or group size (Chapter 4), and task type (Chapter 5). These chapters develop work presented in Satar and Wigham (2020) and Wigham and Satar (2021), and address the following research questions:

Chapter 3: Are instruction-giving higher- and lower-level actions dependent on task repetition? In other words, do instruction-giving higher-level actions and their multimodal composition differ when the same teacher repeats the same task with another pair of learners?

Chapter 4: Are instruction-giving higher- and lower-level actions dependent on the number of learners? In other words, do instruction-giving higher-level actions and their multimodal composition differ when the same teacher repeats the same task with only one learner?

Chapter 5: Are instruction-giving higher- and lower-level actions task dependent? In other words, do instruction-giving higher-level actions and their multimodal composition differ when the same teacher gives instructions for a different type of task?

Finally, in Chapter 6, we conclude with a summary of theoretical and methodological contributions, explore limitations and future research directions, and offer pedagogical perspectives that result from our analysis.

Before we start, however, we would like to set expectations on what we will *not* do in this book: (1) an analysis of recipient design (conversation analysis); (2) treating instructions as fragments (i.e. as perceived by Markee, 2015); (3) exploration of instructional conversations; and (4) judgements on instruction efficacy.

The first issue of recipient design relates to our methodological approach. We acknowledge that instruction-giving is not a one-way process but interactive (Somuncu & Sert, 2019) and collaborative in nature. This may lead to co-construction of instructions (St. John & Cromdal, 2016) as teachers remain responsive to learner feedback and revise their instructions in situ (Badem-Korkmaz & Balaman, 2020). In our analyses, whilst documenting the interactive nature of instruction giving where relevant, our objective is not the identification of the architecture or the sequential organisation of interaction, nor how instructions are co-constructed, which would have necessitated a conversation analytic approach (Seedhouse, 2005). Indeed, Multimodal Conversation Analysis (MCA) is a micro-analytic approach designed to investigate the sequential progression of actions, how an actor plans and modifies their actions based on the actions of others, and legitimate forms of interaction in a given institutional setting. Instead, our interest is the key social actor within instruction giving, that is, the teacher "acting with/through mediational means" (Norris & Pirini, 2016, p. 21). Multimodal (Inter)action Analysis (Norris, 2004, 2019, 2020) enables a single focus on a social actor and the methodological tools to dissect this social actor's (inter)actions.

Second, the inspiration to our work was Markee's (2015) identification of six instruction-giving fragments: how learners will be working; what resources they will need; what task(s) they must accomplish; how they will accomplish the task(s); how much time they will have; and why they should complete the task(s). In this work, we refer to instruction-giving components not as fragments, but we perceive instructions as mediated through and constitutive of higher-level, lower-level, and frozen mediated actions, in line with Multimodal (Inter)action Analysis. This allows us to understand instructions within a dynamic taxonomy where different elements of instructions are not fragmented segments of talk but are compositional higher-level actions constituting a whole. It also enables us to understand the multimodal composition

Preface and introduction xv

and configuration of higher-level actions by lower-level and frozen actions, and the interplay between them.

Third, our understanding of instructions is similar to, but not the same as, instructional conversations (Meskill & Anthony, 2007; Tharp & Gilmore, 1991). Instructional conversations are a pedagogy of teaching through dialogue and interaction, which requires the teacher to initiate conversations, elicit talk from the learners, and tailor the dialogue to meet learner needs (Tharp & Gilmore, 1991). This type of facilitation is in line with sociocultural approaches to language learning, which takes place through interaction (Lantolf, 2001) as well as Thornbury's (2000) dogme perspective, which prioritises teacher-learner interaction as the most authentic interaction available to learners. In this sense, instructional conversations are social, engaging, and pleasurable interactions that lead to learning. Yet, in task-based approaches (Ellis, 2003; Nunan, 2004), task completion through interaction among the learners is underscored whereby teachers strive to minimise teacher-talk time and provide clear and concise task instructions. Meskill and Anthony (2007) offer an understanding of instructional conversation which aligns better with the task-based language teaching approach as the ways in which instructors "set up the language learning task and orchestrate instructional conversation around that task" (p. 11). By examining the first element in this formula, that is, how teachers 'set up the language learning task' we are able to concentrate on one social actor's, the teacher's, higher-level actions in their task instructions without a concern for their role as a task facilitator or the impact of the task on interactional outcomes and dynamics. We do, however, acknowledge and observe that not all teachers may follow this approach, and there could be times when teachers do not clearly set boundaries between setting up and orchestrating the task, for instance, by presenting instructions in small stages, or incorporating social and authentic interactions within instructions (see Chapter 5). Our framework of teachers' higher-level actions in task instructions-as-process (Satar & Wigham, 2020, and revised in Chapter 6) take these actions into account. We further describe our analytical approach in Chapter 2.

Finally, we recognise the demand for research with simple, practical, pedagogical outputs and recommendations. We approach such requests with caution: common pedagogical advice tends to follow suggestions for minimising teacher-talk and offering rehearsed, succinct, and unambiguous instructions (Seedhouse, 2008; Tomlinson & Masuhara, 2017), which contradicts the instructional conversations and dogme approaches. Future comparative, experimental research might shed light on which approach to follow based on a measure of instruction effectiveness. However, without established success criteria, we believe it premature to make judgements on the effectiveness of instruction-giving practices. Instead, our approach is exploratory, focusing on the case of three experienced online teachers. We work from the perspective that their practices are functional, as reflected in their positive learner evaluations, and try to depict variety and provide in-depth, rich descriptions of the multimodal contexts.

The journey of our work on language teachers' instruction-giving (inter) actions began at the EuroCALL 2015 conference in Padova, Italy, when Prof Nicholas Guichon, within the framework of the ISMAEL project (*InteractionS et Multimodalité dans l'Apprentissage et l'Enseignement d'une Langue*), encouraged us to organise a research visit for Müge to Lyon. This visit culminated in co-authoring a journal article in *System* exploring the ISMAEL dataset and then the collection of the dataset studied here. Subsequent research visits resulted in publications in *Alsic* and *ReCALL* journals and conferences and seminars in Italy, Chile, Turkey, and Sweden. By 2019, it was clear that we wanted to answer three more research questions from our data set. We are grateful for the opportunity to present our work in this short monograph.

July 2022, France

References

Badem-Korkmaz, F., & Balaman, U. (2020). Third position repair for resolving troubles in understanding teacher instructions. *Linguistics and Education, 60*, 100859.

Ellis, R. (2000). Task-based research and language pedagogy. *Language Teaching Research, 4* (3), 193–220.

Guichon, N. (2009). Training future language teachers to develop online tutors' competence through reflective analysis. *ReCALL, 21* (2), 166–185.

Guichon, N. (2013). Une approche sé mio-didactique de l'activité de l'enseignant de langue en ligne: Réflexions méthodologiques. *Education & Didactique, 7* (1), 101–115. Retrieved from https://educationdidactique.revues.org/1679

Guichon, N., & Wigham, C. R. (2016). A semiotic perspective on webconferencing supported language teaching. *ReCALL, 28* (1), 62–82.

Kern, R. (2015). *Language, literacy, and technology*. Cambridge: Cambridge University Press.

Kunitz, S. (2021). Instruction-giving sequences in Italian as a foreign language classes: An ethnomethodological conversation analytic perspective. In S. Kunitz, O. Markee, & O. Sert (Eds.), *Classroom-based conversation analytic research: Theoretical and applied perspectives on pedagogy* (pp. 133–161). Springer International Publishing.

Lantolf, J.P. (2001). Sociocultural theory and SLA. In R. B. Kaplan (Ed.), *Handbook of applied linguistics* (pp. 109–119). Oxford: Oxford University Press.

Markee, N. (2015). Giving and following pedagogical instructions in task-based instruction: An ethnomethodological perspective. In P. Seedhouse & C. Jenks (Dir.), *International perspectives on the ELT classroom* (pp. 110–128). Basingstoke: Palgrave MacMillan.

Markee, N. (2015). Giving and following pedagogical instructions in task-based instruction: An ethnomethodological perspective. In P. Seedhouse & C. Jenks (Dir.), *International perspectives on the ELT classroom* (pp. 110–128). Basingstoke: Palgrave MacMillan.

Meskill, C., & Anthony, N. (2007). Learning to orchestrate online instructional conversations: A case of faculty development for foreign languages. *Computer Assisted Language Learning, 20 (1),* 5–19.

Norris, S. (2004). *Analyzing multimodal interaction: A methodological framework*. London: Routledge.
Norris, S. (2004). *Analyzing multimodal interaction: A methodological framework*. London: Routledge.
Norris, S. (2019). *Systematically working with multimodal data: Research methods in multimodal discourse analysis*. Hoboken, NJ: John Wiley and Sons.
Norris, S. (2020). *Multimodal theory and methodology: For the analysis of (inter)action and identity*. Abingdon: Routledge.
Norris, S. (2019). *Systematically working with multimodal data: Research methods in multimodal discourse analysis*. Hoboken, NJ: John Wiley and Sons.
Norris, S. (2020). *Multimodal theory and methodology: For the analysis of (inter)action and identity*. Abingdon: Routledge.
Norris, S. (2020). *Multimodal theory and methodology: For the analysis of (inter)action and identity*. Abingdon: Routledge.
Norris, S., & Pirini, J. (2016). Communicating knowledge, getting attention, and negotiating disagreement via video conferencing technology: A multimodal analysis. *Journal of Organizational Knowledge Communication, 3* (1), 23–48.
Nunan, D. (2004). *Task-based language teaching*. Cambridge: Cambridge University Press.
Satar, H. M., & Wigham, C. R. (2017). Multimodal instruction-giving practices in web-conferencing-supported language teaching. *System, 70*, 63–80.
Satar, H. M., & Wigham, C. R. (2020). Delivering task instructions in multimodal synchronous online language teaching. *ALSIC* (Rubrique Recherche), *23* (1).
Seedhouse, P. (2005). Conversation analysis and *language learning. Language Teaching, 38*(4), 165-187.
Seedhouse, P. (2008). Learning to talk the talk: Conversation analysis as a tool for induction of trainee teachers. In S. Garton & K. Richards (Eds.), *Professional encounters in TESOL: Discourses of teachers in training* (pp. 42–57). Basingstoke: Palgrave Macmillan.
Somuncu, D., & Sert, O. (2019). EFL trainee teachers' orientations to students' non-understanding: A focus on task instructions. In H. T. Nguyen & T. Malabarba (Eds.), *Conversation analytic perspectives on English language learning, teaching, and testing in global contexts* (pp. 110–131). Bristol: Multilingual Matters.
St. John, O., & Cromdal, J. (2016). Crafting instructions collaboratively: Student questions and dual addressivity in classroom task instructions. Discourse Processes, 53 (4), 252–279.
St. John, O., & Cromdal, J. (2016). Crafting instructions collaboratively: Student questions and dual addressivity in classroom task instructions. *Discourse Processes, 53* (4), 252–279.
Tharp, R., & Gallimore, R. (1991). The instructional conversation: Teaching and learning in social activity. Research Report: 2. National Center for Research on Cultural Diversity and Second Language Learning. https://escholarship.org/uc/item/5th0939d
Thornbury, S. (2000). A Dogma for EFL. *IATEFL Issues*,153,2.
Tomlinson, B., & Masuhara, H. (2017). *The complete guide to the theory and practice of materials development for language learning*. Oxford: Wiley-Blackwell.
Watson Todd, R., Chaiyasuk, I., & Tantisawatrat, N. (2008). A functional analysis of teachers' instructions. *RELC Journal*, 39, 25–50.
Wigham, C. R., & Satar, M. (2021). Multimodal (inter)action analysis of task instructions in language teaching via videoconferencing: A case study. *ReCALL, 33* (3), 195–213.

1 Online language teaching and giving task instructions

In this chapter, we first present online language teaching as a semio-pedagogical activity requiring distinct pedagogical skills and competencies. We then discuss instructions within a task-based language teaching pedagogy and the role of social interaction in language teaching, both of which underpin the context and the pedagogical activities we describe in our dataset (Chapter 2). We introduce the literature on task instructions, specifically in online synchronous multimodal teaching via videoconferencing, summarise our work in this area, and identify the research gap this study addresses.

1.1 Online language teaching as a semio-pedagogical activity

Distance education, or distance learning, has a long history with various delivery methods of teaching and means of learner-teacher correspondence. These include printed material, postal services, radio and cassettes, television, video tapes, and of course computers and mobile phones connected via the Internet. A defining characteristic of distance learning delivered online is that teachers and students are not physically but virtually present using computer-mediated communication technologies.

According to Kentnor (2015, p. 22), "online education is no longer a trend, but mainstream." It has traditionally been attractive for its flexibility in learning time and space and, thus, been a viable alternative for learners who have daytime jobs, have mobility-related limitations, prefer learning in quiet individual spaces, live in remote areas, or wish to learn less frequently taught languages not available in their physical vicinity. As such, online language education widens accessibility and caters for various learning styles. High-quality online foreign/second language teaching offers upskilling without boundaries and can have sizeable socio-economic impact on societies.

Online language teaching became especially popular in the first decade of the 21st century (Blake, 2008) with better and wider access to media over the Internet. Today, it is growing exponentially with digital and physical worlds of learners becoming inextricably intertwined. Particularly, the Covid-19 pandemic forced stakeholders to experience online education at unprecedented speeds. With videoconferencing technologies becoming our principal means of communication for social, professional, and educational purposes, online language schools, education providers, and one-to-one language teaching using videoconferencing software are here to stay.

However, online teaching also suffers from high levels of attrition (Rovai, 2003). Recent research also shows that teaching skills developed for face-to-face classrooms are not directly transferable to online contexts, especially when teaching is delivered via videoconferencing technologies (e.g. Develotte, Guichon, & Vincent, 2010; Hampel & Stickler, 2005; Hampel & Stickler, 2012; Kozar, 2016a; Guichon, 2013; Guichon, 2017; Guichon & Cohen, 2014; Satar & Wigham, 2017, 2020; Cohen & Wigham, 2018; Wigham & Satar, 2021). Online teaching platforms bring their "own material properties, feel and techniques of use, affordances and limitations" (Chun, Kern, & Smith, 2016, p. 65). As such, online language teaching offers unique affordances but also challenges which make pedagogical interactions distinct from face-to-face teaching.

First, online teachers must engage with and manage two notions specific to mediated online communication; *semiotic lag* and *semiotic (mis) alignment* (Wigham & Satar, 2021). *Semiotic lag* refers to the time difference between when a social actor communicates a message and when it is received by the other party due to online transmission delay. For example, the teacher may laugh but the learners may receive the visual and/or the audio of the laughter at a later point, largely due to weak Internet connections. Not all learners may receive the actions at the same time either. Indeed, *semiotic lag* can be the main cause for silence and overlapping speech (Kozar, 2016a).

Semiotic (mis)alignment refers to different levels of access to and availability of semiotic means for each social actor. First, *semiotic misalignment* may occur due to social actors' different software and/or hardware configurations. For example, the teacher may be using a computer that runs a Windows operating system with learners connecting on other devices, such as an Android phone, an iPad, etc. The features of the online platform used to deliver teaching may be presented differently on these various devices with different layout, screen design, or menu items. Some platforms may also allow users to modify their individual layout. Whilst it may be possible to focus on different elements of the online teaching platform on a large computer screen, it may not be feasible or as easy to type, view textchat or see all webcam images when connecting using a smaller mobile device. Second, *semiotic misalignment* may occur when the teacher and learners have access to different resources that are not visible or accessible to others, for example, online dictionaries, other applications, communication platforms, or notes. While the teacher may assume that all learners focus on the online teaching platform, the learners could be engaged with some other resource(s). This may not be apparent to the teacher. The reverse would also be true.

Online language teaching and giving task instructions 3

This unique online context requires teachers to effectively utilise "various semiotic and technological resources" (Guichon, 2017, p. 57). Online language teachers need to orchestrate a wide range of modes presented and controlled on the computer screen (Hampel & Stickler, 2012),including head movement, posture, gaze, physical distance (proxemics), and spoken language which demand *critical semiotic awareness* (Guichon, 2013; Kern, 2015), that is, "a high level of consciousness regarding all the information they are conveying when they interact with their learners" (Guichon & Wigham, 2016, p. 67) during a *semio-pedagogical activity* (Guichon, 2013).

More specifically, multimodal synchronous online language teaching imposes restrictions on the visual frame, that is, the meanings communicated within the visual space transmitted through social actors' webcams. Guichon and Wigham (2016, p. 70) identified four visual framing types: extreme close-up shot, close-up shot, head-and-shoulders shot, and head-and-torso shot. We have found that the experienced online language teachers in our dataset also employed different visual framing, which impacted their instruction-giving practices (Satar & Wigham, 2020). Relatedly, investigating semiotic resources within a specific visual frame, Cohen and Wigham (2018) found that webcam images enable users to produce semantically rich descriptions through embodiment of referential properties of lexical items. Other studies have examined the role of multimodality accessible within the visual frame on negotiation of meaning (Lee, Hampel, & Kukulska-Hulme, 2019), teaching vocabulary (Wigham, 2017), and social presence (Satar, 2016, 2020).

Another salient difference in the delivery of teaching via videoconferencing concerns gaze utilisation. While mutual gaze attainment is almost impossible in videoconferencing, it is not always easy to identify social actors' gaze direction either (Satar, 2013). Satar (2013) identified five gaze types learners employ in videoconferencing (fixed, free, strategic, averted, and directed gaze). Using eye-tracking methodology, Shi, Stickler, and Lloyd (2017) found that less experienced teachers spend more time looking at the technical control areas of online teaching platforms and attend less to social and pedagogic aspects of interaction.

A particular characteristic that distinguishes online multimodal synchronous language teaching from face-to-face teaching is the print mode, which is largely manifested as a semiotic resource within the textchat functionality of most online communication and teaching platforms. Textchat use has been found to complement meaning expressed in the spoken language mode with written language and visuals (Meskill & Anthony, 2015). Hampel and Stickler (2012) observed that experienced language teachers and learners employ text-chat for four reasons: to provide comments on other participants' verbal input without interrupting the speakers; to check and confirm vocabulary items; as a private communication channel; and, finally, to compensate for the lack of a blackboard. Kozar (2016b) explored learners' reactions to experienced teachers' use of textchat and found that learners were more likely to incorporate the teacher's text message if "(a) it introduced new vocabulary, and (b) if it was produced bimodally (speaking and typing)" (p. 231).

To conclude, within the semio-pedagogic activity, online language teachers employ multiple modes as part of four teaching competencies: socio-affective, pedagogical, semiotic, and technological (Guichon, 2009). The focus of this book, giving task instructions, require skills in all four competencies. Pedagogical competencies involve offering "clear and concise instructions, providing positive and negative feedback and deploying an array of strategies to facilitate second-language learning" (Guichon, 2009, p. 169). Socio-affective competencies relate to the establishment and maintenance of a relationship with the learners, and ability to project and interpret social presence (Satar, 2015, 2016, 2020). As we observe in our dataset, task instructions-as-process can involve authentic communication and support socio-affective engagement through personal examples provided by the teacher. Finally, semiotic and technological competencies concern the effective use of communication and meaning-making tools to optimise learning potentials. This set of skills and competencies require a specific focus on how task instructions are delivered multimodally.

1.2 What are instructions and why are they important in task-based multimodal online language teaching?

Among many approaches to language learning in applied linguistics, while cognitive approaches focus on changes in an individual's cognitive state, the social or socio-cultural tradition emphasises the process of learning and interaction. Within this latter view, language is regarded as a mode of action, and not just a means to relay information (Seedhouse, Walsh, & Jenks, 2010). Learners are, thus, believed to learn *in* interaction, not *through* interaction as "the ends and the means become one and the same" (Seedhouse et al., 2010, p. 7). Communicative language teaching (CLT) is one approach to language teaching that embraces this view. While CLT is considered a "broad, philosophical approach.... Task-based language teaching represents a realization of this philosophy at the levels of syllabus design and methodology" (Nunan, 2004, p. 10). In task-based language teaching (TBLT), learners' immediate personal experience is the departure point for learning. Thus, tasks designed to facilitate language learning bear close relationships to real-world activities, offering learners experiences similar to those they can participate in outside the classroom. In the language classroom, it is important to maximise learner-talk time and minimise teacher-talk time to allocate ample opportunities for learner interaction during task completion. In learner-learner interaction, meaning negotiation and exchange has precedence over linguistic form, and task completion towards the assigned goal is primary (Ellis, 2000; Nunan, 2004). TBLT tasks typically involve "(1) some input (i.e. information that learners are required to process and use);

and (2) some instructions relating to what outcome the learners are supposed to achieve" (Ellis, 2000, p. 195). In this book, we analyse data collected from online language lessons in which teachers used materials designed following TBLT principles. The focus of the book lies in the second aspect of tasks, that is, instructions.

The word *instruction* can refer to different concepts. Lindwall, Lymer, and Greiffenhagen (2015) distinguish between three types of instructions: instructions as *education*, *directives*, and *written texts* (such as user guides). In our work, we regard instructions as advice and information about how to perform a task, that is, directives that contain *procedural* information targeted at "setting up tasks and making them followable" (St. John & Cromdal, 2016, p. 253).

Procedural instructions for language tasks can be given in three forms: written (Tomlinson & Masuhara, 2017), spoken (Markee, 2015, Seedhouse, 2008), or a spoken instantiation of written instructions (Ha & Wanphet, 2016). Tomlinson and Masuhara (2017) in their work on written instructions identified 11 criteria, including *succinctness*, that is, presentation of instructions "in the briefest and most concise way" (p. 348); *specificity* of instructions clarifying what to do and how to do it; and *unambiguity*, that is, avoiding pronouns, synonyms, and using clear referrals.

While Ha and Wanphet (2016) describe written instructions are "static, pre-arranged and planned," spoken instructions are "dynamic, spontaneous, and unplanned" (p. 152). Seedhouse (2008) also underlined this seemingly spontaneous nature of instructions describing how successful experienced teachers employ instructions to "create a pedagogical focus . . . to get students to do what they want, in an apparently effortless manner" (2008, p. 42) defining successful instructions as being as "full and explicit as possible whilst presenting a single, undiluted focus" (2008, p. 55).

Ha and Wanphet's (2016) study of two English-as-a-Foreign language classes during which teachers provided instructions for the same task describes how verbal instructions complement instructions written on the materials and facilitate learner understanding of the task requirements. They illustrate that teachers' spoken reformulation of written instructions serves several functions, including calling students' attention, checking understanding, giving options and ideas, emphasising important information, helping process the instructions, and creating interaction.

In another study of spoken instructions, Markee (2015) investigated an experienced teacher's face-to-face teaching and identified six task instruction fragments. These inform learners about: (1) how they will be working (in dyads or small groups), (2) what resources are required, (3) what tasks they must accomplish, (4) how to accomplish the tasks, (5) how much time they have to accomplish these tasks, (6) why they should do something.

Procedural instructions for language tasks are important for several reasons. First, successful task completion "is often predicated on the effectiveness of [the] instructions" (Watson Todd, Chaiyasuk, & Tantisawatrat, 2008,

6 *Online language teaching and giving task instructions*

p. 26). Second, language learning happens in meaning-focused interaction (Nunan, 2004) and instructions offer opportunities for authentic communication (Watson Todd et al., 2008), and foster "immediate situational feedback" (Tomlinson & Masuhara, 2017, p. 343). Third, instruction giving is part of task-based teaching competencies (Raith & Hegelheimer, 2010). Finally, instructions may constitute a significant amount of teacher talk time (Ha & Wanphet, 2016). Ha and Wanphet (2016) describe spoken procedural instructions as unplanned. However, drawing on Breen (1987), while teachers can plan task instructions as part of their designed task (what we term *instructions-as-workplan*), the actual instructions they deliver in interaction with the learners (*instructions-as-process*) might differ from the planned instructions. In this book, our focus is on instructions-as-process that we frame as higher-level actions (HLAs, see Chapter 2).

1.3 Previous studies that set the ground work

Two initial research studies set the groundwork for this book. In Satar and Wigham (2020), we firstly explored experienced language teachers' pedagogical instructions to build on Markee's (2015) identification of six instruction-giving fragments and identify HLAs comprising task instructions-as-process. Secondly, we analysed the multimodal elements that operated in the same HLAs employed by the three different teachers. In this section, as we summarise this earlier work, we draw upon Multimodal (Inter)action Analysis (MIA, Norris, 2004, 2009, 2019, 2020, see Chapter 2).

In Satar and Wigham (2020), Grounded Theory analysis (Strauss & Corbin, 1998) allowed us to identify then illustrate 13 HLAs in task instructions-as-process (Figure 1 in Satar & Wigham, 2020) with corresponding definitions and examples from our data set (Appendix C, ibid). The study set the groundwork for the analyses presented here as well as the revised framework of HLAs in task instructions-as-process that we propose in Figure 6.1.2 In particular, we identified that MANAGING RESOURCES presented challenges in the videoconferencing context due to lack of shared artefacts and physical interactional space, and occupied around a quarter of the instruction-giving sequence in two of the three lessons examined and comprised several sub-categories: SENDING THE RESOURCE, ALLOCATING THE RESOURCE, RECEIVING THE RESOURCE, OPENING THE RESOURCE, CONFIRMING ACCESS TO THE (CORRECT) RESOURCE, DESCRIBING THE CONTENT OF THE RESOURCE, and READING THE RESOURCE. In instructions, teachers also highlighted different task steps (FORMULATING TASK STAGES), making them salient through summarising previous task steps and forward-organising subsequent steps. Further HLAs included COMMUNICATING KEY TASK INFORMATION, for example, key vocabulary or learner roles; ACTIVATING SCHEMATA to contextualise and personalise the tasks, and checking learner understanding before launching the tasks (CHECKING UNDERSTANDING OF TASK).

Online language teaching and giving task instructions 7

Our multimodal micro-analyses of the lower-level actions (LLAs) that operate in task instructions-as-process demonstrated that each teacher employed different levels of multimodality. We illustrated that the manner in which HLAs unfolded in the interaction was linked to teachers' preferred choice of visual framing (Guichon & Wigham, 2016) which allowed teachers to capitalise upon the affordances of different modes. A choice of head-and-torso shot, for example, allowed one teacher to effectively mobilise hand gestures, as well as her posture in sideway shifts, and changes in posture to achieve emphasis. A head-and-shoulders shot adopted by another teacher foregrounded facial expression over gestures (which were not always visible) and allowed them to achieve emphasis through changes in gaze and eyebrow movement. The third teacher, who opted for a close-up shot in which their shoulders and hands were rarely visible, predominantly employed the spoken language mode accompanied by gaze shifts, head nods, head tilts, and smiles. This related to her previous online teaching experience in audiographic platforms without the webcam. The combination of different LLAs allowed the teachers to achieve increased modal density in their instructions and, thus, present them as the focal point of attention, foregrounding them in the learners' awareness/attention (Norris, 2004) and potentially enabling all learners to successfully complete the task regardless of differences in how instruction delivery. Thus, our findings emphasised the importance of teacher training especially regarding semio-pedagogical competence, which relates to teaching competencies and skills in employing "various semiotic and technological resources" (Guichon, 2017, p. 57).

In Wigham and Satar (2021), we used the case study of one experienced online language teacher to explore use of the print mode (resource sheets, URLs, textchat, Google Docs [online document hereafter]) in instruction-giving practices and illustrated how modal configuration and density vary when the print mode is employed. Our case study identified that the print mode was employed for the HLAs SENDING THE RESOURCE, ALLOCATING THE RESOURCE, DESCRIBING THE CONTENT OF THE RESOURCE, and CONFIRMING ACCESS TO THE RESOURCE. Task resource sheets were electronically shared with learners during instructions. As the teacher read aloud the contents of the online documents, they presented the instructions bimodally (through the spoken language and print modes), and facilitated task accomplishment by ensuring joint attention (Ricci Bitti & Garotti, 2011). Textchat was also employed to summarise decisions made during previous micro-tasks, again, to facilitate task accomplishment.

The different artefacts in the print mode were frequently embodied and disembodied when participants moved back and forth between different resources (online documents and text chat). For example, the teacher would embody a URL in a previously created online document by copying it before sending it to the learners via textchat. Once sent, the link became disembodied for learners to embody when opening the resource.

MIA allowed us to disassemble the modes employed in combination with the print mode. Our analysis highlighted that participants interacted both visually and verbally when employing the print mode as an integral part of the interaction. Gaze direction and shifts were a salient signal of the teacher's engagement with the print mode during the lesson, whereas for the HLA SENDING THE RESOURCE, object handling combined with the print mode assumed high prominence.

1.4 Research gap

We identify two main research gaps in the area of synchronous online language teaching generally, and specifically related to the research on instruction giving presented here: (1) methodological and (2) contextual.

The study of multimodal interaction within applied linguistics research is relatively new (e.g. de Silva Joyce & Feez, 2018). Literature on the multimodal analysis of in-person classroom interaction predominantly employs multimodal conversation analysis to understand the turn-by-turn sequential organisation of interaction. Conversation analysis (CA) is a powerful tool to investigate social interaction and understand how interaction is multimodally co-constructed. For instance, Hellermann and Pekarek Doehler (2010) explored multimodal signalling of task launch in foreign language classrooms and found that posture shifts and mutual posture alignment were instrumental signals. Likewise, Markee (2015) showed how language learners in the classroom employ eye gaze, gestures, and cultural artefacts to signal collaborative mutual orientation to group actions. However, CA is guided by recipient design and, thus, does not enable researchers to focus on mediation or the multimodal complexity of a single social actor's actions. With a specific focus on micro-analysis, it also does not lend itself to the investigation of intermediate and macro actions.

Compared to studies investigating in-person classroom interaction, synchronous online language learning-teaching research demonstrates methodological variety. Whilst some studies offer largely descriptive commentaries of multimodal interaction, others employ a discourse analytic approach analysing instances of certain concepts (e.g. negotiation of meaning, language-related episodes), offer quantitative analysis, or data commentary drawing on concepts of CA. Thus, we see the gap in the application of a method that enables a focus on mediation, as well as the modal density (complexity and intensity) of actions taking place in synchronous online language teaching. The method we employ for our analysis – MIA (Norris, 2004, 2019, 2020) – fills this methodological gap.

Regarding context, we observe two gaps in the literature related to instruction giving. First, a lack of research investigating instruction giving in online language teaching settings. As outlined above, few studies have examined teachers' instruction-giving practices in the physical classroom (e.g.

Markee, 2015; Somuncu & Sert, 2019), and apart from our previous work (Section 1.3), we only identified two other studies that explored instruction giving in synchronous online teaching. Codreanu and Combe Celik (2012) report how online teachers pre-prepare their instructions and copy-and-paste them in textchat to launch activities quickly. These pre-prepared instructions also enable teachers to sustain a pedagogical focus. Cappellini and Combe (2017) compares instruction giving in asynchronous and synchronous online teaching. They highlight that when instructions are delivered synchronously, they are negotiated with the learners in interaction. They also show how teachers shift focus from pedagogy to technical instruction to demonstrate access to task resources. Neither study, however, offers multimodal micro-analyses of instruction giving, nor explores different actions comprising instructions.

The second contextual gap relates to the experience level of the teachers. Satar and Wigham (2017) and Cappellini and Combe (2017) explore the multimodal practices of trainee teachers. While Markee (2015), Somuncu and Sert (2019), Codreanu and Combe Celik (2012) and two of our previous publications (Satar & Wigham, 2020; Wigham & Satar, 2021) analyse data collected from experienced teachers, only our previous work offers insights into how experienced synchronous online language teachers give task-instructions. It is indeed within this specific context that this book fills a niche in the literature. Building on our previous work, we present original comparative multimodal analyses illustrating the impact of contextual factors of task repetition, number of learners and task type on task instructions. We depict similarities and differences in the multimodal composition of task instructions when delivered by the same teacher for a second time to a different group of learners (task repetition, Chapter 3), when delivered by the same teacher for a second time to only a single learner (number of learners, Chapter 4), and when the teachers give instructions for a different type of task (task type, Chapter 5).

1.5   Chapter summary

This preliminary chapter presented online synchronous language teaching and its multimodal complexity due to computer mediation. We described our focus on teachers' instruction-giving actions, which fills both methodological and contextual research gaps. Our earlier research (Satar & Wigham, 2020; Wigham & Satar, 2021) set the scene for the work we present here. We also offered a brief review of the research in the area and defined instructions.

Notes

1 'Figure 1: Higher-level actions in task instructions-as-process' and 'Appendix C: Instruction fragments, examples, and observations' can be consulted at https://journals.openedition.org/alsic/4571?lang=en

2 All full-size Figures, Extracts and Tables are available in colour at https://doi.org/10.25405/data.ncl.20315142

References

Blake, R. (2008). Distance learning for second and foreign language teaching. In N. H. Hornberger (Ed.), *Encyclopedia of language and education*. Boston, MA: Springer.

Breen, M. P. (1987). Learner contributions to task design. In C. N. Candlin & D. Murphy (Eds.), *Language Learning Tasks* (Vol. 7, pp. 5–22). Lancaster Practical Papers in English Language Education. London: Prentice-Hall International and Lancaster University.

Cappellini, M., & Combe, C. (2017). Analyser des compétences techno-sémio-pédagogiques d'apprentis tuteurs dans différents environnements numériques: résultats d'une étude exploratoire. *ALSIC*, *20*(3). Retrieved from http://journals.openedition.org/alsic/3186

Chun, R., Kern, R., & Smith, B. (2016). Technology in language use, language teaching, and language learning. *The Modern Language Journal*, *100*, 64–80. https://doi.org/10.1111/modl.12302

Codreanu, T., & Combe Celik, C. (2012). La médiation de l'interaction pédagogique sur une plateforme de visioconférence poste à poste. *ALSIC*, *15*(3). Retrieved from https://journals.openedition.org/alsic/2572

Cohen, C., & Wigham, C. R. (2018). A comparative study of lexical word search in an audioconferencing and a videoconferencing condition. *Computer Assisted Language Learning (CALL Journal)*, *32*(4), 448–481.

de Silva Joyce, H., & Feez, S. (Eds.). (2018). *Multimodality across classrooms: Learning about and through different modalities*. Routledge.

Develotte, C., Guichon, N., & Vincent, C. (2010). The use of the webcam for teaching a foreign language in a desktop videoconferencing environment. *ReCALL*, *23*(3), 293–312.

Ellis, R. (2000). Task-based research and language pedagogy. *Language Teaching Research*, *4*(3), 193–220.

Guichon, N. (2009). Training future language teachers to develop online tutors' competence through reflective analysis. *ReCALL*, *21*(2), 166–185.

Guichon, N. (2013). Une approche sémio-didactique de l'activité de l'enseignant de langue en ligne: Réflexions méthodologiques. *Education & Didactique*, *7*(1), 101–115. Retrieved from https://educationdidactique.revues.org/1679

Guichon, N. (2017). Sharing a multimodal corpus to study webcam-mediated language teaching. *Language Learning & Technology*, *21*(1), 55–74.

Guichon, N., & Cohen, C. (2014). The impact of the webcam on an online L2 interaction. *Canadian Modern Language Review*, *70*(3), 331–354.

Guichon, N., & Wigham, C. R. (2016). A semiotic perspective on webconferencing-supported language teaching. *ReCALL*, *28*(1), 62–82.

Ha, C. B., & Wanphet, P. (2016). Exploring EFL teachers' use of written instructions and their subsequent verbal instructions for the same tasks. *Nordic Journal of English Studies*, *15*(4), 135–159.

Hampel, R., & Stickler, U. (2005). New skills for new classrooms: Training tutors to teach languages online. *Computer-Assisted Language Learning*, *18*(4), 311–326.

Hampel, R., & Stickler, U. (2012). The use of videoconferencing to support multimodal interaction in an online language classroom. *ReCALL, 24*(2), 116–137.

Hellermann, J., & Pekarek Doehler, S. (2010). On the contingent nature of language-learning tasks. *Classroom Discourse, 1*(1), 25–45.

Kentnor, H. (2015). Distance education and the evolution of online learning in the United States. *Curriculum and Teaching Dialogue, 17*(1&2). Retrieved April 9, 2021, from https://digitalcommons.du.edu/law_facpub/24/

Kern, R. (2015). *Language, literacy, and technology.* Cambridge: Cambridge University Press.

Kozar, O. (2016a). Teachers' reaction to silence and teachers' wait time in video and audioconferencing English lessons: Do webcams make a difference? *System, 62,* 53–62.

Kozar, O. (2016b). Text chat during video/audio conferencing lessons: Scaffolding or getting in the way? *CALICO Journal, 33*(2), 231–259.

Lee, H., Hampel, R., & Kukulska-Hulme, A. (2019). Gesture in speaking tasks beyond the classroom: An exploration of the multimodal negotiation of meaning via Skype videoconferencing on mobile devices. *System, 81,* 26–38.

Lindwall, O., Lymer, G., & Greiffenhagen, C. (2015). The sequential analysis of instruction. In N. Markee (Ed.), *The handbook of classroom discourse and interaction* (pp. 142–157). Malden, MA: Wiley-Blackwell.

Markee, N. (2015). Giving and following pedagogical instructions in task-based instruction: An ethnomethodological perspective. In P. Seedhouse & C. Jenks (Dir.), *International perspectives on the ELT classroom* (pp. 110–128). Basingstoke: Palgrave MacMillan.

Meskill, C., & Anthony, N. (2015). *Teaching languages online* (2nd ed.). Bristol: Multilingual Matters.

Norris, S. (2004). *Analyzing multimodal interaction: A methodological framework.* London: Routledge.

Norris, S. (2009). Modal density and modal configurations: Multimodal actions. In C. Jewitt (Ed.), *The Routledge handbook of multimodal analysis* (pp. 78–90). London: Routledge.

Norris, S. (2019). *Systematically working with multimodal data: Research methods in multimodal discourse analysis.* Hoboken, NJ: John Wiley and Sons.

Norris, S. (2020). *Multimodal theory and methodology: For the analysis of (inter)action and identity.* Abingdon: Routledge.

Nunan, D. (2004). *Task-based language teaching.* Cambridge: Cambridge University Press.

Raith, T., & Hegelheimer, V. (2010). Teacher development, TBLT and technology. In M. Thomas & H. Reinders (Eds.), *Task-based language learning and teaching with technology* (pp. 154–175). London: Continuum.

Ricci Bitti, P. E., & Garotti, P. L. (2011). Non-verbal communication and cultural differences: Issues for face-to-face communication over the Internet. In A. Kappas & N. C. Krämer (Eds.), *Face-to-face communication over the Internet* (pp. 81–99). Cambridge: Cambridge University Press.

Rovai, A. P. (2003). In search of higher persistence rates in distance education online programs. *Internet and Higher Education, 6,* 1–16.

Satar, H. M. (2013). Multimodal language learner interactions via desktop videoconferencing within a framework of social presence: Gaze. *ReCALL, 25*(1), 122–142.

Satar, H. M. (2015). Sustaining multimodal language learner interactions online. *CALICO Journal*, *32*(2), 480–507.
Satar, H. M. (2016). Meaning-making in online language learner interactions via desktop videoconferencing. *ReCALL*, *28*(3), 305–325.
Satar, H. M. (2020). L1 for social presence in videoconferencing: A social semiotic account. *Language Learning & Technology*, *24*(1), 129–153.
Satar, H. M., & Wigham, C. R. (2017). Multimodal instruction-giving practices in webconferencing-supported language teaching. *System*, *70*, 63–80.
Satar, H. M., & Wigham, C. R. (2020). Delivering task instructions in multimodal synchronous online language teaching. *ALSIC* (Rubrique Recherche), *23*(1).
Seedhouse, P. (2008). Learning to talk the talk: Conversation analysis as a tool for induction of trainee teachers. In S. Garton & K. Richards (Eds.), *Professional encounters in TESOL: Discourses of teachers in training* (pp. 42–57). Basingstoke: Palgrave Macmillan.
Seedhouse, P., Walsh, S., & Jenks, C. J. (Eds.). (2010). *Conceptualising 'learning' in applied linguistics*. London: Palgrave Macmillan.
Shi, L., Stickler, U., & Lloyd, M. E. (2017). The interplay between attention, experience and skills in online language teaching. *CercleS*, *7*(1), 205–238.
Somuncu, D., & Sert, O. (2019). EFL trainee teachers' orientations to students' non-understanding: A focus on task instructions. In H. T. Nguyen & T. Malabarba (Eds.), *Conversation analytic perspectives on English language learning, teaching, and testing in global contexts* (pp. 110–131). Bristol: Multilingual Matters.
St. John, O., & Cromdal, J. (2016). Crafting instructions collaboratively: Student questions and dual addressivity in classroom task instructions. *Discourse Processes*, *53*(4), 252–279.
Strauss, A. L., & Corbin, J. M. (1998). *Basics of qualitative research: Techniques and procedures for developing grounded theory* (2nd ed.). London, Thousand Oaks, and New Delhi: SAGE.
Tomlinson, B., & Masuhara, H. (2017). *The complete guide to the theory and practice of materials development for language learning*. Oxford: Wiley-Blackwell.
Watson Todd, R., Chaiyasuk, I., & Tantisawatrat, N. (2008). A functional analysis of teachers' instructions. *RELC Journal*, *39*, 25–50.
Wigham, C. R. (2017). A multimodal analysis of lexical explanation sequences in webconferencing-supported language teaching. *Language Learning in Higher Education. Journal of the European Confederation of Language Centres in Higher Education (CercleS)*, *7*(1), 81–108. Retrieved from www.degruyter.com/view/journals/cercles/7/1/article-p81.xml
Wigham, C. R., & Satar, M. (2021). Multimodal (inter)action analysis of task instructions in language teaching via videoconferencing: A case study. *ReCALL*, *33*(3), 195–213.

2 Methods

In this chapter, we describe our participants, data collection methods, and the original approach for data analysis which draws upon Grounded Theory (Strauss & Corbin, 1998) and employs Multimodal (Inter)action Analysis (Norris, 2004, 2019, 2020).

2.1 Context

The analysis chapters in this book (Chapters 3–5) stem from a larger project which employed a mixed-methods research design to study instruction-giving practices (Mackey & Bryfonski, 2018). Two data types are employed in our qualitative analysis: a semi-controlled corpus (Tellier, 2013) of the screen-recordings of a sequence of three 30- to 60-minute online English-as-a-foreign-language classes conducted by three different teachers and post-sequence teacher and learner interview data.

2.1.1 Participants

In Spring 2018, three experienced online English teachers (one male, two female) were recruited from the online language teaching providers: iTalki < www.italki.com> and SpeakPlus <www.speakplus.fr/en/learner/>. Selection was based on their teaching qualifications and online teaching experience (Table 2.1). British English was the first language of all three teachers. They all held teaching qualifications and had a minimum of two years online teaching experience. They regularly taught lessons using the videoconferencing platform Skype (Microsoft, 2021).

The volunteer teachers were renumerated at their hourly teaching rate and a £20 e-commerce voucher compensated them for the time spent completing the post-sequence interview.

Nine volunteer language learners (four male, five female) of B1–B2 CEFR level (Council of Europe, 2001) were recruited. All were studying a foundation-level English course at a higher education institution in Turkey. Their motivation to participate was the opportunity to practise speaking skills

14 Methods

Table 2.1 Teacher profiles and teacher-learner participants' groupings and gender

Teacher pseudonym	Craig (m)	Karen (f)	Sarah (f)
Teaching qualification(s)	TEFL Certificate Cambridge TKT units 1–3	TEFL certificate 20hr Grammar awareness course	TEFL certificate
Face-to-face teaching experience prior to moving to online teaching	18 months (Spain)	24 months (China)	Some (France)
Teaching online since	2016	2013	2007
Online lessons completed on iTalki	1454	4638	n/a
iTalki learner rating	5-star	5-star	n/a
Learner pseudonym			
First iteration	Eda (f) & Didem (f)	Gonca (f) & Erol (m)	Sevil (f) & Demet (f)
Second iteration	Kuzey (m)	Hasan (m) & Mete (m)	n/a

because they did not have many opportunities for such practice in their face-to-face classes. The learners completed the pedagogical sequence outside of their institutional setting and it was not the object of evaluation. Dyad matching was based on learners availability. All three teachers (Craig, Karen, Sarah) completed the sequence with a learner dyad (Table 2.1). In order to observe variance in instruction-giving practices as regards task repetition and group size (number of learners), Karen repeated the sequence with a different learner dyad and Craig repeated the sequence with an individual learner.

2.1.2 Pedagogical organisation

Lessons were conducted via the videoconferencing platform Skype (Microsoft, 2021). Lesson 1 was an introductory lesson in which teachers used their preferred activities. For the subsequent lessons, teachers were provided with the same task resources (task-as-workplan) via email (Appendices 1 and 2). No additional instructions were shared; the teachers could introduce the tasks in the way(s) that suited their own practices.

The materials design for the lessons adopted a TBLT approach to engage learners in authentic language use during a meaningful task and elicit linguistic output (Ellis, 2000). Tasks are characterised by a primary focus on meaning, the need for participants to choose the linguistic resources necessary to complete the task, and clearly defined, non-linguistic outcomes. They typically involve some input and instructions (Chapter 1). Pica, Kanagy, and Falodun

Methods 15

(1993) identified five task types (information gap, jigsaw, problem-solving, decision-making, opinion exchange), and predicted that information-gap and jigsaw tasks would stimulate a higher number of meaning-negotiations, thus, increasing language learning opportunities. Opinion-exchange task, however, are not expected to yield as many negotiation episodes since they neither necessitate a single outcome, convergent goal orientation, nor required interactions. While information-gap tasks require detailed task input and instructions, opinion-exchange tasks can be more flexible regarding detail needed. Thus, participating teachers were presented with an information gap (convergent task, Lesson 2) and an opinion-exchange task (divergent task, Lesson 3) to create maximum opportunities to observe variance in their instructions.

For Lesson 2, teachers used the convergent task for which learners were encouraged to reach a consensus in order for a reasonable solution to be produced (Wegerif, Mercer, & Dawes, 1999). This required learners to reach a single outcome collectively, meaning that they both needed to understand the task information and instructions correctly. The task was divided into two micro-tasks: an information exchange activity during which learners had to compare two gift-package deals for a colleague's leaving present and decide upon one; and a collaborative email writing activity asking other colleagues for financial contributions towards the purchase of the gift package (Appendix 1). Lesson 3 had a divergent task design, which allow individuals to perform differently leading to different outcomes (Swan, 2005). There is no correct answer as task responses depend on the participants' viewpoints and/or experience (Nielsen, Bayard, Pickett, & Simonton, 2008). The task topic was vegetarianism. Firstly, learners were asked to describe vegetarianism, discuss foods vegetarians do /do not eat, and share whether they knew any vegetarians. Secondly, learners were asked to express their opinion of vegetarianism and reasons for following this diet. Some discussion ideas were provided. Lastly, leaners were asked to visually summarise their discussion using a collaborative whiteboard application (Appendix 2).

2.1.3 Data collection procedures

The semi-controlled corpus comprised screen recordings of the online lessons using Snagit (Tech Smith, 2021) by the teachers and, where possible, by a researcher who participated as a silent observer with muted microphone and camera. Some learners also screen recorded the lessons and/or provided screen shots during the lessons. Table 2.2 presents a description of the semi-controlled corpus including recording lengths that ranged from 25 to 63 minutes.

The analyses presented in Chapters 3–5 relate to lesson segments involving teachers' higher-level actions (HLAs) in their task instructions until learners engage with the task. The primary video source was the teachers' screen recordings, and where available we referred to learner or researcher screen recordings for validation or clarification. One teacher, Sarah, was unable to

16 Methods

Table 2.2 The semi-controlled corpus of screen recordings and recording length

Learners	Lesson	Screen recording by	Length of recording
Gonca, Erol	1	A student (Erol)	63 mins
	2	The teacher (Karen)	61 mins
	3	The teacher (Karen)	60 mins
		The researcher	61 mins
Hasan, Mete	1	The teacher (Karen)	61 mins
		The researcher	61 mins
	2	The teacher (Karen)	60 mins
		The researcher	60 mins
	3	The teacher (Karen)	25 mins
		The researcher	62 mins
Sevil, Demet	1	The researcher (Sarah)	32 mins
	2 – Take 1	The researcher	49 mins
	2 – Take 2[1]	The researcher	37 mins
	3	The researcher	30 mins
Eda, Didem	1	The researcher	60 mins
	2	The teacher (Craig)	61 mins
		The researcher	61 mins
	3	The teacher (Craig)	62 mins
		The researcher	60 mins
Kuzey	1	The teacher (Craig)	57 mins
		The researcher	56 mins
	2	The teacher (Craig)	61 mins
		The researcher	62 mins
	3	The teacher (Craig)	57 mins
		The research	53 mins

screen record, thus, extracts from her lessons represent her actions as received on the researcher's screen. Consequently, we are unable to present Sarah's interactions with other resources on her computer.

Post-sequence interviews with each teacher and four learners (Eda, Erol, Hasan, Sevil) were conducted by one researcher via Skype up to three days following their last lessons. An emotionalist approach (Silverman, 2013) was adopted to seek the participants' perceptions, understandings, and viewpoints to better understand their thoughts on the teachers' task instructions. The interviews followed a semi-structured interview guide (Appendix 3). Teacher interviews were divided into five sections focusing on the teachers' background, experience of different online teaching platforms, lesson-planning practices for online teaching, and task instructions. A final section was specific to individual teachers' actions during the lessons completed: researcher notes taken during the lessons formed the basis for these questions. Learner post-sequence interviews focused on their understanding of instructions and any difficulties they had understanding task explanations. The interviews lasted between 13 minutes (Eda) and 50 minutes (Karen).

Ethical approval and informed consent were obtained from all participants and Newcastle University ethics committee. Pseudonyms and blurred images, according to participant preferences, are used throughout.

2.2 Methodological framework

Multimodal (Inter)action Analysis (MIA) established and described by Norris (2004, 2019, 2020) constitutes the methodological framework of this study. MIA enables researchers to focus on a single actor's actions (in our case, the teacher) as well as the mediational qualities of these actions through multiple modes. It allows us to unpack the hierarchical organisation of higher-level (HLA), lower-level (LLA), and frozen actions (FA) that comprise teachers' instructions and explore multimodal complexity in delivering instructions.

2.2.1 Grounded Theory

While MIA offers guidance on how to demarcate HLAs (see Section 2.2.2), it does not offer a systematic approach to ensuring all identified HLAs are mutually exclusive. In our demarcation of HLAs, we followed a bottom-up, grounded approach to analysis, watching screen-recordings multiple times, identifying HLAs, and writing descriptions for these actions. Following Grounded Theory (Strauss & Corbin, 1998), we tagged teachers' instructions using the multimodal transcription software ELAN (Sloetjes & Wittenburg, 2008). First, for the open-coding stage, we grouped similar HLAs to reach theoretical saturation by refining the categories of actions until no new categories could be identified. Second, we actively looked for variation between and within the categories through constant comparison (see Satar & Wigham, 2020).

Grounded Theory analytical principles (Strauss & Corbin, 1998) were also employed to systematically analyse interview data. Considering our focus on the multimodal aspects of teachers' instructions, we do not present a detailed analysis of the themes that emerged from the interviews, but rather use the interview data as and when relevant to illuminate and strengthen our analyses and interpretations of the multimodal actions.

2.2.2 Multimodal (Inter)action Analysis (MIA)

MIA (Norris, 2004, 2019, 2020) is "a holistic analytical framework that understands the multiple modes in (inter)action as all together building one system of communication" (Norris & Pirini, 2016, p. 24). It considers interactions between social actors and other social actors, objects, or the environment as actions. It offers a broad socio-cultural perspective which is compatible with detailed micro-analysis of interaction, whilst also allowing the researcher, when required, to address the macro and intermediate (Norris & Pirini, 2016). We now summarise the key analytical tools from MIA employed in our analytical approach.

2.2.2.1 Mediated actions and communication modes

The unit of analysis in MIA is the mediated action "defined as a social actor acting with/through mediational means" (Norris & Pirini, 2016, p. 24). Mediated actions are composed of HLAs and lower-level actions (LLAs). LLAs are "the smallest interactional meaning unit" (Norris, 2004, p. 11) comprising interactional meaning units that draw on nine communication modes: spoken language, proxemics, posture, gesture, head movement, gaze, layout, music, and print (Norris, 2004). HLAs are "a chain of lower-level actions, with an opening and a closing" (Norris & Pirini, 2016, p. 25) and can be embedded in various other HLAs. For example, *engaging in conversation* is a HLA, which constitutes LLAs comprising, for instance, nods (head movement mode), hand movements (gesture mode) and utterances (spoken language mode). This conversation could occur among friends within other HLAs, such as *walking* and/ or within the HLA of *vacationing together* (Wigham & Satar, 2021).

A third type of actions are frozen actions (FAs). FAs are HLAs performed by social actors prior to the HLA currently being performed and that are now entailed in disembodied modes, for example, within printed material, layout of an environment or material objects (Norris, 2004). Norris and Makboon (2015), for example, illustrate the FA of *raising children* as evoked by a self-made photo calendar present in an office and telling of the participant's identity of a working mother.

2.2.2.2 Site of engagement

The "'real time window' opened through the intersection of social practices and mediational means that enables a mediated action to occur" (Norris & Jones, 2005, p. 139) is described in MIA as the site of engagement in which HLAs, LLAs, and FAs are performed. It comprises the social actors and the mediated actions in which they are engaged, as well as the FAs entailed in disembodied modes and material objects within the interactional setting.

2.2.2.3 Modal configuration, modal density, and attention/ awareness continuum

Modal configuration (the hierarchical organisation of LLAs) allows the analysis of a HLA in terms of the (chains of) LLAs (e.g. gesture units, utterances, printed materials occurring as an ensemble) that constitute it and the relationships between them (Norris, 2004). In this process "[t]he lower-level actions that are most important to the meaning produced are defined as most important to the construction of the higher-level action" (Norris & Pirini, 2016, p. 26).

Following the analysis of a HLA's modal configuration, its modal density can be mapped out. Modal density is measured through *intensity* and *complexity*. When a mode is absolutely necessary for the completion of a HLA, it carries *high modal intensity*. When the mode is discontinued, if it changes the HLA only slightly, it has *medium modal intensity*; and when it does not change the HLA, it carries *low modal intensity* (Norris, 2004). A specific interaction will determine which communication modes take on particular intensity. For example, during a telephone conversation, the spoken mode is strongest. Although a speaker might doodle or make gestures as they speak, these two modes (print and gesture) carry less intensity: if discontinued, they do not change the HLA. However, should someone in the speaker's physical space point at a clock which, in turn, prompts the speaker to *end the phone conversation*, the gesture mode (pointing at a clock) carries high intensity and when discontinued prompts a change in HLA (Wigham & Satar, 2021).

Modal complexity, diversely, "refers to the interplay of numerous communicative modes that make the construction of a higher-level action possible . . . [when the modes are] intricately intertwined" (Norris, 2004, p. 87). For example, for the HLA *baking a cake*, the recipe book contains text and images in the print mode. The layout mode concerns the positioning of different kitchen appliances within the room, ingredients and utensils on the kitchen worktop, and the person's posture towards these. There are also embodied modes of the social actor (gaze, gesture, head movement, facial expression, posture, proxemics). These modes together enable the HLA *baking a cake*.

Any given HLA is therefore considered modally dense when either (a) a mode plays a central role (modal intensity), or (b) an action can only be performed by multiple modes being inextricably linked (modal complexity).

Modal density is also a measure of social actors' phenomenological attention/awareness (Norris & Pirini, 2016). Norris (2020) describes that attention and awareness, considered as two different sides of the same concept, can be analysed as a continuum: foreground – mid-ground – background. The foreground presents focused attention whereas the background refers to the level to which a performer pays least attention and/or is least aware. Social actors can pay "various levels of attention to simultaneously performed higher-level mediated actions" (Norris, 2019, p. 247). Modal density determines the relative position of the actions in the social actors' attention/awareness continuum. When the HLA carries high modal density, the performer (person A) is more focused upon that action (Norris & Pirini, 2016), which is foregrounded in their attention/awareness. Norris also proposes the notion of (inter)actional attention whereby interlocutors "read off the verbal and nonverbal actions that a person performs" (2020, p. 12) as

20 *Methods*

expressions of what the performer (person A) experiences, perceives, thinks, and feels and, then in turn, the interlocutor (person B) performs particular actions in relation to how they perceive person A's performed actions. Focused attention/awareness in a social actor's action may, thus, increase the relative position of the action in the interlocutor's attention/awareness. For example, when a teacher foregrounds actions through modal density this may increase the relative position of the action on the attention/awareness continuum of their learner(s).

2.2.3 Operationalising Multimodal (Inter)action Analysis (MIA)

In identifying the comparative arguments presented in Chapters 3–5, our unit of analysis was mediated actions. We started from the macro perspective and identified similarities and differences in HLAs across selected lessons. Subsequently, we focused on the similarities and differences at micro-level in LLAs and FAs enacted within the HLAs. Our analyses remained grounded in the data throughout as we constantly viewed and re-viewed the recordings along with multimodal annotations. We then annotated sections of the data as our initial observations emerged. Through comparing and revising sections where the same observations were made, we refined our arguments and selected extracts for detailed micro-analysis. The selection was based on illustrative examples that were succinct enough to be presented within the space of this book. Both researchers were actively involved in this analytical process discussing and resolving instances and analyses where opinions diverged.

Data annotation began with the transcription of the spoken language mode, and then proceeded to identifying and annotating the HLAs related to task instructions-as-process identified in Satar and Wigham (2020). We then annotated LLAs in the spoken language, gesture, proxemics, gaze, posture, head movement, print, and layout modes. Spoken language was transcribed using the transcription conventions reported in Satar and Wigham (2020). To annotate the gesture mode, we drew upon McNeill's (1992) schema to categorise communicative gestures as iconic, metaphoric, deictic, and beats, to which we added the category of emblems (Kendon, 1982) to refer to culturally-specific gestures (see Satar & Wigham, 2017 for further description).

Proxemics, describing the interactional spatial behaviour in relation to other individuals (Andersen, 2008) or to relevant objects (Norris, 2009) was annotated with respect to the distance participants placed between themselves and the webcam. The ways in which the teacher participants positioned their bodies towards the webcam in the interactions (posture mode) was also annotated. We annotated posture shifts during which the teachers changed the directional position of the body.

Gaze, considered as "the direction of orientation that people display through the positioning of their head, notably their eyes, in relation to their environment" (MODE, 2020), was annotated with relation to Satar's (2013) identification of five gaze types in videoconferencing mediated interactions: fixed, free, strategic, averted, and directed gaze.

Finally, we examined head movements, facial expressions, and use of the print and layout modes when relevant. Regarding head movements, we annotated simple lateral (horizontal) or sagittal (vertical lowering or raising) movements and directional shifts. We described facial expressions that included smiles, grimaces, and looks of surprise. Regarding the print mode, we examined the use of textchat, written resources, and online documents. Layout was relevant when, for example, a participant shifted between different computer screen windows or with reference to the different versions of the videoconferencing platform used.

Working from these multimodal transcriptions then allowed us to analyse modal configuration and density. In identifying the multimodal organisation of LLAs, our guiding principle was to discern "what is absolutely necessary to perform this very action and what is not," as well as modal density to determine the place of the HLAs within the social actors' attention/awareness (Norris, 2019, p. 246). The analytical tools of modal density, modal configurations, and the foreground-background continuum of attention/awareness (Norris, 2019) were employed.

For micro-analysis, we produced multimodal transcripts (Norris, 2019) taking a screenshot from the data whenever a change in LLA was observed and creating a series of frames demonstrating the dynamic nature of interaction. As Guichon (2017) underlines, multimodal data poses representational challenges including what information to include in the transcript and "the necessary tradeoff between rendering all the aspects of the data and keeping the transcript readable" (pg. 69). Our process was, thus, selective depending on the LLAs that were central to the argument being made. For instance, when the argument related to teachers' LLAs within the gesture mode, a screenshot was taken each time a gesture shift was observed. Given that our annotations for movement cannot be captured in single frames, the frames were sometimes annotated (e.g. using arrows) to make movement across the stills more salient to the reader, and allowing us to embed aspects of analysis. For example, in Extract 5.1, as Norris (2019) advises, we merged some images that were very close in time, particularly when the frames were the only difference in order to reduce the final transcript length and ensure its readability. Higher-resolution, colour, versions of all Figures, extract transcripts (Extracts), and Tables can be viewed in an online data repository https://doi.org/10.25405/data.ncl.20315142.

In MIA, Norris (2019) transcribes the spoken interaction multimodally to illustrate and represent intonation, using waves for example to show the rhythmic pattern of speech, font size to demonstrate loudness and layout

22 *Methods*

space to illustrate timing, overlaps and speech contractions. When producing transcripts of short interactions, often in which only one participant partakes in the spoken language mode, we adopted this method (e.g. Extract 3.3). However, for longer transcripts and those in which several participants interact in the spoken language mode, for example, Extract 5.1, we added the spoken language and timestamps with frame numbers under the images to enhance readability. Timestamps allow us to communicate how quickly or slowly the interaction proceeds.

We also had to make a practical decision as regards the proportion of the site of engagement visible in the still frames. Although we would have liked to present the whole site of engagement in all frames, when placed together on a single printed page, the size of each frame had to be quite small. This made it difficult for the reader to see the data particularly when we focused on modal shifts in one small section of the frame presented in our argument and data commentary. Therefore, the proportion of the site of engagement represented in various extracts (and at times in various frames within the same extract) differs in an attempt to select and present the most salient features to the reader while providing sufficient evidence to our arguments and, thus, "highlight specific phenomenon and create a 'shared focus' among audience and analyst" (Ten Have, 1999, p. 33).

2.3 Chapter summary

In this chapter, we described our context (including participants, tasks used in the lessons, and dataset), and provided explanations regarding our analytical procedures. Namely, Grounded Theory and MIA for which we detailed the key analytical tools. In the following three analytical chapters, we address research questions in relation to variance in experienced teachers' actions in task instructions-as-process as regards task repetition (Chapter 3), number of learners (Chapter 4), and task type (Chapter 5).

Note

1 This lesson was completed over two separate occasions, which we label as Take 1 and Take 2 here. During Take 1, one of the learners was late for the lesson, they experienced technical problems, and thus had difficulty understanding what to do. The teacher had already sent the task resource to the students, so she allowed them time to study the task individually and rescheduled the lesson at a later time (Take 2).

References

Andersen, P. A. (2008). *Nonverbal communication: Forms and functions*. Waveland Press.
Council of Europe. (2001). *Common European framework of reference for languages: Learning, teaching, assessment*. Cambridge: Cambridge University Press.

Ellis, R. (2000). Task-based research and language pedagogy. *Language Teaching Research*, 4 (3), 193–220.
Guichon, N. (2017). Sharing a multimodal corpus to study webcam-mediated language teaching. *Language Learning & Technology*, 21(1), 55–74.
Kendon, A. (1982). *Nonverbal communication, interaction and gesture*. New York: Mouton.
Mackey, A., & Bryfonski, L. (2018). Mixed methodology. In A. Phakiti, P. De Costa, L. Plonsky, & S. Starfield (Eds.), *The Palgrave handbook of applied linguistics research methodology* (pp. 103–121). London: Palgrave MacMillan.
McNeill, D. (1992). *Hand and mind: What gestures reveal about thought*. Chicago and London: University of Chicago Press.
Microsoft. (2021). *Skype*. Retrieved April 26, 2021 from www.skype.com
MODE. (2020). *Glossary of multimodal terms*. Retrieved April 26, 2021, from https://multimodalityglossary.wordpress.com/
Nielsen, H., Bayard, M., Pickett, C., & Simonton, D. (2008). Conceptual versus experimental creativity: Which works best on convergent and divergent thinking tasks? *Psychology of Aesthetics, Creativity and the Arts*, 2(3), 131–138.
Norris, S. (2004). *Analyzing multimodal interaction: A methodological framework*. London: Routledge.
Norris, S. (2009). Modal density and modal configurations: Multimodal actions. In C. Jewitt (Ed.), *The Routledge handbook of multimodal analysis* (pp. 78–90). London: Routledge.
Norris, S. (2019). *Systematically working with multimodal data: Research methods in multimodal discourse analysis*. Hoboken, NJ: John Wiley and Sons.
Norris, S. (2020). *Multimodal theory and methodology: For the analysis of (inter)action and identity*. Abingdon: Routledge.
Norris, S., & Jones, R. H. (2005). Introducing sites of engagement. In S. Norris & R. H. Jones (Eds.), *Discourse in action: Introducing mediated discourse analysis* (pp. 139–140). Abingdon: Routledge.
Norris, S., & Makboon, B. (2015). Objects, frozen actions, and identity: A multimodal (inter)action analysis. *Multimodal Communication*, 4(1), 43–59.
Norris, S., & Pirini, J. (2016). Communicating knowledge, getting attention, and negotiating disagreement via video conferencing technology: A multimodal analysis. *Journal of Organizational Knowledge Communication*, 3(1), 23–48.
Pica, T., Kanagy, R., & Falodun, J. (1993). Choosing and using communication tasks for second language instruction. In G. Crookes & S. Gass (Eds.), *Tasks and language learning: Integrating theory and practice* (Vol. 1, pp. 9–34). Clevedon: Multilingual Matters.
Satar, H. M. (2013). Multimodal language learner interactions via desktop videoconferencing within a framework of social presence: Gaze. *ReCALL*, 25(1), 122–142.
Satar, H. M., & Wigham, C. R. (2017). Multimodal instruction-giving practices in web-conferencing-supported language teaching. *System*, 70, 63–80.
Satar, H. M., & Wigham, C. R. (2020). Delivering task instructions in multimodal synchronous online language teaching. *ALSIC*, 23.
Silverman, D. (2013). *Doing Qualitative Research: A Practical Handbook*. Sage Publications.
Sloetjes, H., & Wittenburg, P. (2008). Annotation by category – Elan and ISO DCR. In N. Calzolari, K. Choukri, B. Maegaard, J. Mariani, J. Odijk, S. Piperidis, & D. Tapias

(Eds.), *Proceedings of the 6th international conference on language resources and evaluation* (pp. 816–820). Marrakech: ELRA.

Strauss, A. L., & Corbin, J. M. (1998). *Basics of qualitative research: Techniques and procedures for developing grounded theory* (2nd ed.). London, Thousand Oaks, and New Delhi: SAGE.

Swan, M. (2005). Legislation by hypothesis: The case of task-based instruction. *Applied Linguistics, 26*(3), 376–401.

Tech Smith. (2021). *Snagit.* Retrieved from www.techsmith.fr/capture-ecran.html

Tellier, M. (2013). De l'usage du corpus semi-contrôlé dans la recherche en didactique des langues. *Cahiers de l'Asdifle, 24*, 39–47.

ten Have, P. (1999). *Doing conversation analysis.* London: Sage Publications.

Wegerif, N., Mercer, N., & Dawes, L. (1999). From social interaction to individual reasoning; an empirical investigation of a possible socio-cultural model of cognitive development. *Learning and Instruction, 9*, 493–516.

Wigham, C. R., & Satar, M. (2021). Multimodal (inter)action analysis of task instructions in language teaching via videoconferencing: A case study. *ReCALL, 33*(3), 195–213.

3 Task repetition

Do teachers' instructions change when they repeat the same lesson with different learners?

One teacher, Karen, delivered two iterations of the three lessons with two different pairs of learners. Her first iteration was with Gonca and Erol. The second iteration with Hasan and Mete. For these lessons, the teacher followed the same guidance from the researchers. All students were studying the same foundation-level English course at the same institution and were of similar age and English language level. The only difference was in gender: students in the second pair were male. Yet, overall, no impact of gender on the interactions was observed. The pairs of learners knew each other before the online lessons but met the teacher for the first time online.

In this chapter, we investigate similarities and differences in the teacher's higher- and lower-level actions in task instructions-as-process, as well as the multimodal composition of Karen's instructions, for the information-gap task used in the second lesson (see Chapter 2) with both pairs of learners. Our research question is:

Are instruction-giving higher- and lower-level actions dependent on task repetition? In other words, do instruction-giving higher-level actions and their multimodal composition differ when the same teacher repeats the same task with another pair of learners?

This chapter is organised in four sections. We first compare Karen's instruction-giving higher-level actions (HLAs) in both iterations of the same task instruction delivery (Section 3.1). We then explore how certain lower-level actions (LLAs) were similar or different, focusing on use of gesture and posture shifts for the HLAs of SENDING THE RESOURCE, ALLOCATING TASK ROLES, COMMUNICATING KEY TASK INFORMATION, and LAUNCHING THE TASK (Section 3.2). In the third section, we investigate the multimodal configuration of Karen's instructions comparing the modal density of her actions. We demonstrate instances of *semiotic misalignment* (Wigham & Satar, 2021) which may fragment or distort the shared interactional space in online learning. We show how LLAs foregrounded for the teacher and the learners can differ, subsequently proposing the concept of *modal density misalignment*. Finally, section 3.4 summarises our findings, which we discuss in Chapter 6. All full-size Figures, Extracts and Tables are available in colour at https://doi.org/10.25405/data.ncl.20315142.

26 *Task repetition*

3.1 Task repetition: higher-level actions in task instructions-as-process

To understand the similarities and differences in Karen's HLAs between the first and second iterations of the same task instructions, we focus on the HLAs present in the information-exchange task (Lesson 2): comparing and contrasting two gift-package deals for a colleague's leaving present to decide which one to purchase (Chapter 2 and Appendix 1). Table 3.1 shows, in chronological order, Karen's HLAs in task instructions-as-process for both iterations. In the first column, we have assigned numbers to each HLA. The second and fourth columns give the timestamps taken from the teacher's screen recordings indicating the onset of each HLA. Columns three and five show the types of HLAs. These are colour-coded to increase readability and make patterns more salient.

Immediately visible in Table 3.1 is that there are fewer (22) instruction-giving HLAs in the second iteration which took about 14 minutes to deliver, compared to 64 HLAs in the first iteration, which took around 22 minutes to deliver. Given both instruction-giving sequences led to successful task completion, the second iteration of instruction delivery appears more efficient. Further data analysis reveals patterns that explain this difference.

First, we note that Karen initiated instructions in the second iteration with the HLA ACTIVATING SCHEMATA. Here, Karen referred to the first lesson where she had introduced what the learners would do in Lesson 2 by saying: "Excellent, now can you remember what I said we were going to do in this lesson?" Karen then engaged with the HLAs of FORMULATING TASK STAGES by giving an overview of what learners would do in this task, FOCUSING ON STUDY SKILLS (which transpired as identification of background information and instructions in the task resource sheet), and COMMUNICATING KEY TASK INFORMATION (i.e., that each learner would receive a document in which some information would be similar and some would be different). This preparation for *work-to-come* (Heyman, 1986), lasting 3 minutes 17 seconds, as well as an explanation of what to find in the resource appeared to assist Karen in MANAGING RESOURCES (SENDING THE RESOURCE, CONFIRMING ACCESS TO THE (CORRECT) RESOURCE, READING THE CONTENT OF THE RESOURCE) and DEFINING LEARNER ROLES (acting as Student A and Student B). Once the learners received their electronic resource sheets, Karen scaffolded their comprehension of the information by asking them to identify the background information and instructions. She also performed the HLAs of COMMUNICATING KEY TASK INFORMATION again and SUGGESTING WAYS INTO TASK, that is, how learners could start and complete the task. Karen then LAUNCHED THE TASK that led to successful completion.

In the first iteration, we see that Karen employed almost the same HLAs as in the second iteration, yet in a different order. Instructions began with the

Table 3.1 Karen's higher-level actions in task instructions-as-process for Lesson 2, Micro-task 1

No	Time	with Gonca-Erol (first iteration)	Time	with Hasan-Mete (second iteration)
1	00:07:26.930	Managing resources	00:04:40.240	Activating schemata
2	00:07:31.710	Formulating task stages	00:04:56.760	Formulating task stages
3	00:07:35.250	Defining roles	00:05:01.110	Focusing on study skills
4	00:07:45.950	Managing resources	00:05:14.060	Communicating key task information
5	00:08:43.895	Defining roles	00:05:31.500	Focusing on study skills
6	00:08:49.208	Formulating task stages	00:07:33.286	Defining roles
7	00:09:34.380	Checking understanding (of task)	00:07:57.234	Managing resources
8	00:09:44.194	Defining roles	00:08:07.100	Defining roles
9	00:09:48.552	Focusing on study skills	00:08:17.205	Managing resources
10	00:10:54.849	Stating task outcome	00:08:57.616	Defining roles
11	00:11:08.746	Communicating key task information	00:09:11.469	Managing resources
12	00:11:12.081	Stating task outcome	00:11:05.355	Focusing on study skills
13	00:11:55.059	Checking understanding (of task)	00:11:10.705	Checking understanding (of task)
14	00:12:21.507	Communicating key task information	00:12:37.264	Communicating key task information
15	00:12:44.835	Checking understanding (of task)	00:12:46.499	Focusing on study skills
16	00:12:58.650	Stating task outcome	00:14:42.200	Communicating key task information
17	00:13:22.910	Communicating key task information	00:15:11.550	Focusing on study skills

(*Continued*)

Table 3.1 Continued

No	Time	with Gonca-Erol (first iteration)	Time	with Hasan-Mete (second iteration)
18	00:13:51.430	Focusing on task accomplishment	00:16:22.603	Focusing on task accomplishment
19	00:14:35.880	Managing resources	00:16:54.600	Suggesting ways into task
20	00:14:58.150	Focusing on task accomplishment	00:17:00.450	Communicating key task information
21	00:15:15.955	Focusing on study skills	00:17:06.900	Suggesting ways into task
22	00:15:47.432	Focusing on task accomplishment	00:18:50.077	Launching the task
23	00:16:40.280	Checking understanding (of task)		
24	00:16:42.552	Focusing on task accomplishment		
25	00:17:10.388	Managing resources		
26	00:17:16.134	Stating task outcome		
27	00:17:33.298	Communicating key task information		
28	00:17:39.029	Focusing on task accomplishment		
29	00:17:54.297	Managing resources		
30	00:18:02.835	Focusing on task accomplishment		
31	00:18:26.440	Checking understanding (of task)		
32	00:18:30.610	Focusing on task accomplishment		

33	00:18:39.387	Focusing on study skills
34	00:19:05.300	Focusing on task accomplishment
35	00:21:52.780	Checking understanding (of task)
36	00:21:54.447	Focusing on study skills
37	00:21:59.984	Checking understanding (of task)
38	00:22:02.715	Focusing on study skills
39	00:23:34.537	Focusing on task accomplishment
40	00:23:43.447	Checking understanding (of task)
41	00:23:45.830	Managing resources
42	00:23:50.253	Defining roles
43	00:23:57.551	Managing resources
44	00:24:06.014	Focusing on task accomplishment
45	00:24:09.283	Checking understanding (of task)
46	00:24:11.149	Launching the task
47	00:24:12.528	Learners' attempt at initiating the task
48	00:25:32.950	Allocating time
49	00:25:39.764	Learners' attempt at initiating the task
50	00:25:46.984	Checking understanding (of task)
51	00:26:37.919	Learners' attempt at initiating the task

(Continued)

Table 3.1 Continued

No	Time	with Gonca-Erol (first iteration)	Time	with Hasan-Mete (second iteration)
52	00:26:55.530	Checking understanding (of task)		
53	00:27:21.764	Focusing on task accomplishment		
54	00:27:43.787	Defining roles		
55	00:27:50.663	Focusing on task accomplishment		
56	00:27:53.574	Communicating key task information		
57	00:27:57.441	Focusing on task accomplishment		
58	00:28:12.326	Checking understanding (of task)		
59	00:28:13.681	Suggesting ways into task		
60	00:28:28.523	Focusing on task accomplishment		
61	00:28:37.245	Suggesting ways into task		
62	00:28:47.016	Communicating key task information		
63	00:28:56.097	Suggesting ways into task		
64	00:29:09.081	Launching the task		

HLAs of MANAGING RESOURCES (SENDING THE RESOURCE) and DEFINING ROLES. We then observe cycles of FOCUSING ON STUDY SKILLS, CHECKING UNDERSTANDING (OF TASK) (11 times, compared to one in the second iteration), FOCUSING ON TASK ACCOMPLISHMENT (14 times, compared to one in the second iteration) and COMMUNICATING KEY TASK INFORMATION before Karen's first HLA LAUNCHING THE TASK. Between lines 46–51 learners attempted to initiate the task three times but were interrupted by further instructions as it was revealed that the learners had not fully understood the task. In both iterations, Karen engaged with COMMUNICATING KEY TASK INFORMATION and SUGGESTING WAYS INTO TASK before finally LAUNCHING THE TASK. While in the first iteration, Karen suggested one way of how learners could compare and contrast the information upon a learner request (line 59), in the second iteration she offered this information unsolicited (line 19).

Thus, this change in order of initial HLAs in task instructions-as-process in the second iteration (i.e., SENDING THE RESOURCE and DEFINING ROLES following a preamble by ACTIVATING SCHEMATA, FOCUSING ON STUDY SKILLS, and COMMUNICATING KEY TASK INFORMATION) appears to determine the efficiency of instructions. We acknowledge that learner variation could have impacted this. However, given the learners were highly homogenous, this appears unlikely. On the contrary, because learners were similar, Karen could set certain expectations in the second iteration that enabled her to predict and pre-empt problematic areas in her instructions.

> Karen (interview, 34:02): "So yes, (100%) the second class I was much more confident, I roughly knew what answers (cause) they are from the same country, roughly the same age, so I kind of knew what was coming so I was able to adapt to that. They weren't identical, but they followed roughly the same format."

Further interview data indicated that Karen reflected on her instruction-giving practice in the first iteration and made modifications in the subsequent iteration. Karen's comments support our argument that instructions appear to be more efficient when they are initially contextualised within work-to-come (Heyman, 1986) prior to the delivery of electronic resources and allocation of roles.

> Karen (interview, 19:03): "And another thing that I do, I kind of fail (first one I really forgot is) you gotta explain the instructions before sending any resources, and I didn't do that. I sent the resources and then did the explanation because if you send the resources they will start reading what you sent them and will not be listening to you. (inaudible) I don't know why, I usually say what we are going to do and then send the website. And then I say it again. I didn't do that with the first set of students, you probably noticed that one."

> Karen (interview, 34:45): "I did notice that, which always happens the second time I teach something, is (quicker) so we (inaudible) everything, I think (inaudible) it was much quicker (inaudible) familiar also with actually using

with students the resources that you gave and knowing the students' reactions, so (inaudible) I had to concentrate on, but again it's one of the things that, reflecting, I think I do the reflection automatically."

Karen (interview, 37:40): "I am tending to get them to think about what the task was coming, what they would need to be able to do it (and) trying to get them to do it."

One further explanation relates to learner dynamics and how learners can influence each other's reactions (or demonstrate conformity to each other's responses).

Karen (interview, 37:42): "When you have two students it's so different from one. One would have a go, and it's amazing how if one gets it how the other one suddenly will understand even though nothing more (was) explained. Whereas if one says no, the other one would automatically, very quickly say no I don't know either."

Thus, further research would help understand whether and how teachers' HLAs change as they deliver the same task instructions a number of times, or with different numbers of learners (Chapter 4).

3.2 Task repetition: lower-level actions in task instructions-as-process

We now focus on the similarities and differences in Karen's LLAs. Our findings indicate that Karen's LLAs and her practices were largely similar in both iterations. In this section, we present evidence for six related arguments:

1. Karen utilised gestures to complement her meaning expressed in the spoken language mode and ensured that her gestures were centred and sustained longer within the webcam frame, particularly when repeating instructions upon learner requests for clarification (Section 3.2.1);
2. When COMMUNICATING KEY TASK INFORMATION (i.e. stating that there will be Student A and Student B, and that each will receive similar but different resources), Karen always used the same gesture types (iconic and metaphoric), with occasionally exactly the same gestures (Section 3.2.2);
3. Karen's deictic gestures when referring to different learners within the HLA SUGGESTING WAYS INTO TASK were oriented towards the position of the learners' webcam images as displayed on her own screen (Section 3.2.3);
4. Karen signalled the HLA LAUNCHING THE TASK in the spoken language mode ("okay off you go") accompanied by a slight shift in posture by moving away from the screen, thus, reducing her proximity to the camera and the learners, and a downwards gaze shift, indicating her removal from the interaction (Section 3.2.4);

5. Karen employed the textchat as she bimodally (spoken language and print mode) delivered four HLAs: MANAGING RESOURCES, FOCUSING ON STUDY SKILLS, FOCUSING ON TASK ACCOMPLISHMENT, and COMMUNICATING KEY TASK INFORMATION. During task accomplishment, written language in the print mode (frozen actions) functioned as reminders of task instructions delivered at an earlier stage, thus, offering scaffolding (Section 3.2.5);
6. Karen's webcam framing, screen layout and gaze patterns were consistent across the two iterations even when she was not physically in the same location (Section 3.2.6).

Although these arguments elaborate on modes other than the spoken language mode, we acknowledge that the spoken language mode had high modal intensity in all extracts and was central to meaning-making. Both the teacher and the learners reported a high level of awareness of the teacher's employment of the spoken language mode compared to other modes. For instance, they represented awareness of shorter but full sentences, simpler words, slower pace, and word stress to clarify meaning.

> Karen (interview, 23:30): "If I had to explain something again I would have slowed down . . . sometimes it's shortening and emphasising the words I want them to pay attention to. . . . I always try and use full sentences."

> Erol (interview, 08:29): "I think she used simpler words that we know, and she repeated the instructions . . . she also spoke more slowly."

Yet, as we document the teacher's concomitant use of other modes with the spoken language mode, the relevance of these other modes (such as gestures, proximity, print) become apparent. Although the participants did not explicitly report their awareness of modes other than the spoken language within specific HLAs in task instructions-as-process, they acknowledged and exemplified salient utilisation of other modes in general. For instance, both Hasan and Karen reflected on Karen's effective use of gestures when explaining sentence structure. Karen also reported how her use of gestures improves each time she delivers the same lesson. Erol suggested that they were all able to signal and read non-understanding from each other's facial expressions, that the teacher was also attentive to their facial expressions, and offered clarifications without any explicit requests in the spoken language mode. Karen confirmed this and added that she adopts a particular facial expression when expecting a learner response.

> Karen (interview, 52:12): "I think my students do appreciate when I move my hands . . . that really helps the students to understand [sentence structure] and then with the conjunction in the middle, I turn my hand upside,

34 *Task repetition*

> the other way round, so I kind of do the first clause and then the conjunction upside down, facing downwards and then the third one facing upwards. So yeah that's a good example because you use them so much, and you do them so much, each time I do it I improve it and improve it and improve it, which is why I really like my IELTS lessons now because they just improve every time I've done them."
>
> Erol (interview, 05: 25): "When we both focus on distance, we know that we didn't understand. That's what we always do, we look afar when we don't understand. That's how I gathered that Gonca didn't understand either. Then we laughed, and the teacher explained what she said again. When we both laughed at the same time, the teacher would explain again right away even when we had not requested an explanation."

3.2.1 Sustained and central hand gestures following learners' lack of understanding

In their interviews, learners stated that they understood a large amount of Karen's instructions, and reported challenges during the information-exchange task.

> Hasan (interview, 14:15): "When comparing spa packages, I did not understand it in the instructions first, that was when Mete and I asked a few times. Apart from that, I understood most instructions."
>
> Erol (interview, 07:27): "For example, in the last lesson, she asked us about what vegetarians eat and what they do not eat. We both understood these instructions easily. But in the first lesson . . . we both had spa centre information. She had asked us to compare the information, which we didn't understand. We understood it the second time Karen explained it."

When learners failed to understand or misunderstood the instructions, Karen offered a repetition, with slower pace and simpler sentences, as mentioned earlier. In both iterations, we also observed that Karen utilised hand gestures to complement the meaning expressed in the spoken language mode. Karen's gestures were more central and sustained longer within the webcam frame when instructions were repeated upon learner clarification requests or when learners signalled misunderstanding. Extracts 3.1 and 3.2 show Karen's LLAs in the two iterations. In both lessons, learners request clarification of the HLA SUGGESTING WAYS INTO TASK. Our analytical focus is on Karen's gestures when she repeats this HLA.

In the first iteration with Gonca and Erol (Extract 3.1 – first time), Karen's first attempt at presenting SUGGESTING WAYS INTO TASK takes 13 seconds with a

Task repetition 35

First time

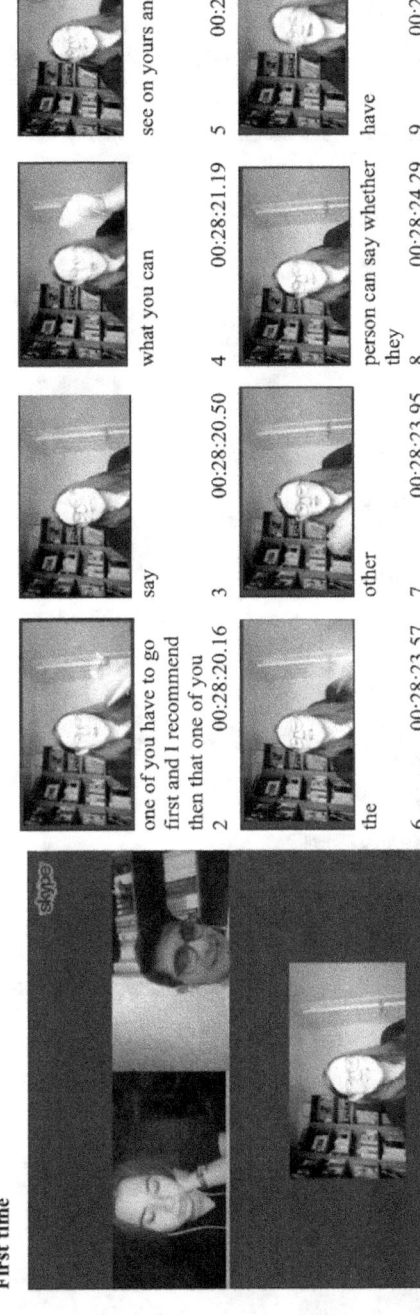

so why dom'- hehhehh why-
1   00:28:13.73

one of you have to go first and I recommend then that one of you	say	what you can	see on yours and
2 00:28:20.16	3 00:28:20.50	4 00:28:21.19	5 00:28:21.71

the	other	person can say whether they	have
6 00:28:23.57	7 00:28:23.95	8 00:28:24.29	9 00:28:26.0

the	same	thing or something different	
10 00:28:26.26	11 00:28:26.60	12 00:28:26.64	

Extract 3.1 SUGGESTING WAYS INTO TASK – iteration 1: Gonca & Erol

36 Task repetition

Second time upon learner request to repeat

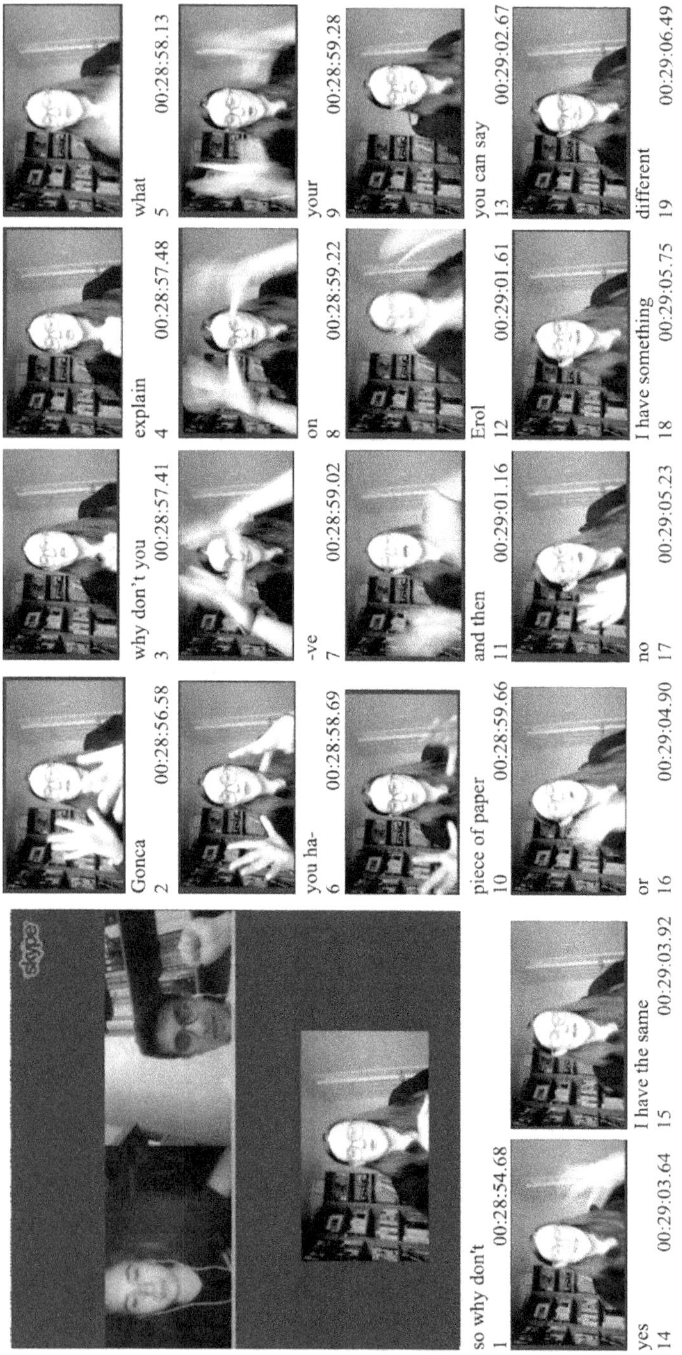

so why don't	Gonca	why don't you	explain	what
1 00:28:54.68	2 00:28:56.58	3 00:28:57.41	4 00:28:57.48	5 00:28:58.13

you ha-	-ve	on	your
6 00:28:58.69	7 00:28:59.02	8 00:28:59.22	9 00:28:59.28

piece of paper	and then	Erol	you can say
10 00:28:59.66	11 00:29:01.16	12 00:29:01.61	13 00:29:02.67

yes	I have the same	or	no	I have something	different
14 00:29:03.64	15 00:29:03.92	16 00:29:04.90	17 00:29:05.23	18 00:29:05.75	19 00:29:06.49

Extract 3.1 (Continued)

total of 12 gesture shifts. While Karen's hand gestures are visible (Frames 2, 4, 6, 7, 10, and 12), they are not sustained within the webcam frame but rather are displayed in quick successions; held in the frame for about half a second at most. Except Frames 2 and 4, Karen's hand gestures are not foregrounded or centralised within the webcam frame, while we observe only slight lateral head or posture shifts oriented in the same direction as her hand gestures (Frames 9, 11, and 12).

This first attempt at SUGGESTING WAYS INTO TASK was followed by Karen reminding learners to take notes and asking who would like to start explaining their task resource sheet information. Seven seconds of silence followed ending with Gonca asking Erol, in Turkish, whether he understood what to do. Perceiving this correctly as orientation to a lack of comprehension of the instructions by the learners, Karen quickly repeated her instructions by stressing KEY TASK INFORMATION (i.e., that each student has different information). Following confirmation from both learners, Karen reintroduced the HLA SUGGESTING WAYS INTO TASK with some changes in the spoken language mode (using learner names instead of "one of you" and "the other person") along with foregrounded and sustained gestures, accompanied by marked lateral posture shifts. This time the HLA SUGGESTING WAYS INTO TASK took 12 seconds and included 19 gesture shifts. In Extract 3.1 – second time, Karen's hands are visible in all frames except 13, 15, 18, and 19, demonstrating a continuation of sustained but dynamic gesture movements for about 11 seconds. Gestures are foregrounded at all times, held high up, central to the webcam frame (Frames 2, 5, 6, 7, 8, 9, 11, 12, 14, 16, and 17). Karen's posture shifts are more pronounced in the same direction as the position of her hand gestures (Frames 12, 15, 16, and 17). In Frame 19, Karen's posture shifts away from the computer screen, reducing her virtual proximity to the learners, and signalling her removal from the interaction and, thus, end of instruction giving. Following learner confirmation of comprehension, Karen then moves into the HLA LAUNCHING THE TASK.

We observe a similar pattern in the second iteration of task instruction giving. Again, the first time Karen introduces the HLA SUGGESTING WAYS INTO TASK her hand gestures are not visible within the webcam frame (Extract 3.2 – first time). Except a slight rightwards lateral head movement (Frame 3), and a slight sagittal head movement (vertical lowering, Frame 4), Karen does not employ any other embodied modes. The HLA takes about 24 seconds with four gesture shifts.

Karen's instruction in this extract was immediately followed by confirmations from both learners, and then an instruction repetition request from Mete:

38 Task repetition

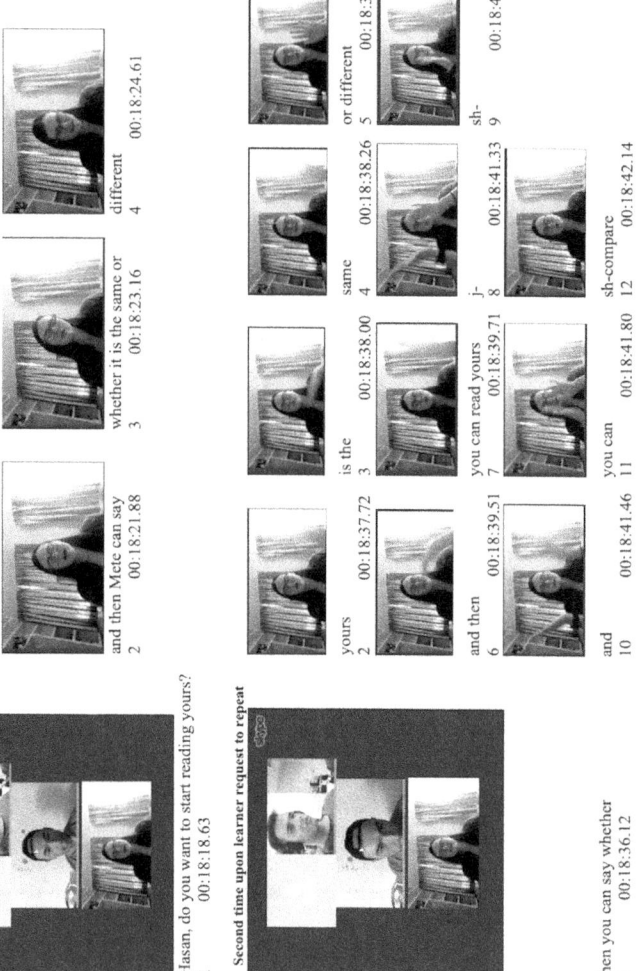

Extract 3.2 *Suggesting ways into task* – Iteration 2: Hasan & Mete

Hasan okay

00:18:28.363–00:18:29.059

Mete okay

00:18:29.000–00:18:29.460

Mete please repeat

00:18:30.120–00:18:31.430

Karen uhm so Hasan will read his

00:18:31.913–00:18:34.436

Karen he will start reading his then you can say whether yours is the same or different and then you can read your's just- and you can sh- compare

00:18:34.969–00:18:43.123

Following this repetition request, in the spoken language mode, Karen explained that Hasan will start by reading his document, and then directly addressed Mete whilst utilising concomitant LLAs in the gesture mode with sustained and central hand gestures (Extract 3.2 – second time). In Frames 2, 3, and 4, Karen uses an iconic gesture to represent the concept of *sameness* (palm inwards) followed by another iconic gesture to represent the concept of *difference* (palm outwards, Frame 5). In Frames 6 and 7, she repeats the gesture produced in Fames 2–4 to refer to Mete's information once more ("your's"). Karen's metaphoric gestures (Frames 8–11) constituting dynamic, brisk hand movements shifting sideways, represent the concept of *comparing the information* in the two resource sheets. The HLA takes six seconds and involves 12 gesture shifts. Both learners then confirm understanding and initiate the task.

Thus, in both iterations, Karen demonstrated heightened use of hand gestures, as well as posture and head movement shifts, following learners' claim of a lack of full comprehension of task instructions. However, during her interview, Karen appeared not to be semiotically aware of the support her gestures lend to clarification of spoken instructions. Rather, she alluded to the possibility to observe learners' reactions and adapt her behaviour accordingly.

Interviewer (interview, 32:22): "Do you think your gestures and facial expressions are useful when you're explaining what to do?"

Karen (interview, 32:52): "I have no idea, you have to ask the students that. I hope so, because that's the difference between a video call and an audio call. Video calls are so much easier than because you get feedback from the students and I look at the students' faces a lot to know whether they understand something or not. So, I think so, but I mean I use their facial expressions, so I assume they use my facial expressions, so when I'm asking a question, I'm looking like I want an answer. Perhaps, but, that's an excellent question, I think I would like to know the answer to that one."

Interestingly, one learner, Erol, also mentioned that he could understand Karen's feedback delivered through her LLAs (e.g., facial expressions), but also demonstrated awareness of modal complexity when instructions are presented bimodally using spoken language and gesture modes. Erol stated that teacher gestures which accompanied spoken language facilitated concentration. We interpret this as an indication that the modal complexity of Karen's HLAs foregrounded instructions in Erol's attention/awareness.

Erol (interview, 09:33): "Karen always used her gestures and facial expressions like teachers do when teaching, but . . . If there were no words, I definitely wouldn't have understood, but when the teacher uses their gestures, I can focus better . . . teachers' gestures help me (focus), like opening her hands/arms and moving them around."

Erol (interview, 10:23): "Yes, sometimes I would pronounce a word wrongly, and by her facial expressions, I could understand that I was wrong. . . . Her gestures were sometimes within the screen and other times outside the screen. The bits I could see helped me focus because some teachers never show their arms, just move their lips. I think that distracts the learner."

3.2.2 Same gestures or same type of gestures in both iterations

In this section, we again direct our focus to the mode of gesture but within the HLA COMMUNICATING KEY TASK INFORMATION. We observed that Karen used deictic and iconic gestures to refer to different students and resource sheets, and at times these gestures were exactly the same.

3.2.2.1 Communicating key task information: there is student A and B

In the information exchange activity, key task information was the fact that learners did not have access to some part of the information required to complete the convergent task and, thus, must interact to obtain the missing information. In both lesson iterations, Karen completed the HLA COMMUNICATING KEY TASK INFORMATION by informing the learners, in the spoken language mode, that there would be a Student A and a Student B and by asking for a volunteer to fill the first role (Extract 3.3). Her use of LLAs in the gesture mode is very similar for both iterations.

Task repetition 41

Extract 3.3 COMMUNICATING KEY TASK INFORMATION: there is Student A and B

In Extract 3.3 – first iteration, Karen employs iconic gestures, with her palms turned towards the webcam to represent Students A and B: first, using her right hand to represent Student A (Frames 2 and 3); second, using her left hand to represent Student B whilst simultaneously withdrawing her first iconic gesture (Frame 4). This key task information becomes the focal point of attention through modal complexity offered by the combination of gesture and spoken language modes. In this extract, Karen then elicits a volunteer to be Student A (Frames 5 and 6). Frame 5 shows her relaxed body movements: scratching behind her ear with a free gaze direction away from the camera and then, in Frame 6, directing her gaze towards the screen again addressing the learners. The modal aggregate, combining LLAs in the posture (directly facing the camera), gaze (directed towards the screen), facial expressions (still), sagittal head movement (vertical raising), and spoken language (question followed by a pause) modes form this elicitation.

Extract 3.3 – second iteration illustrates similar LLAs that inform the learners of the same key task information. In the spoken language mode, Karen produces almost identical utterances with only "There is going to be" replaced by "There is." In the gesture mode, Karen, again performs two iconic gestures as she vocalises "Student A" (Frame 2) and "Student B" (Frame 3), yet in this second iteration of the same instructions, the form of the iconic gestures differs. Rather than hands representing different roles, Karen represents Student A with her index finger and Student B with her index and middle fingers as if to enumerate the two roles, even though in the spoken language mode she refers to them using letters. As she invites one learner to take the role of Student A (Frame 5), we observe the same posture and gaze direction facing the learners. These LLAs again appear to draw learners' awareness/attention to this information. In her interview, Karen explained that she pays particular attention to her facial expressions.

> Karen (interview, 33:28): "I use their [learners'] facial expressions, so I assume they use my facial expressions, so when I'm asking a question, I'm looking like I want an answer."

Thus, we conclude that for the same HLA COMMUNICATING KEY TASK INFORMATION, Karen produced almost identical LLAs in the spoken language, posture, gaze, and facial expression modes. She also produced the same type yet different form of gestures (iconic) concomitantly with the same utterances in the spoken language mode in both iterations.

3.2.2.2 Communicating key task information: different information

In Extract 3.4, we observe Karen's delivery of the HLA COMMUNICATING KEY TASK INFORMATION; specifically, that each learner's information is different. This is achieved by multiple LLAs. In the spoken language mode, Karen delivers the key task information linguistically and para-linguistically, uttering the

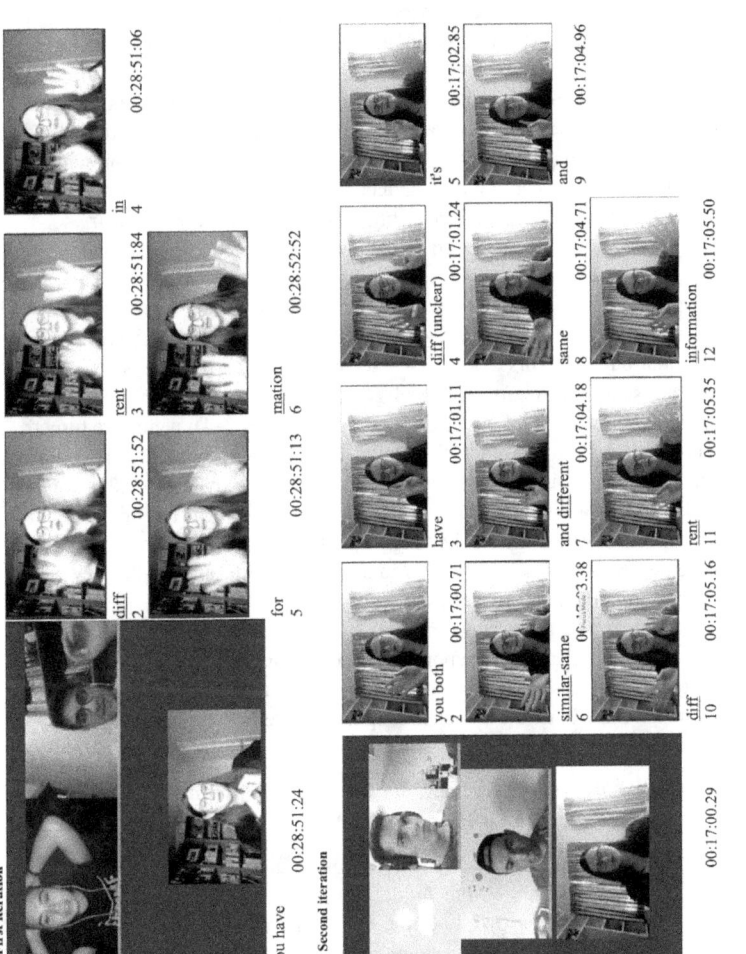

Extract 3.4 COMMUNICATING KEY TASK INFORMATION: different information

word "different" and placing a stress on this word. The notion of difference is also foregrounded in the gesture mode.

In Extract 3.4 – first iteration, starting from a neutral position (Frame 1), Karen employs metaphoric gestures with her palms turned towards the webcam within which the gestures are well framed. The notion of *contrast* (different) is marked by metaphorically separating the hands in the gestural space. In Frames 3–6, Karen then renders the gestures dynamic: she moves her hands in counterbalance forward and backwards in coordination with the different syllables in the spoken language mode, using opposite directions in the gestural space. The quick, coherent, and rhythmic movements also constitute beat gestures, increasing the saliency of the key idea of *difference*, representing the relationship between the two students/resources, that is, each learner has a resource, which includes different information. The HLA COMMUNICATING KEY TASK INFORMATION is, thus, achieved by the joint employment of spoken language and static and dynamic metaphoric gestures, resulting in high modal density.

During the second iteration, whilst expressing the same HLA COMMUNICATING KEY TASK INFORMATION, Karen again introduces the notion that the resources are similar but different (Extract 3.4 – second iteration). In doing so, she employs the same metaphoric and beat gestures as in iteration one to accompany the utterance "you both have different" (Frames 2–4): palms are turned towards the webcam and metaphorically separated in the gestural space, the gestures are well framed, and the gestures are rendered dynamic with a counterbalance forward-backwards movement (Frames 4–12). The high modal density, in the gesture and spoken language modes for the notions of *similarity* and *difference*, allows the teacher to increase the relevance of this key task information in learners' awareness/attention.

To convey and foreground the notion of difference as part of key task information, these extracts demonstrate Karen using exactly the same metaphoric and beat gestures, posture, head movement, and proximity, and employing similar LLAs in the spoken language mode in both iterations.

3.2.3 Alignment of the teacher's spoken language, gesture, gaze, and posture with the layout mode

We now focus on alignment of Karen's spoken language, gesture, gaze, and posture modes with her layout mode across the two iterations within the HLA SUGGESTING WAYS INTO TASK. In the first iteration, this HLA is embedded within another level of HLA *exchanging information*, whereas in the second iteration, the same HLA is embedded with the HLA *writing collaboratively*. Extract 3.5 illustrates how Karen's deictic gestures, as well as LLAs in the modes of spoken language, gaze, and posture, were oriented towards the position of the learners' webcam images, as displayed on her own screen, when referring to different learners.

Task repetition 45

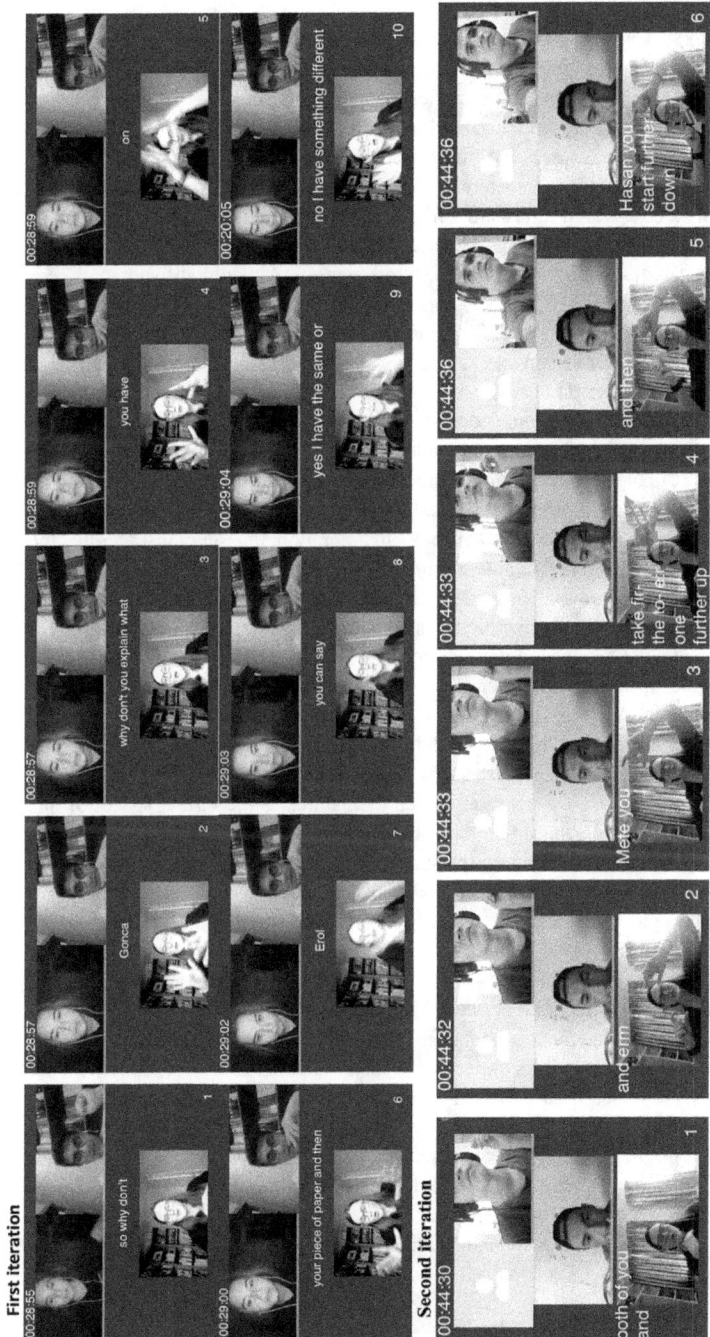

Extract 3.5 SUGGESTING WAYS INTO TASK: why don't

46 Task repetition

Extract 3.5 – first iteration is taken from the first micro-task: the information gap activity. In Frame 1, Karen uses the discourse marker "so" in the spoken language mode to signal moving into a new HLA: SUGGESTING WAYS INTO TASK. Karen nominates different learners through vocatives and pronouns in the spoken language mode, combined with deictic gestures and postural shifts. When Karen addresses the first learner, Gonca, using her name in Frame 2, her deictic gesture and posture are oriented towards the learner's image on her own screen. Karen returns to a more neutral body position (Frame 3) before re-employing the same LLAs to accompany "you" (Frame 4) and "your piece of paper" (Frame 6) in the spoken language mode. Although difficult to discern in the transcript of Extract 3.5 – first iteration, it is clear in the video recordings that Karen's free gaze direction follows her posture and head direction and orients towards her screen area where Gonca's webcam image is visible. Karen's orientation towards Gonca can be contrasted with the multimodal configuration in Frame 7 where she addresses the second learner, Erol, whose webcam image is displayed on the right side of Karen's screen. Here, Karen employs the LLAs of a deictic gesture, combined with a posture and gaze shift directed towards the right, that is, towards the space where Erol's webcam image appears on her own screen. Extract 3.5 – first iteration, thus, demonstrates that the teacher's multimodal expression in her own physical and virtual interactional space moves along a horizontal axis, representing the horizontal organisation of the learners' images within her mediated interactional space (layout mode).

Extract 3.5 – second iteration is taken from Karen's instruction-giving sequence for the second micro-task: writing an email to inform colleagues of the leaving gift chosen and asking for financial contributions. Prior to this extract, Karen displays two model texts using an electronic document (print mode) and requests learners to use the same document to write their texts. In Extract 3.5 – second iteration, Karen then allocates the virtual spaces of this document, requesting Mete to write in the space directly below the example texts, and Hasan to write in the space below Mete's writing. As illustrated in Frame 1, Mete's webcam image is displayed above that of Hasan's, that is, in the second iteration, the learners' webcam images are positioned on a vertical axis in the visual organisation of Karen's layout. Interestingly, we again observe alignment in Karen's employment of gesture, spoken language, and gaze modes in line with her layout mode. In Frame 3, as Karen refers to Mete in the spoken language mode, using a vocative and the second person singular pronoun, her gaze shifts upwards, her hands are positioned vertically with her left hand raised high up in her webcam frame with an iconic gesture of a C shape representing the space on the document in which Mete is to write.

In Frame 4, Karen allocates Mete his writing space while her iconic gesture is rendered dynamic with a forward and backwards movement and, thus, takes on the properties of a beat gesture emphasising the top position of both the writing space in the document and the learner's webcam image on the teacher's screen. In the spoken language mode, Karen's utterance "further up" perfectly

Task repetition 47

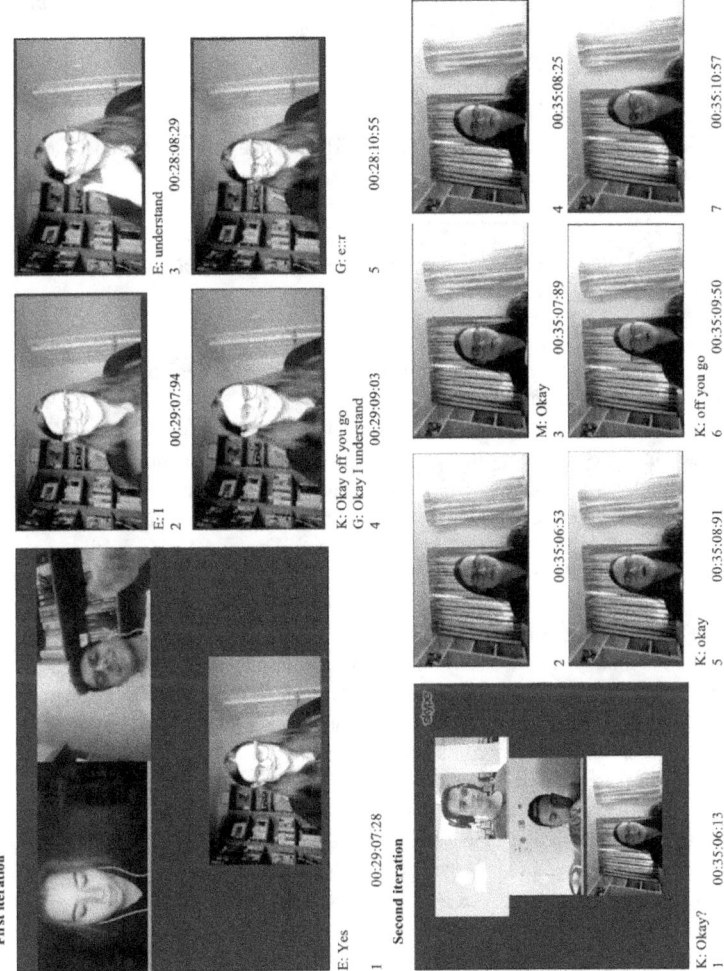

Extract 3.6 Off you go

aligns with top position references in the gesture, layout, and gaze modes. Karen then allocates Hasan the role to write in the space below Mete's writing (Frame 6), again signalled by alignment across the gesture (right hand positioned at the bottom of her webcam frame and rendered dynamic with back-and-forth movements), use of a vocative and a second person singular in the spoken language mode to address the learner, and "further down" to allocate the space on the document. This is accompanied by a gaze shift downwards.

Overall, Extract 3.5 evidences Karen's reliance on learner image positions (vertical or horizontal) in her own layout mode to orchestrate the modes of spoken language, gesture, gaze, and posture when ALLOCATING LEARNER ROLES within the HLA SUGGESTING WAYS INTO TASK. Throughout this interaction, Karen does not have access to the layout of the learners' displays nor where exactly each actor's webcam image is positioned on their screens.

3.2.4. Signalling removal from interaction in the proxemics/posture mode

Extract 3.6 reveals similarities in Karen's LLAs in both iterations for the HLA LAUNCHING THE TASK. Here, we specifically focus on the spoken language, proxemics, posture, and gesture modes.

Extract 3.6 – first iteration is the continuation of the instructions that follow Extract 3.5 – first iteration. In this extract, Erol expresses his understanding of the instructions and Karen confirms this through an emblem gesture, that is, a thumbs up, which is centrally positioned in the webcam frame (Frame 3). In Frame 4, Gonca also expresses her understanding and Karen, in the spoken language mode with the utterance "okay off you go," confirms student understanding and moves into the HLA LAUNCHING THE TASK. She completes this HLA in Frame 5 by leaving the interactional space to the learners in the proxemics mode: she physically moves away from the webcam and adopts a neutral straight posture. Karen's gaze also shifts downwards and complements the modal configuration. We, thus, note an increase in the interpersonal space (Andersen, 2008) (Frame 5 compared to Frame 3). Following Frame 5, we observed that Karen focused on the task resource sheet and shifted her attention away from the videoconferencing window. Although not signalled to the learners, Karen's site of engagement demonstrated an increased distance from the interactional space and reduced attention/awareness towards the learners.

Karen's proxemic shift, as a LLA to achieve LAUNCHING THE TASK, is also clear in her second iteration (Extract 3.6 – second iteration). In the spoken language mode, Karen performs a confirmation check "okay?" (Frame 1) and waits for learner response (Frames 2–3). She then employs the same LLA in the spoken language mode ("okay off you go', Frames 5 and 6) as in iteration one, both as confirmation of understanding and to mark moving into LAUNCHING THE TASK. Frame 6 shows a LLA in the proxemics mode whereby Karen moves away from the webcam. In Frames 6 and 7, we again observe a downward gaze shift. As in iteration one, we observed Karen switch her screen to the task sheet following Frame 7.

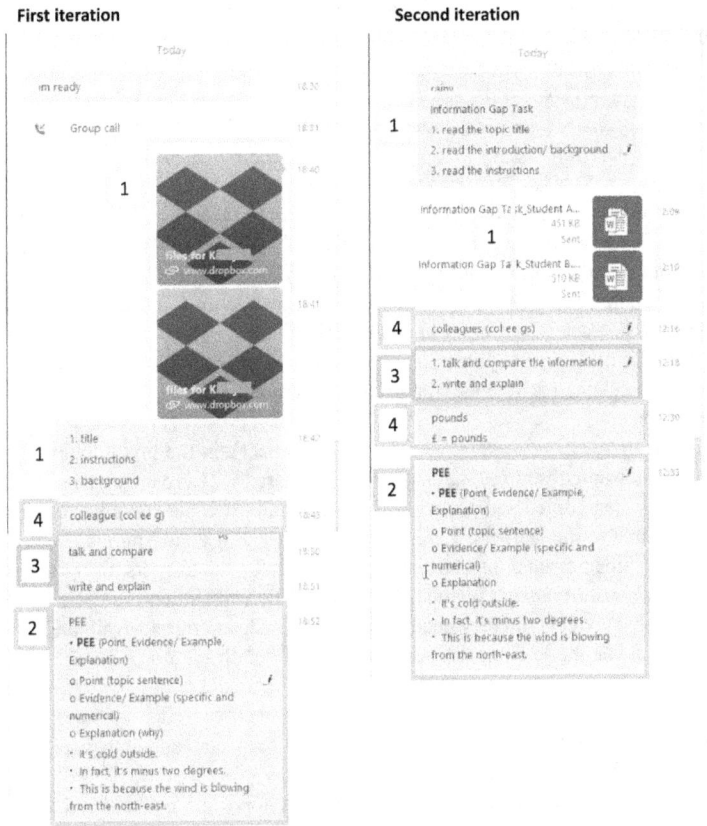

Extract 3.7 Giving instructions in the print mode

Thus, in both iterations, the modal configuration of 1) "okay off you go" in the spoken language mode, 2) downward gaze shift, and 3) reduced proximity constitute the LLAs which enable the teacher to achieve the HLA LAUNCHING THE TASK and leave the interactional space in the spoken language mode open to the learners.

3.2.5 Bimodal instruction giving in the modes of spoken language and print

For her second lesson with both pairs of learners, Karen utilised the print mode (textchat) as an additional mode to express four HLAs: MANAGING RESOURCES, FOCUSING ON STUDY SKILLS, FOCUSING ON TASK ACCOMPLISHMENT, and COMMUNICATING KEY TASK INFORMATION. These HLAs were presented at least bimodally with a spoken language and print mode aggregate: Karen systematically verbalised the content of her textchat messages.

First, the print mode (textchat) was employed to achieve the HLA MANAGING RESOURCES (SENDING THE RESOURCE, READING THE RESOURCE, and *describing the content of the resource*) in both iterations (Extract 3.7 – Frame 1). Whilst in the first iteration, SENDING THE RESOURCE was accomplished first followed by READING THE RESOURCE; in the second iteration, DESCRIBING THE CONTENT OF THE RESOURCE was presented first, as the teacher explained what resource the learners would receive and described the contents, followed by *sending the resource*. In both iterations, textchat was used to record key elements learners should focus upon when READING THE RESOURCE (title, instructions, introduction/background; Extract 3.7 – Frame 1) and during the HLA FOCUSING ON STUDY SKILLS (PEE: Point, Evidence/Example, Explanation; Extract 3.7 – Frame 4) when Karen explained a method for giving structured extended responses to a question.

For SENDING THE RESOURCE (Extract 3.7, Frame 1), in the first iteration, for each electronic resource, Karen generated a shared URL from a cloud storage service, then copied and pasted the URL into the textchat. These LLAs were not visible to the learners: Karen had access to and used a semiotic resource in her online personal interactional space unseen by the learners, thus causing *semiotic misalignment* (Wigham & Satar, 2021). Only when the URLs were sent in the textchat did they become visible to the learners, and available to be embodied as the learners accessed or downloaded the resource (in the HLA RECEIVING THE RESOURCE). In the textchat, the semiotic representation of the URLs was automatically changed by the videoconferencing software: both were demonstrated as links to files on www.dropbox.com and both displaying the same file name ("files for Karen").

In contrast, in the second iteration, Karen stored the resource sheets locally on her computer, had renamed them to correspond to the task type and student, and sent the resources via the textchat as electronic files. The semiotic representation of the files in the textchat included a symbol representing file type (Microsoft Word), file size, and file title ("Information-Gap Task_Student A. . . ." and "Information-Gap Task_Student B . . ."). The teacher's pre-lesson preparation, in renaming the files could have contributed to higher efficiency in the delivery of task instructions, which may have allowed the HLA ALLOCATING THE RESOURCE to be a simpler process. Again, once the files were sent and received on textchat, all social actors had access to the required resources, which remained available throughout the lesson in the shared interactional space.

In a similar manner, Karen embodied the textchat in both iterations within the HLA DESCRIBING HOW TO ACCOMPLISH THE TASK (Extract 3.7 – Frame 3) to reinforce the instructions by typing key instruction words: "talk and compare," "write and explain." For all HLAs, these LLAs became frozen in the print mode and could then be referred back to during the lesson.

Task repetition 51

A final pedagogical use of LLAs in the textchat was within the HLA *CLARI-FYING KEY TASK VOCABULARY* (Extract 3.7 – Frame 4). In both iterations, Karen offered bimodal feedback for key task vocabulary (e.g., colleague). In the interviews, both the teacher and the learners reflected on their *critical semiotic awareness* of the employment of print mode, especially in the form of textchat, particularly during the instruction-giving HLA *CLARIFYING KEY TASK VOCABULARY*. For example, Karen reflected on her use of textchat during her lessons and stated a preference towards the affordances of Skype textchat compared to, for instance, Zoom textchat. The former enables participants to access the textchat after the synchronous session is over and to edit the text and change its style (e.g., bold, italics) after being sent. One of the learners confirmed Karen's frequent use of textchat, especially for *CLARIFYING KEY TASK VOCABULARY* during the instruction-giving sequence and beyond.

Karen (interview, 32:30): "I use text chat a lot. . . . I don't like using the Zoom chat because (a) it doesn't remember the messages, and (b) I don't like the layout it. . . . Now, another useful thing with Skype is that you can edit the messages."

Karen (interview, 15:40): "You can also, unlike Zoom, I like Skype because you can put some messages in bold, you can put some messages in italics. So, there is different ways of making notes in Skype which my students find quite useful."

Hasan (interview, 09:40): "She used chat frequently, in order to explain the vocabulary we did not know . . . She wrote most things on chat . . . When we asked vocabulary we did not know, . . . she explained them in the chat right away, which was good."

However, the learners did not always appear to be aware that the HLAs of *CLARIFYING KEY TASK VOCABULARY, DESCRIBING HOW TO ACCOMPLISH THE TASK,* or *FOCUSING ON STUDY SKILLS* formed part of the teacher's instructions. When asked whether Karen wrote task instructions on textchat, Hasan replied as follows:

Hasan (interview, 11:26): "No, she usually told us those kind of things. She wrote on the chat windows only for definitions and when we did not understand. As long as we understood things, she only talked to us. . . . She could have written some of the instructions on the chat window. . . . It is more difficult for me to listen. I learn by reading. And also because it is English, therefore it was a little challenging."

3.2.6 Site of engagement and semiotic misalignment: *layout, webcam framing, gaze patterns*

Despite being in different physical spaces, Karen's site of engagement was persistent across both iterations (Figure 3.1 – Frames 1 and 2). This included

52 Task repetition

(1) similar webcam framing: head-and-torso shot (in which her face, shoulders and torso can be seen, see Guichon & Wigham, 2016) which allowed gestures to be visible, (2) free gaze patterns largely directed at the on-screen interaction (Satar, 2013), and (3) similar layout predominantly with the Skype interface at the centre of Karen's attention/awareness and her contacts list on the left, textchat on the right, and the similar-sized interlocutor webcam images central. In Figure 3.1, we do not see Karen's contacts window due to the smaller screen area that the teacher chose to record iteration one. Yet, Karen confirmed that she always has the contacts list visible.

> Karen (interview, 11:55): "The screen as you saw it that is what I usually use. I always have the text box open for Skype on the right. And then my other students (will be available) on the left. I kind of just (inaudible) how Skype is laid out."

While in Figure 3.1 we see that Karen's site of engagement involves similar-size webcam images, in the interviews, the learners indicated that within their site of engagement/layout their own webcam images were smaller.

> Erol (interview, 06:23): "Because you [researcher] didn't have a video, but only a picture, I minimised your video and mine, which were displayed at the bottom of the screen. Gonca's and Karen's images were large. On the right-hand side, I had the chat window."

> Hasan (interview, 05:25): "The chat window was visible at all times. It was on the right. My video was on the right bottom, Karen was on the left and Mete was on the right. My video was smaller and theirs' were bigger."

Due to technical difficulties, only one of the learners (Erol) was able to screen record the first lesson with Karen. Figure 3.1 – Frame 3 shows Erol's site of engagement during this lesson, which corroborates his statement of layout. We also notice that Gonca and Karen's webcam images were displayed vertically with Gonca's image on top.

Finally, Figure 3.1 shows the multimodal composition of the teacher's screen (Frame 2) compared to what was seen by the researcher who was also recording the lesson (Frame 4) at the same moment during the lesson (also mentioned in Extract 3.3 – second iteration, Frame 2). In the researcher's site of engagement, whilst the vertical organisation of the learners' webcam images on the researcher's screen is similar to that of the teacher's, webcam image sizes differ; the teacher's image taking up the largest space in the layout. Yet, we observe a mirror effect: as the teacher's image is flipped on its horizontal axis, the textchat is not available, and the wide-angle/narrow-angle view of the teacher's webcam image differs. One result of this *semiotic misalignment* is varying access to the teacher's LLAs in the

Task repetition 53

1 Karen's site of engagement, lesson 2, first iteration, 10:51

2 Karen's site of engagement, lesson 2, second iteration, 07:45

4 Researcher's site of engagement, lesson 2, second iteration, 07:45

3 Erol's site of engagement lesson 1, first iteration, 20:42

Figure 3.1 Social actors' site of engagement

gesture mode: Karen's iconic gesture representing Student A with her index finger (Frame 2) is no longer visible on the researcher's screen (Frame 4).

Equally, some of the teacher's gestures that are directed towards specific learners' webcam images in Karen's site of engagement (e.g. Extract 3.5) may be difficult to interpret because the webcam images positioning can differ in other social actors' layout modes. An actor's interpretation of gaze patterns may also be affected. Thus, differences in how each social actor views the interactional space may cause *semiotic misalignment* (see Wigham & Satar, 2021). Although all actors may be present in the same virtual interactional space, variations in hardware and software specifications and screen layout may result in the shared interactional space being viewed differently, depending on the multimodal composition of each individual's site of engagement. This may impact, firstly, the multimodal aggregates available to the social actors, resulting in a loss of a common "site of display" (see Jones, 2009, p. 115). Secondly, the modes that carry high or low modal density for each participant may differ resulting in instances of *modal density misalignment* in which the participants do not have access to the same hierarchy of modes to communicate and interpret meaning. We elaborate on this concept in the following sections.

3.3 Modal configuration and modal density

Despite Karen being in different physical interactional spaces for the two iterations, we observed very little variety in her multimodal organisation of LLAs (modal configuration) and the intensity and complexity of the different modes (modal density). When Karen interacted within the videoconferencing window, HLAs were achieved through a combination of LLAs principally in the spoken language, gesture, and gaze modes. Figure 3.2 – Frames 1 and 2 show this predominant configuration. The example in Frame 1 is taken from iteration one in which Karen is performing the HLA *FOCUSING ON STUDY SKILLS*. Karen performs a modal aggregate that comprises spoken language including a pause, an iconic gesture, and gaze shift towards the screen (learners' images). All of these LLAs carry medium modal intensity: they would impact the HLA should they be discontinued. Frame 2 shows a similar modal configuration taken from iteration two. Although the HLA differs (*DEFINING ROLES*), LLAs in the same three modes form the modal aggregate and all modes carry similar intensity.

However, when Karen interacted with the electronic resources, during HLAs relating to *MANAGING RESOURCES*, her modal configuration was somewhat different. For both iterations (Figure 3.2. – Frames 3 and 4), when the electronic resource became the focal point of the teacher's attention, the HLAs related to resources were achieved through LLAs in the print and spoken language modes. Frame 3 shows an example of the HLA from iteration one of

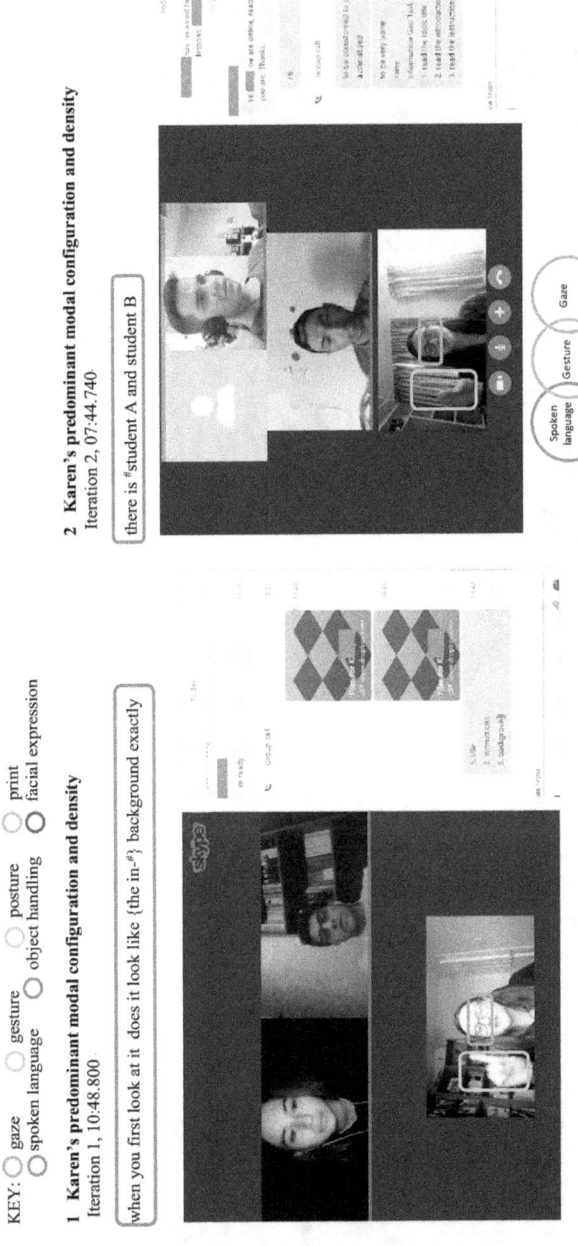

Figure 3.2 Karen's predominant modal configuration and density

56 Task repetition

3 Karen's modal configuration and density while following learner responses during instruction giving
Iteration 1, 07:27.120

so I will send you# the exercise

4 Karen's modal configuration and density while following learner responses during instruction giving
Iteration 2, 08:45.110

so are they opening/#

Figure 3.2 (Continued)

MANAGING RESOURCES (SENDING THE RESOURCE) and Frame 4 the HLA from iteration two of MANAGING RESOURCES (CONFIRMING ACCESS TO THE (CORRECT) RESOURCE). In both extracts, the teacher had sent an electronic resource to learners via textchat. In iteration one, this online resource was a shared document to which the teacher was connected but the learners had yet to do so. In iteration two, Karen had sent word-processor files via textchat and had opened the online resource as a word-processor document locally on her own computer.

3.4 Semiotic misalignment and modal density misalignment

In Section 3.2.6, we illustrated variety in social actor's devices and, thus, their site of engagement in the virtual interactional space, which can lead to *semiotic misalignment*. Here, we illustrate social actor's ability to change their virtual or on-screen site of engagement without any significant shift in their embodied modes, and how this lack of shared access to all social actors' virtual sites of engagement can lead to *semiotic misalignment*. We then explore what this means for modal density as experienced by different social actors. Our example comes from the first iteration of Karen's Lesson 2.

At the onset of Extract 3.8, Erol had just volunteered to take on student role A. In Frame 1, Karen begins to engage with two HLAs: SENDING THE RESOURCE and ALLOCATING THE RESOURCE to a specific learner. The move into these HLAs is marked by the hesitation marker "okay" in the spoken language mode accompanied by the action of pasting a URL link into the textchat (object handling). In Frame 2, whilst the URL is loading and, thus, not yet visible to the other actors, Karen uses a deictic gesture to point to the space in the layout mode in which the URL appears on her screen. In Frame 3, when she pronounces "this one," Karen has already moved back from the videoconferencing window to the electronic resource and has highlighted a second URL. Karen then returns to the videoconferencing window where the URL in the shared interactional space was, accompanied by the hesitation marker "u::hm" before using a vocative addressing the learner to which the resource is not allocated (Frame 4). This is followed by a second hesitation marker "e:rr" and vocative "Erol clicks" accompanied by a deictic gesture towards the textchat as Karen corrects herself and allocates the resource to Erol (Frame 5). As Karen instructs the second learner to not click on the resource through a vocative "Gonca" accompanied by another deictic gesture directed towards the learner's webcam image (Frame 6), she moves back to another electronic resource (Frame 7), highlights and copies the URL, before pasting it into the textchat in Frame 8 ("this one"). As the URL is transferred to the shared interactional space and changes into a visual icon, Karen asks the learner to click on the latter to access her allocated resource (Frame 9).

In Extract 3.8, we observe *semiotic misalignment*. Karen multitasks and moves between the videoconferencing window to which all actors have access

58 *Task repetition*

and the electronic resources to which, at the current time, only she has access. Karen, thus, shifts the multimodal composition of her site of engagement but the changes into and away from the shared interactional environment are not announced in the spoken language mode which is accessible to the three participants regardless of their on-screen site of engagement

The screen set-up during HLAs related to MANAGING RESOURCES brings the electronic resource to the foreground in Karen's attention/awareness as only one learner's webcam image becomes visible in the small videoconferencing window. During these moments, there is *semiotic misalignment* regarding the semiotic resources to which the social actors have access. Whilst the teacher no longer has access to her own image, the learners do not have access to the electronic resource but have access to the teacher's webcam image and any LLAs performed in the gesture, gaze, facial expression, or posture modes. This configuration, in which the participants have different sites of engagement, does not allow the teacher to monitor her LLAs in the different modes communicated via the webcam: Karen does not have access to her own head-and-torso webcam framing, which provides cues as to the exact content of the frame and the LLAs being projected.

This example of *semiotic misalignment* also allows us to observe *modal density misalignment* depending on the participants: for the teacher, the print mode appears to carry high modal prominence (intensity) and when discontinued will lead to a change in HLA. However, for the learners, who do not (yet) have access to the print mode (which, thus, carries no modal intensity for them), the spoken language mode carries high intensity and discontinuation would impact the HLA. There is no joint focal point of attention other than the spoken language mode.

3.5 Chapter summary

This chapter examined whether HLAs and LLAs in task instructions-as-process were similar or different when the same teacher repeated the same task with different learners. Our analysis demonstrated that task instructions appeared to be more efficient during a second iteration: the number of HLAs was reduced and, overall, instructions were shorter in length. We reported how contextualising a task before turning to the HLA MANAGING RESOURCES helped achieve greater efficiency. Regarding LLAs, we observed many similarities in the iterations as regards the teacher's hierarchical organisation of LLAs (modal configuration) and the intensity and complexity of different modes (modal density). The teacher's predominant configuration was the videoconferencing software layout where HLAs were achieved through a combination of LLAs principally in the spoken language, gesture, and gaze modes. Gestures were centred and sustained longer within the webcam frame, particularly when repeating instructions upon learner clarification requests. Within the HLA COMMUNICATING KEY TASK INFORMATION, the teacher employed the same

Task repetition 59

Extract 3.8 Click on this one please (07:45.870–08:03.440)

types of gestures (iconic and metaphoric) in both iterations. Deictic gestures were oriented towards the position of learners' webcam images as displayed on the teacher's screen. The teacher's webcam framing, with a choice of head and torso shot, screen layout, and predominant use of free gaze patterns were consistent across the two iterations.

References

Andersen, P. A. (2008). *Nonverbal communication: Forms and functions*. IL: Waveland Press Inc.

Guichon, N., & Wigham, C. R. (2016). A semiotic perspective on webconferencing-supported language teaching. *ReCALL*, *28*(1), 62–82.

Heyman, R. D. (1986). Formulating topic in the classroom. *Discourse Processes*, *9*(1), 37-55.

Jones, R. H. (2009). Technology and sites of display. In C. Jewitt (Ed.), *The Routledge handbook of multimodal analysis* (pp. 114–126). London: Routledge.

Satar, H. M. (2013). Multimodal language learner interactions via desktop videoconferencing within a framework of social presence: Gaze. *ReCALL*, *25*(1), 122–142.

Wigham, C. R., & Satar, M. (2021). Multimodal (inter)action analysis of task instructions in language teaching via videoconferencing: A case study. *ReCALL*, *33*(3), 195–213.

4 Number of learners

Do teachers' instructions change when they repeat the same lesson with only one learner?

One teacher in our corpus (Craig) repeated the same task sequence with a single learner (Kuzey). This chapter explores whether and how Craig's higher-level actions (HLAs), as well as the modal configuration and density of his lower-level actions (LLAs) varied as he delivered the instructions for the same task a second time with only one learner. We have shown in Chapter 3 that when a teacher repeats the same task, the instruction-giving HLAs become more efficient and LLAs (spoken language, gesture, gaze, and posture shifts) remain similar. As we explore Craig's data, we expect a comparable impact of task-repetition and will attend to the impact of the number of learners. Our research question, then, is:

> Are instruction-giving higher- and lower-level actions dependent on the number of learners?
>
> In other words, do instruction-giving higher-level actions and their multimodal composition differ when the same teacher repeats the same task with only one learner?

This chapter begins with a description of the site of engagement and how it differs when only one learner is present. We then provide a comparative analysis of the HLAs observed in Craig's first iteration of this lesson with two learners (Eda and Didem) and second iteration with one learner (Kuzey). Next, we select two sets of HLAs: those that were similar and those that were different, to explore how LLAs accomplish the HLAs. This involves, first, an analysis of LLAs for the HLAs of COMMUNICATING KEY TASK INFORMATION, FOCUSING ON TASK ACCOMPLISHMENT, SUGGESTING WAYS INTO TASK, and LAUNCHING THE TASK. Second, in the second iteration, we observe two failed task starts by Kuzey following LAUNCHING THE TASK. We, thus, investigate the LLAs within this HLA to understand the causes of failed task starts, but also the ways in which Craig remedies the problem leading to successful task accomplishment. Chapter 4 ends with a comparison of modal configuration and density analysis to explain the key factors in this process. All full-size Figures, Extracts and Tables that

DOI: 10.4324/9781003274216-4

accompany this chapter are available in colour at https://doi.org/10.25405/data.ncl.20315142.

The main argument we put forth in this chapter is that the teacher's instruction-giving HLAs and LLAs somewhat differed when there was only one learner. First, regarding MANAGING RESOURCES: When teaching two learners, the teacher engaged with the HLA CONFIRMING ACCESS TO THE (CORRECT) RESOURCE early on in the instruction-giving sequence. In the second iteration with one learner, the learner's lack of access to the resource led to *semiotic misalignment* between the teacher and the learner's interactional space. This appeared to be one reason why the learner could not follow the instructions. Second, when teaching a single learner, Craig's instructions-as-process largely foregrounded the print mode in his attention/awareness leading to less intense use of his embodied modes. As such, his interaction with the resource sheet gained higher density in comparison to his interaction with the learner. That said, the teacher's embodied modes were visible on the learner's screen and were foregrounded on his attention/awareness continuum. This mismatch of foregrounded modes in each social actor's attention/awareness appeared to have led to *semiotic density misalignment* (see Chapter 3), and to a failed task launch attempt. Thus, we propose that MANAGING RESOURCES (particularly SENDING THE RESOURCE and CONFIRMING ACCESS TO THE (CORRECT) RESOURCE) is an essential HLA, even when there is only one learner and one resource to be shared.

As we progress with our qualitative analyses, we make other arguments throughout which are not necessarily related to class size but are relevant to instruction-giving in online teaching in general. Chapter 6 provides a summary and discussion.

4.1 Number of learners: site of engagement

As previously shown for the first task iteration with two learners (Wigham & Satar, 2021), a screenshot (Figure 4.1) taken at 28 minutes 42 seconds from the teacher's screen recording allows us to analyse the different social practices within Craig's site of engagement. The primary difference between the site of engagement for Craig's lesson with one learner is that it involves three rather than four social actors [A]: the teacher participant, Craig, and the learner, Kuzey, portrayed in their moving webcam images; and one of the two principal investigators in the research portrayed in the print mode through a generic Skype profile image. The large-scale action of *partaking in a research project* remains evident for Craig through the software icon in the toolbar for a screen-recording programme used to capture the interaction data [B] and the presence of the non-participant researcher [A]. Independent of the number of learners, the participants are engaged in the second large-scale action of *participating in an online language lesson via videoconferencing*. This social practice is shown in the sidebar through the name of the videoconferencing

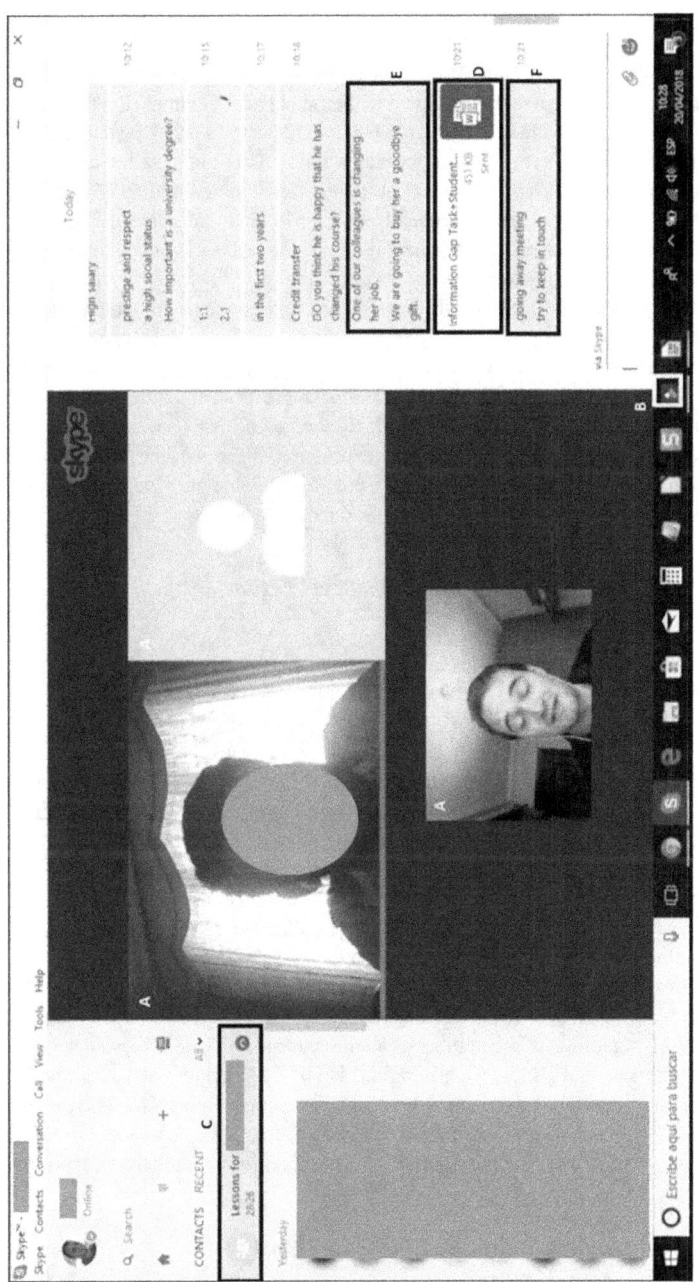

Figure 4.1 The teacher's (Craig) site of engagement when teaching one learner (Kuzey)

call "Lessons for Craig and Kuzey" [C] as well as the participants' (learner and teacher) webcam images [A].

The two HLAs of *completing a language-learning task* and *giving instructions for a convergent task* are evident in the frozen actions entailed in the electronic resources visible in the textchat window that shows a task resource, that is, handout for the learner with information required to complete the task [D], task instructions [E], and some lexical items offered as scaffolding [F]. All of these HLAs were presented bimodally through spoken and written language modes, which then became frozen actions contained in the print mode (textchat).

As Figure 4.1 illustrates, the webcam framing portrays Kuzey [A] with his back to a window with bright light streaming into the room, which meant that Kuzey's face was not clearly visible. At times, Kuzey also experienced technical difficulties: his webcam feed sometimes froze or reverted to a still profile image. This had implications both for the teacher participant in his interactions and later for the social practice of *analysing the research data*. Indeed, the modes of gaze and facial expression and sometimes proxemics, posture, gesture, and head movement were not available or difficult for Craig to draw upon in interaction and for subsequent data analysis.

4.2 Number of learners: higher-level actions in task instructions-as-process

To understand the similarities and differences in Craig's HLAs between the first and second iterations of the same task instructions, we focus on the HLAs present in Lesson 2, Micro-task 1 of the information-exchange task: comparing and contrasting two gift-package deals for a colleague's leaving gift to decide which one to purchase (Chapter 2 and Appendix 1). Table 4.1 shows Craig's HLAs for both iterations. In the first column, we have assigned numbers to each HLA. The second and fourth columns are the timestamps taken from the teacher's screen recordings, indicating the onset of each HLA. Columns three and five show the task instructions-as-process HLAs identified using the framework we present in Figure 6.1. As in the previous chapter, HLAs are colour-coded to increase readability and make patterns salient.

Similar to what we observed in Chapter 3, an exploration of the impact of task repetition on instruction-giving HLAs, Table 4.1 indicates that the second iteration, regardless of the number of learners, is more efficient. *launching the task* with Eda and Didem (first iteration) is HLA 27 taking place after about 6 minutes 30 seconds from the onset of the instruction giving. However, with Kuzey (second iteration), the first task launch occurs at HLA 16 about 4 minutes 15 seconds after the initiation of the instruction-giving mediated actions. Primary HLAs employed in both iterations are:

- ACTIVATING SCHEMATA,
- FORMULATING TASK STAGES,

Table 4.1 Craig's higher-level actions in task instructions-as-process

No	Time	with Eda and Didem (first iteration)	Time	with Kuzey (second iteration)
1	00:15:53.500	Activating schemata	00:20:16.320	Formulating task stages
2	00:16:57.742	Formulating task stages	00:20:47.160	Activating schemata
3	00:17:15.700	Focusing on study skills	00:21:52.454	Managing resources
4	00:17:57.210	Managing resources	00:22:06.409	Activating schemata
5	00:18:20.435	Formulating task stages	00:22:48.759	Managing resources
6	00:18:24.424	Managing resources	00:23:59.893	Focusing on task accomplishment
7	00:18:47.431	Identifying task rationale	00:23:29.460	Managing resources
8	00:8:50.136	Stating task outcome	00:23:54.070	Defining roles
9	00:18:56.333	Communicating key task information	00:23:55.425	Communicating key task information
10	00:19:11.978	Activating schemata	00:23:57.400	Managing resources
11	00:19:22.872	Communicating key task information	00:24:13.990	Communicating key task information
12	00:19:33.331	Formulating task stages	00:24:17.630	Focusing on task accomplishment
13	00:19:34.892	Focusing on task accomplishment	00:24:25.970	Stating task outcome
14	00:19:36.790	Stating task outcome	00:24:30.110	Checking understanding (of task)
15	00:19:42.676	Suggesting ways into task	00:24:31.508	Suggesting ways into task
16	00:19:54.078	Focusing on task accomplishment	00:24:37.292	Launching the task
17	00:19:55.608	Managing resources	00:24:44.070	Task (1st failed attempt)
18	00:20:07.924	Suggesting ways into task	00:25:54.362	Managing resources
19	00:20:11.100	Managing resources	00:25:57.602	Focusing on task accomplishment
20	00:20:44.659	Allocating time (for reading the resource)	00:26:01.277	Managing resources
21	00:20:47.750	Managing resources	00:26:08.541	Launching the task
22	00:20:58.600	Formulating task stages	00:26:14.080	Task (2nd failed attempt)
23	00:21:01.825	Communicating key task information	00:27:08.471	Checking understanding (of task)

(Continued)

Table 4.1 Continued

No	Time	with Eda and Didem (first iteration)	Time	with Kuzey (second iteration)
24	00:21:15.979	Focusing on task accomplishment	00:27:13.716	Managing resources
25	00:21:20.666	Suggesting ways into task	00:28:36.112	Communicating key task information
26	00:22:14.722	Launching the task	00:28:43.150	Launching the task
27	00:22:18.276	Task	00:28:54.470	Allocating time (for reading the resource)
28			00:29:06.357	Communicating key task information
29			00:29:12.213	Focusing on task accomplishment
30			00:29:13.930	Stating task outcome
31			00:29:17.772	Managing resources
32			00:29:45.943	Launching the task
33			00:29:55.190	Task

- MANAGING RESOURCES,
- COMMUNICATING KEY TASK INFORMATION,
- FOCUSING ON TASK ACCOMPLISHMENT,
- STATING TASK OUTCOME,
- SUGGESTING WAYS INTO TASK, and
- LAUNCHING THE TASK.

In Table 4.1, in the second iteration with the single learner, we observe two failed attempts at task initiation. The teacher, Craig, then clarifies the instructions with two additional instruction-giving sequences (HLAs 18–21 and 23–34), following which the learner embarks on the task.

During HLAs 18–21, based on Kuzey's responses regarding cultural differences (i.e. in Turkey, colleagues do not buy gifts for staff who are leaving), Craig explains that gift-giving is common practice in the USA and UK. He makes references to the document (the task resource sheet) [D] sent in the textchat (MANAGING RESOURCES) to illustrate a gift idea, while FOCUSING ON TASK ACCOMPLISHMENT and re-launching THE TASK.

Kuzey's second failed attempt at task initiation involves generation of ideas for the gift, but these differ from the idea presented in the task resource sheet. This prompts Craig to offer further clarification to ensure learner access to the task resource sheet (MANAGING RESOURCES) through which he enacts the HLAs CONFIRMING ACCESS TO THE (CORRECT) RESOURCE, COMMUNICATING KEY TASK INFORMATION, ALLOCATING TIME to read the resource, and re-LAUNCHING THE TASK after repeating FOCUSING ON TASK ACCOMPLISHMENT and STATING TASK OUTCOME (HLAs 23–32).

Post-lesson, Craig attributed interactional trouble (Kuzey's misunderstanding of task instructions) to: (1) student's lack of awareness of the textchat as a semiotic resource (thus, we see the impact of *semiotic misalignment* which we elaborate upon further in this chapter), (2) student's temporal inability to understand the instructions clearly (e.g. *having a bad day, bad connection*), and (3) class size, that is, lack of a second learner (impact of lack of social learning and interaction opportunities).

> Craig (interview, 29:10): "I didn't really have any problems with Eda and Didem because if they didn't understand they had each other from which to bounce off of as well which is great you know they were helping each other and we were moving things along very logically. . . . Kuzey had trouble understanding the information gap activity. He didn't really know firstly that it was an information gap activity because he couldn't see the side board (textchat window) and secondly he didn't really know what was expected so I had to walk him through it a lot slowly than I did with the other ones there but it was apparent from his answers and also his kind of body language and facial activity that he doesn't really understand what's

going on. . . . That's nothing really to do with students it's just like the task, the student could be having a bad day, the connection could be bad something like this. So you occasionally do have that but normally it's not a big problem, you can get there in the end."

While we are unable to interpret Kuzey's potential technical issues on the day (because it was not possible to interview this participant), in the lesson recordings we observe a key difference in the HLA MANAGING RESOURCES, particularly at the secondary-level HLA CONFIRMING ACCESS TO THE (CORRECT) RESOURCE. As shown in Table 4.1 with Eda & Didem, Craig engages with CONFIRMING ACCESS TO THE (CORRECT) RESOURCE early on (HLA 6) as soon as he *sends, allocates,* and *opens the resource* (HLA 4). However, with Kuzey, Craig does not confirm the learner's access as part of his initial instructions (HLAs 3–5), but only does so at HLA 24 when repairing Kuzey's failed second attempt. In Wigham and Satar (2021), we portrayed Craig's engagement with the print mode within MANAGING RESOURCES and highlighted its increased salience when teaching online. Here, we observe that even experienced online teachers may forget to confirm learners' access to the resource, especially when there is a single learner. As such, lack of CONFIRMING ACCESS TO THE (CORRECT) RESOURCE appears to be the most relevant explanation for the reason underlying Kuzey's failed attempts at task accomplishment. In inperson pedagogical settings, CONFIRMING ACCESS TO THE (CORRECT) RESOURCE can be accomplished through object handling and gaze modes: the teacher can physically hand out the resource sheets and then observe whether the learners have access to and are engaged with the task resource. However, when teaching online, CONFIRMING ACCESS TO THE (CORRECT) RESOURCE needs to be accomplished through spoken or written language modes, and often learners' access is not visually evident. Therefore, spoken and/or written language modes essentially have high modal intensity for the accomplishment of this HLA.

4.3 Number of learners: lower-level actions in task instructions-as-process

In this section, we investigate the multimodal configuration of Craig's HLAs during both iterations of Lesson 2 to question whether and in which ways Craig's HLAs were similar or different when delivering the same task instructions a second time but to a single learner. In Section 4.3.1, we analyse two extracts where the instruction-giving HLAs were the same and were presented in the same order. In section 4.3.2, we then investigate the HLA MANAGING RESOURCES to explore LLA configuration, why the missing secondary-level HLA CONFIRMING ACCESS TO THE (CORRECT) RESOURCE in the second iteration with one learner caused trouble, and how it was remedied.

4.3.1 Multimodal composition of similar higher-level actions prior to launching the task with different number of learners

We take two extracts where four task instructions-as-process HLAs were the same and presented in the same order (Table 4.1): Extract 4.1 for the HLAs 23–26 for the lesson with Eda and Didem (first iteration) and Extract 4.2 for the HLAs 11–12 and 15–16 for the lesson with Kuzey (second iteration).

Extract 4.1 demonstrates Craig's HLAs for this instruction-giving sequence consisting of COMMUNICATING KEY TASK INFORMATION (Frames 1–10), FOCUSING ON TASK ACCOMPLISHMENT (Frames 11–15), *suggesting ways into task* (Frames 16–27), and LAUNCHING THE TASK (Frames 28–31). Frame 1 shows the teacher's screen layout with the learners' moving images displayed one above another (Didem above and Eda below), as well as the researcher's still profile image. We also see the textchat window that was visible for the teacher throughout this extract. The extract starts after Craig has shared the task resource sheets and assigned them to each learner. The resource sheets continue to be available in textchat and, thus, the HLAs relevant to MANAGING RESOURCES (including ALLOCATING THE RESOURCE, and CONFIRMING ACCESS TO THE (CORRECT) RESOURCE – see Extracts 4.3 and 4.4) are frozen actions available in the print mode.

For the first HLA COMMUNICATING KEY TASK INFORMATION (Frames 1–10), we observe that Craig employs the following modes:

- Gaze shifts between the learners and the textchat window (most visible at Frames 3 and 8), potentially evidencing his attention to the "similar but different" task resource sheets available in print mode while referring to the documents in the spoken language mode. Although the contents of the documents are unavailable, the document previews show different gift package prices, and document titles involving learner names and the expressions "Student A" and "Student B." The print mode also appears to act as a reminder for the frozen HLAs of Craig adding learner names to the document titles during lesson preparation;
- Spoken language with enunciated pronunciation for the key words "slightly different" (Frame 4), "also good value" (Frame 9), and "different benefits" (Frame 10);
- Head movement (lateral tilt, Frame 8) while referring to "the other" in the spoken language mode;
- Hand (beat) gestures in Frames 8 and 10;
- Accentuated facial expressions, especially raised eyebrows and wide-open eyes, particularly with high intensity in Frames 9 and 10 while emphasising similarity ("also") and "different benefits" included in the different task resources.

70 *Number of learners*

Overall, Frames 8–10 which conclude COMMUNICATING KEY TASK INFORMATION are high in modal complexity, which assists in foregrounding the importance of delivering essential information for task completion within the teacher's attention/awareness continuum. Given all these modes are also available to the learners through the teacher's webcam image, it is likely that the same HLAs are also foregrounded in their attention/awareness (Norris, 2020).

The second HLA, FOCUSING ON TASK ACCOMPLISHMENT (Frames 11–15) demonstrates similar modal complexity as Craig delivers a modally dense summary of how learners should accomplish the task (Frame 15). We observe a quick gaze shift between the textchat (task resources in print mode) and the learners (Frame 14), followed by a modal configuration employing spoken language (with stress on the verb "talk"), facial expressions (raised eyebrows, wide-open eyes, accentuated lip movements), and a small head tilt.

The third HLA SUGGESTING WAYS INTO TASK (Frames 16–27) is that one learner can take the lead by describing the benefits of the gift package using their task resource sheet. Craig employs spoken language mode in all the frames, except Frame 27, with raised intonation in Frames 17 and 20 when he talks about the action ("describe") and the object ("benefits"). Frame 18 shows his head tilt accompanying the phrase "the other" in the spoken language mode. Between Frames 20–26, we observe a sequence of hand gestures delivered with the words "benefits," "package," and "talk" (Frames 20, 22, 25, 26). We also observe dynamic head movements and intense facial expressions (Frames 20, 21, 25, 26) as well as a gaze shift directed towards textchat (Frame 20). Frame 27 shows a silent period of 1.42 seconds during which Craig intensely directs his gaze towards the learners with a slight head tilt, awaiting learner response to his question "Who wants to begin?" (Frame 26).

The final HLA in Extract 4.1, LAUNCHING THE TASK, is accomplished by a combination of four modes. We observe:

1) A gaze shift towards the task resources (Frame 29), followed by a direct gaze;
2) An imperative ("tell us") and a vocative ("Didem") in the spoken language mode, which ends (Frame 30) with 0.30 second silence;
3) A head tilt in head movement mode;
4) A backwards move in the mode of proxemics.

In what follows, Didem embarks on task completion successfully.

In Extract 4.2, we now explore how the same four HLAs were conveyed in Craig's second iteration:

1) COMMUNICATING KEY TASK INFORMATION (Frame 1);
2) FOCUSING ON TASK ACCOMPLISHMENT (Frames 1–3);
3) SUGGESTING WAYS INTO TASK (Frames 5–8);
4) LAUNCHING THE TASK (Frames 9–14).

Number of learners 71

Extract 4.1 First iteration with two learners – teacher's screen

72 *Number of learners*

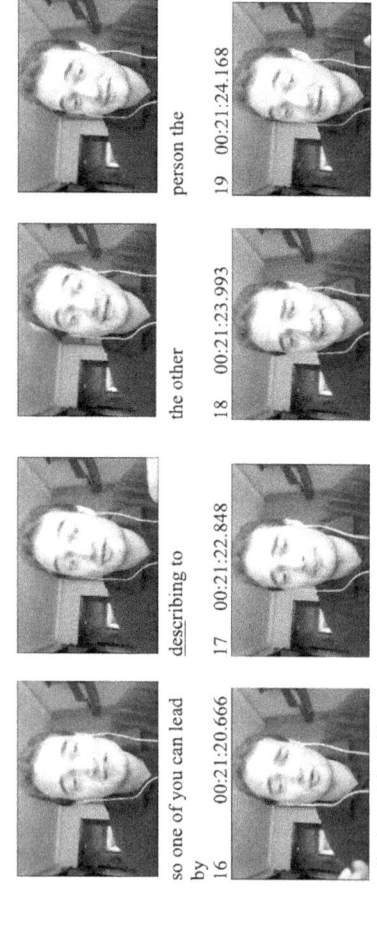

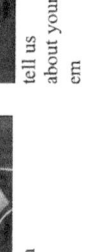

so one of you can lead by   describing to   the other   person the   bene
16 00:21:20.666   17 00:21:22.848   18 00:21:23.993   19 00:21:24.168   20 00:21:25.441

talk about things like   p   rice (0.31) talk about   benefits that they   package (0.16) yeah
                                               things like the   include with the e::r   uhm who wants to
                                                                        with the   begin?
22 00:21:27.317   23 00:21:28.778   24 00:21:28.934   25 00:21:30.596   26 00:21:33.187

fits of the package
(0.20) okay
21 00:21:25.739

(1.42)

27 00:21:35.810   so uhm   tell us
                                                                                    about your package Did
                                                                                    em
                    28 00:21:13.661   29 00:22:14.722   30 00:22:15.966

(0.30)
31 00:22:17.648

((00:21:37.242 - 00:22:13.700: Following learner silence, Craig suggests flipping a coin. Eda indicates that she is having an internet connection problem. Craig establishes that Eda can still hear them and dedicates Didem as the person to start ("Didem you're the person that leads off yeah") while Eda waits for her connection to restabilise.))

Extract 4.1 (Continued)

Compared to these equivalent HLAs in the first iteration, we observe that the print mode is foregrounded in Craig's attention/awareness throughout the first three HLAs. During these frames, Craig's own webcam image is not visible on his screen, while Kuzey's webcam image does not show his facial expressions or gaze due to bright background. Therefore, the print mode carries high intensity for Craig with some object handling as the teacher scrolls up and down the resource sheet (Frames 2–4) and clicks on the URL for the online document needed for the next micro-task (Frame 5). Frames 3 and 4 demonstrate two other HLAs – which we did not observe in the first iteration – STATING TASK OUTCOME ("and then we'll talk about whether your gift or my gift is the best one to buy for Anne") and CHECKING UNDERSTANDING (OF TASK). The print mode remains foregrounded in Craig's attention/awareness during these two HLAs.

There are two relevant points to be made based on the comparison of Extracts 4.1 and 4.2.

First, as later revealed (Extract 4.5), Kuzey did not have access to the print mode (task resource sheet) during Extract 4.2. In the first iteration, Craig engaged with CONFIRMING ACCESS TO THE (CORRECT) RESOURCE early on (Table 4.1, HLA number 6), whereas in the second iteration, prior to Extract 4.2, this HLA was yet to be completed. During Frames 1–8, Craig did not screen share, nor explicitly instruct Kuzey to open the document sent on textchat. (We examine when and how he did the latter in Extract 4.5.) Thus, the teacher appears to have assumed that, potentially because there was only one learner, once he shared the document on textchat, the learner would automatically see and have access to the resource. However, it is highly likely that the leaner never noticed the document being sent, resulting in *semiotic misalignment* (Wigham & Satar, 2021) between the teacher and the learner's interactional space and leading to an unsuccessful task initiation (Table 4.1, row 17).

Second, in Extract 4.2, Frames 1.1–1.4, 2.1, 3.1–3.7, and 6.1–6.2 show Craig's webcam image as recorded by the researcher participant, which represents what the learner potentially had access to during these frames. Compared to Craig's pronounced facial expressions, gestures, and intonation in Extract 4.1, we observe in Extract 4.2 that these were less intense while the print mode was foregrounded in Craig's attention/awareness, except when he repaired a mistake in his instructions (Frames 3.4 and 3.5). While in Extract 4.1, Craig's gaze shifts briskly between textchat, which displays the task resource sheets, and the learners; in Extract 4.2, we observe fewer and less frequent gaze shifts with less animated eye and eyebrow movements.

In Extract 4.2 Frames 9–14, the final HLA LAUNCHING THE TASK is delivered differently. The print mode is no longer foregrounded in Craig's attention/awareness as he moves back to the videoconferencing window. His gestures, gaze, facial expressions, body movements, and head tilts become more animated, similar to those in Extract 4.1. Relatedly, in Extract 4.2, we observe Craig employing the following LLAs to accomplish this HLA:

1) Hand gestures (Frames 9–12);
2) Eyebrow movements in the mode of facial expression for emphasis (Frames 9–12);
3) Head tilts in head movement mode and an accompanying gaze shift (Frames 13–14);
4) In the spoken language mode, an imperative ("describe to me," Frame 9) followed by a silence of 2 minutes 37 seconds (Frames 13–14).

Therefore, the LLAs for LAUNCHING THE TASK were similar in both iterations. However, with one learner, Craig foregrounded the print mode in his attention/awareness during the other HLAs, which led to less intense use of his embodied modes. As such, his interaction with the resource sheet gained higher density for him compared to his interaction with the learner. That said, the learner's lack of access to the same resource sheet meant that only the teacher's embodied modes were visible on the learner's screen and his interaction with the teacher was foregrounded in his attention/awareness continuum. This mismatch of foregrounded modes in each social actor's attention/awareness appears to have led to *semiotic density misalignment* (see Chapter 3) and a failed task launch attempt.

4.3.2 Multimodal composition of managing resources with different number of learners

We now explore how the LLAs were configured across the two iterations for the HLA MANAGING RESOURCES. We first focus on the different ways in which the teacher achieved the secondary-level HLA SENDING THE RESOURCE with two learners (Extract 4.3, Frames 1–21) and with a single learner (Extract 4.4, Frames 1–13). We then explore ways in which the secondary-level HLA CONFIRMING ACCESS TO THE (CORRECT) RESOURCE was accomplished (Extract 4.3, Frames 22–29 and Extract 4.4, Frames 14–21). During the lesson with two learners, this HLA took place before *reading the content of the resource*. Whereas during the lesson with one learner, CONFIRMING ACCESS TO THE (CORRECT) RESOURCE was initially skipped and only acted upon when remedying the learner's misunderstanding of task instructions following two failed task initiation attempts (Extract 4.5).

Extract 4.3, Frames 1–21 show the HLA SENDING THE RESOURCE in the first iteration. It is completed in gaze, print and object handling modes, while other HLAs accompanying the action of *sending* are achieved in gaze, facial expression, gesture, and spoken language modes. In Frames 1–3, Craig initiates SENDING THE RESOURCE following ANNOUNCING NEXT TASK STAGE as he informs the learners that they will receive some information. In the spoken language

Number of learners 75

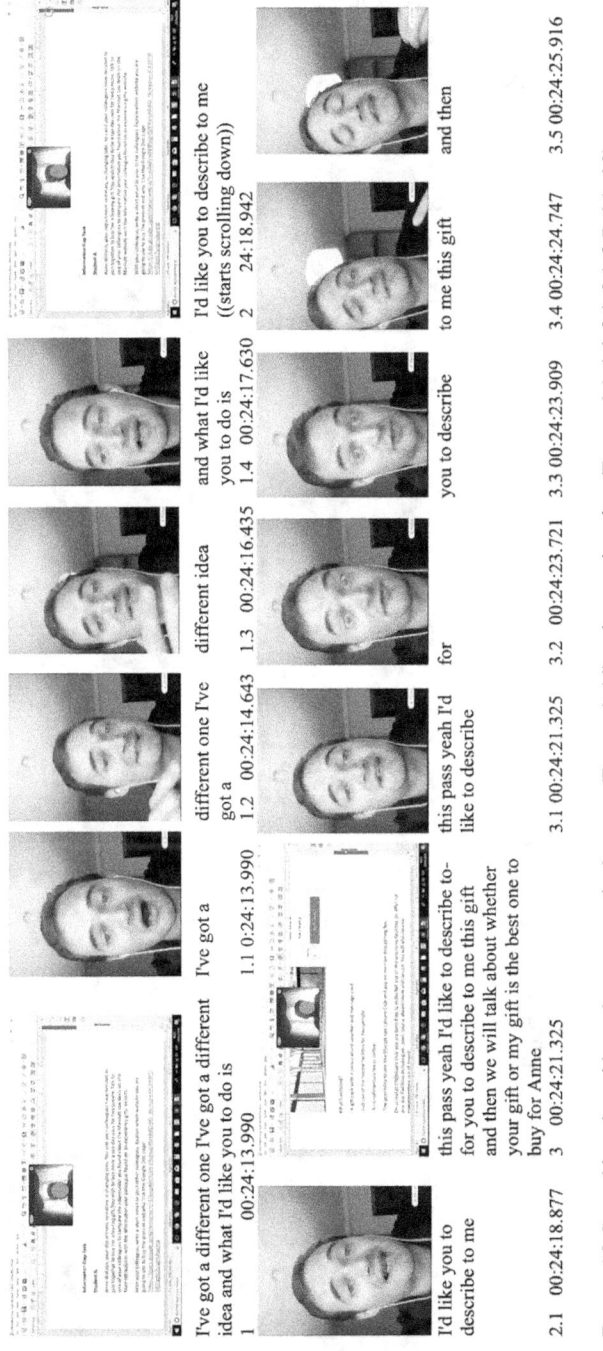

Extract 4.2 Second iteration with one learner – teacher's screen (Frames 1–14) and researcher view (Frames 1.1–1.4, 2.1, 3.1–3.7, 6.1–6.2)

76 *Number of learners*

Extract 4.2 (Continued)

mode, he emphasises the word "send" and produces a metaphoric gesture (Frame 2). These appear to reinforce the message for the action of *sending* a resource. In the gaze and object handling modes, however, Craig looks downwards (Frame 1) then upwards (Frame 2) as he moves his mouse and attention/awareness away from the videoconferencing window to his browser window (Frame 3) to access the electronic resource to be sent. As Frame 4 illustrates, the electronic resources are documents available online on a collaborative writing platform.

In Frames 4–14, Craig engages in SENDING and ALLOCATING THE RESOURCE sheets to each learner. SENDING THE RESOURCE again is achieved in the modes of gaze, print, and object handling: Craig looks downwards and locates (Frame 4), highlights, and copies (Frame 5) the URL from the first document, moves back to the videoconferencing window (Frame 6), pastes the URL in textchat (Frame 7), then sends it (Frames 12–13). The URL/resource becomes available to the learners in Frame 14. Next, in Frames 15–21, the same actions are repeated for SENDING THE RESOURCE for the other learner. In Frame 15, Craig selects the URL on the online document, copies it (Frame 17), moves to the videoconferencing window (Frame 18), pastes the URL in textchat (Frame 19), and sends it (Frame 20). The URL/resource becomes accessible to the learners in Frame 21.

During these frames, the mode of gaze is significant: the shift in gaze accompanying the spoken language mode indexes actions where Craig is solely interacting with the learners. In Frames 4–7, while SENDING THE RESOURCE, we observe a second HLA taking place ALLOCATING THE RESOURCE to one of the learners in the spoken language mode as Craig explains that he will first send the information for Eda. However, before allocating the second resource, Craig highlights whom the first resource is *not* sent for, that is, he tells the other learner, Didem, not to look at this first resource (Frames 8–12). In doing so, he raises his head, directs his gaze forwards, uses an iconic gesture (Frame 9) and intense facial expressions (raised eyebrows and wide-open eyes), while in the spoken language mode addressing the learner with a vocative. From Frames 8 to 12, he is not engaged in the print mode nor object handling, hence there is only one HLA foregrounded in his attention/awareness: ALLOCATING THE RESOURCE. Frame 16 demonstrates the success of this single-focus modal aggregate: Didem covers her face with her hand and turns away from her screen, signalling her understanding that the first instantiation of the HLA SENDING THE RESOURCE was addressed to her peer and that she should "not look at" the document.

In Frame 13, in the spoken language mode, Craig continues the HLA ALLOCATING THE RESOURCE. He repeats that the resource sent is for Eda (Frame 13), and that the one for Didem is to follow (Frames 14–16).

In Frames 16–19, while still utilising gaze, print, and object handling modes for SENDING THE RESOURCE, in the spoken language mode Craig completes the HLA DESCRIBING THE CONTENT OF THE RESOURCE and in Frames 20–21 ANNOUNCING NEXT TASK STAGE ("we'll read the context, we read the information") and FOCUSING ON TASK ACCOMPLISHMENT ("together"). Craig's gaze shift towards the learners in Frame 21 marks the end of SENDING THE RESOURCE.

Extract 4.4, Frames 1–13 demonstrate SENDING THE RESOURCE in the second iteration. Here, we also observe two HLAs taking place simultaneously. In Extract 4.3, while these were mainly related to MANAGING RESOURCES, in Extract 4.4, Frames 1–13, the overlapping HLAs are ACTIVATING SCHEMATA and SENDING THE RESOURCE. At the onset of Extract 4.4, in the spoken language mode, Craig is listening to Kuzey's response to a question regarding Turkish leaving-gift traditions addressed as part of the HLA ACTIVATING SCHEMATA. Yet, in the modes of gaze and object handing, we observe that Craig is engaged in SENDING THE RESOURCE (Frames 1–7) as he chooses to send the electronic resource file as an offline document via the document-sharing function of the textchat.

In Frame 1, we see Craig's gaze directed towards textchat and his mouse cursor over the attachment sign in the textchat window. In Frame 2, Craig selects the option to send a file, which triggers the file explorer window on his screen. In Frames 4 and 5, Craig navigates the file explorer window and selects the electronic resource to be sent. Selecting the file initiates the sending process (Frame 6) and the file is sent in Frame 7. During this time, Craig's gaze is downwards and appears to monitor the textchat window, that is, the process of resource sending, which is most evident in Frame 6. His facial expressions are not animated and he does not use the spoken language mode.

Once the resource sent (Frame 7), Craig produces a backchannel ("yeah") in the spoken language mode, his gaze returns to a more central position, which is accompanied by a head tilt. This signals that listening to the learner response is once again foregrounded in his attention/awareness. Unlike the first iteration, in which Craig uses a URL on a shared document on his browser and has access to at least one of the learners' moving images during SENDING THE RESOURCE; in the second iteration, the file browser becomes the sole focus in his attention/awareness while locating and sending the resource sheet. This causes *semiotic* and *modal density misalignment* since the teacher no longer has access to the videoconferencing window and the learner's and his own moving images.

Between Frames 7 and 8, the participants engage in further conversation related to Kuzey's response. Then, in the spoken language mode (Frames 8 and 9), Craig engages with the HLA SUMMARISING PREVIOUS TASK STAGE to indicate that he has sent the information needed ("well I've just sent you the activity yeah"). In Frame 10, he proceeds with the HLA OPENING THE RESOURCE as he requests Kuzey to do so. In Frames 11 and 12, he engages with ANNOUNCING THE NEXT TASK STAGE ("we'll read the information") and FOCUSING ON TASK ACCOMPLISHMENT ("together"). During these frames, his gaze shifts between right (Frames 8, 10, 12) and left (Frames 9, 11, 13), potentially between the learners

Extract 4.3 MANAGING RESOURCES: SENDING THE RESOURCE (Frames 1–21) and CONFIRMING ACCESS TO THE (CORRECT) RESOURCE (Frames 22–29) – first iteration with two learners

Extract 4.3 (Continued)

moving image and the textchat window, where the HLA SENDING THE RESOURCE is now frozen in the print mode and contains the reference to information mentioned in the spoken language mode, that is, the contents of the resource.

In both iterations, the modal configuration of SENDING THE RESOURCE is similar and is achieved in the gaze, object handling, and print modes. However, unlike the first iteration with two learners – where Craig first announces that he will send the resource as part of ANNOUNCING NEXT TASK STAGE and sends it while ALLOCATING and DESCRIBING THE CONTENT OF THE RESOURCE– in the second iteration with one learner, the announcement of the HLA SENDING THE RESOURCE in the spoken language mode comes in the form of the HLA SUMMARISING PREVIOUS TASK STAGE after the resource has been sent.

Another difference is that in Extract 4.3, Frames 1–21, Craig is actively engaged with the learners during SENDING, ALLOCATING, and DESCRIBING THE CONTENT OF THE RESOURCE in the modes of spoken language, gaze, gesture, and facial expressions, while simultaneously being engaged in object handling and print modes. This appears to ensure *modal density alignment:* the HLAs are not only foregrounded in Craig's attention/awareness but also potentially in the attention/awareness of the learners. However, in Extract 4.4, Frames 1–13, Craig is not engaged with the learner in his embodied modes during SENDING THE RESOURCE and quietly selects and sends the document in textchat while *responding to the teacher's question* was foregrounded in the learner's attention/awareness, thereby leading to *modal density misalignment.*

As we move on to the HLA CONFIRMING ACCESS TO THE (CORRECT) RESOURCE, we observe other differences between the two iterations. Extract 4.3, Frames 22–29 demonstrate how this HLA was achieved with two learners. Extracts 4.4, Frames 14–21 and 4.5 come from the iteration with a single learner demonstrating what happened when Craig did not confirm access right after SENDING THE RESOURCE and how he remedied this following two failed task initiation attempts.

In Extract 4.3, Frames 22–29, as soon as the resource is sent, Craig moves into the HLA CONFIRMING ACCESS TO THE (CORRECT) RESOURCE: his gaze is directed straight towards his screen (i.e. the learners in Frame 24), while in the spoken language mode he asks whether the learners have access to what has been sent. In Frame 25, he continues to look towards the screen with a tilted head allowing for a silence of 1 minute 19 seconds. In object handling, his cursor moves over the browser icon which shows a preview of one of the resource sheets that was sent (the resource sent for Student A, Eda). In Frame 25, Craig employs the HLA OPENING THE RESOURCE, and his utterance in the spoken language mode ("it takes a moment loading the Google documents yeah") acts as a signal for the learners to indicate with which action he is engaged. This utterance also demonstrates Craig's *critical semiotic awareness* (Guichon, 2013) regarding a potential *semiotic lag* (Wigham & Satar, 2021, p. 9), that is, that opening the electronic resource may take some time depending on the Internet connection speed and that the receiving actor(s) may have access to

82 *Number of learners*

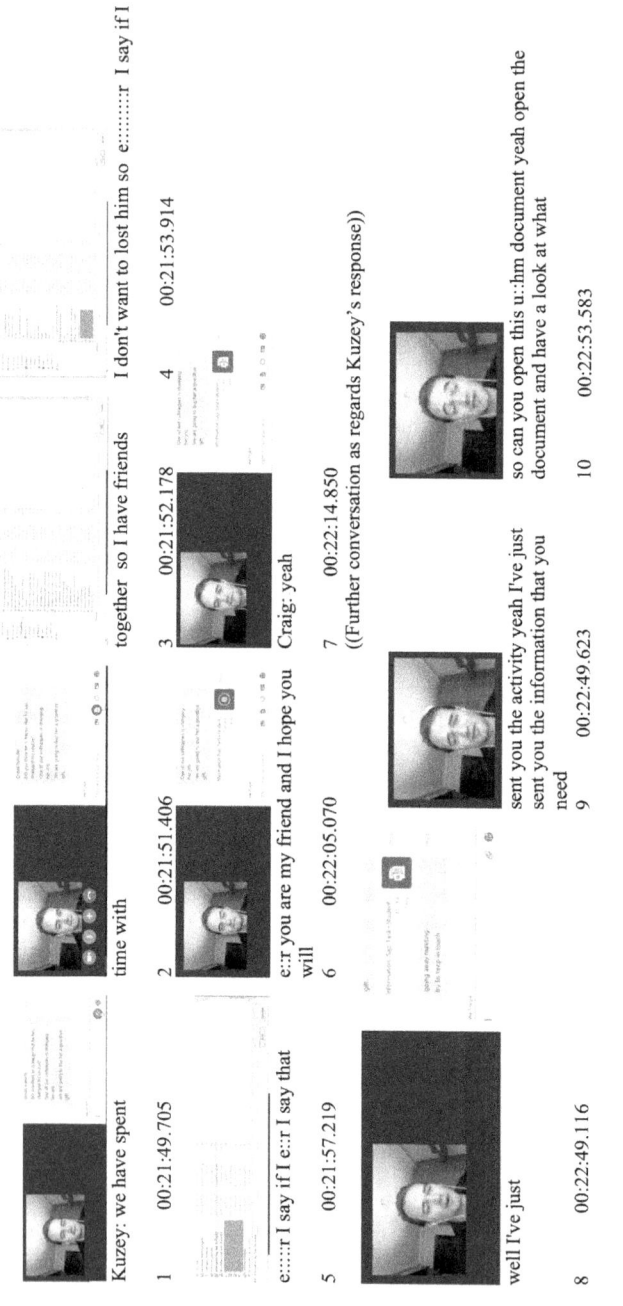

Kuzey: we have spent time with so I have friends together I don't want to lost him so

1 00:21:49.705   2 00:21:51.406   3 00:21:52.178   4 00:21:53.914

e:::::r I say if I e::r I say that e::r you are my friend and I hope you will   e:::::::r I say if I

5 00:21:57.219   6 00:22:05.070   Craig: yeah

7 00:22:14.850

((Further conversation as regards Kuzey's response))

well I've just sent you the activity yeah I've just sent you the information that you need   so can you open this u::hm document yeah open the document and have a look at what

8 00:22:49.116   9 00:22:49.623   10 00:22:53.583

Extract 4.4 MANAGING RESOURCES: SENDING THE RESOURCE (Frames 1–13) and CONFIRMING ACCESS TO THE (CORRECT) RESOURCE (Frames 14–21) – second iteration with one learner

it says and we'll read	the information	together before we do the activity	a u:::hm one of the e:r
11 00:11:480.141	12 00:23:00.661	13 00:23:01.758	14 00:23:17.739

Information Gap Task

Student A.

Anne Watson, your department secretary, is changing jobs. You and your colleagues have decided to join together to buy her a leaving gift. You wish to buy Anne a spa day pass for two people. Talk to one of your colleagues to compare the information you found about the Marriott spa deals on the Marriott website with the information your colleague found on an experience gifts website.

activities yeah we'd like to have a look at it together so	here is the u: here is the::: scenario the background yeah Anne Watson this is just a person she is our department secretary so she kind of looks after our department's administration yeah	she is changing jobs she is moving to a different company and we have decided that we want to buy her a leaving gift okay u::hm we want to buy Anne a spa day pass for two people so she can take a friend or maybe her husband to uhm the spa yeah so we're gonna talk together because we have discovered two possible ideas I've sent you one idea
15 00:23:20.479	16 00:23:23.304	17 00:23:36.486

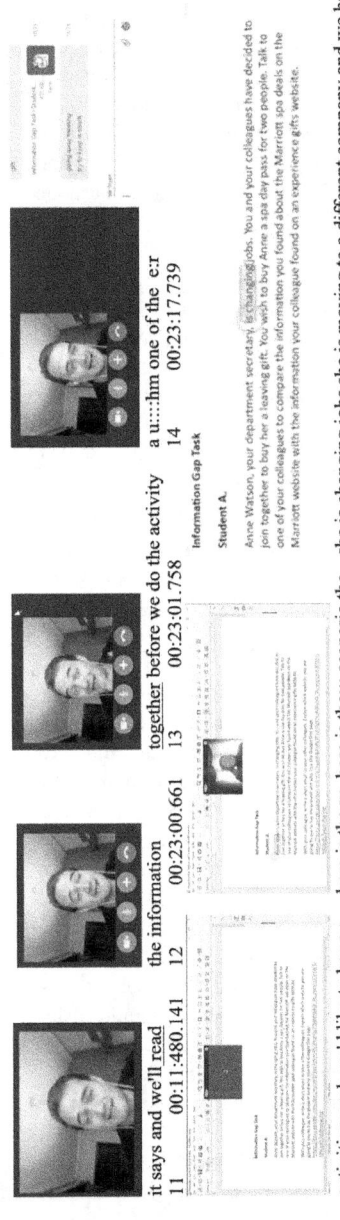

so if you scroll down if you scroll down	here you'll see the spa day pass	that you have okay? and it's got lots of information it's got where it is it's got the price who it is and it's got what's included in the price yeah	uhm I've got a different one I've got a different idea
18 00:23:59.501	19 00:24:01.679	20 00:24:04.224	21 00:24:13.308

Extract 4.4 (Continued)

the document at a different moment in interaction than its temporal position in the sending actor's attention/awareness.

In Frame 25, Didem (Student B) confirms access to the resource. Only then does Craig proceed with READING THE CONTENT OF THE RESOURCE. Visual confirmation, however, is only available in Frame 29 when a pink user icon appears in the top right corner showing that the learner (Eda) now has access.

The HLA READING THE CONTENT OF THE RESOURCE is foregrounded in Craig's attention/awareness as he articulates which part of the page he will read (Frame 26), and as he places his cursor at the top of the page in the print and object handling modes. Likewise, in Frame 27, he embodies the print mode and highlights the section he will read.

In this extract, we again see that when Craig is interacting with the learners, his gaze is directed towards the screen (Frames 23–24). Yet, when engaged in MANAGING RESOURCES, his gaze direction is predominantly downwards.

In the second iteration (Extract 4.4, Frames 14–21), Craig does not perform the HLA CONFIRMING ACCESS TO THE (CORRECT) RESOURCE but rather follows SENDING THE RESOURCE with the HLAs of ANNOUNCING NEXT TASK STAGE ("one of the activities, yeah," Frame 14), FOCUSING ON TASK ACCOMPLISHMENT ("look at it together," Frame 15), OPENING THE RESOURCE (Frame 15), DESCRIBING THE CONTENT OF THE RESOURCE ("here is the scenario, the background," Frame 16), READING THE CONTENT OF THE RESOURCE (Frames 16 and 17), FOCUSING ON TASK ACCOMPLISHMENT ("we're gonna talk together," Frame 17), ALLOCATING THE RESOURCE ("I've sent you one idea:," Frame 17), DESCRIBING THE CONTENT OF THE RESOURCE (Frames 18–20) and, ALLOCATING THE RESOURCE ("I've got a different one," Frame 21).

Except OPENING THE RESOURCE (Frame 17) – the multimodal construction of which involves object handling and gaze – all the HLAs in Extract 4.4, Frames 14–21, involve the spoken language mode. Similar to Extract 4.3, Frames 22–29, while READING THE CONTENT OF THE RESOURCE, Craig embodies the print mode as he selects and highlights (object handling) information he reads aloud (Frames 16–17). Print mode and object handling is again utilised for DESCRIBING THE CONTENT OF THE RESOURCE (Frames 18–20) as Craig scrolls up and down. This action enables him to foreground relevant information in his attention/awareness alongside the description in the spoken language mode. Therefore, the HLAs and LLAs accomplished in both iterations appear to be largely similar. Yet, although this proved to be a useful strategy in the first iteration (Extract 4.3, Frames 22–29), where Craig immediately sought confirmation of access upon sending the resource, in the second iteration with Kuzey (Extract 4.4, Frames 14–21), it is not yet clear whether the learner has access to the resource. As Craig does not screen share, highlighting information displayed in the print mode only serves to foreground the information for himself, and not for the learner.

Extract 4.5 shows how Craig engaged with the available modes to remedy the missing HLA CONFIRMING ACCESS TO THE (CORRECT) RESOURCE. In Frame 1,

Number of learners 85

Extract 4.5 MANAGING RESOURCES: CONFIRMING ACCESS TO THE (CORRECT) RESOURCE – second iteration with one learner

86 Number of learners

Extract 4.5 (Continued)

in the spoken language mode, Craig reminds Kuzey that he has sent a document, directing his attention to the textchat window in the spoken language and gesture modes (Frame 2). Frames 3 and 4 are the first time Craig delivers CONFIRMING ACCESS TO THE (CORRECT) RESOURCE in the spoken language mode with stress on the word "see" and raised eyebrows. In Frame 5, Craig waits for a confirmation with silence in the spoken language mode, sideways tilted head movement, and direct gaze towards the screen.

When, in Frame 6, Kuzey expresses his failure to locate the document, Craig explains that it is in the "message bar" as his gaze shifts towards textchat. In Frame 8, we see Craig holding the same listening posture. Kuzey still cannot locate the document, and in Frames 9–11, Craig refers to an icon on the videoconferencing window that will reveal the textchat. This is achieved through the spoken language and object handling modes as he moves his cursor towards this icon, gesture mode as he points to the icon, and facial expression mode as he raises his eyebrows. In Frames 12–16, his dynamic gestures (moving his hand back and forth in Frame 13) and explanation of how to use the icon in the spoken language mode foreground FACILITATING USE OF THE RESOURCE in his attention/awareness. This appears to assist Kuzey in locating the resource sheet: in Frame 16 the learner responds in the spoken language mode with "okay."

Yet, Craig seeks further clarification in the same mode and rearticulates the required action of *clicking* through shifts in gaze, spoken language, and facial expression (Frames 17–19). After waiting for about two seconds with the same head movement and facial expression modes as before (Frame 20), he embarks on DESCRIBING THE CONTENT OF THE RESOURCE (Frames 20–24). In Frame 22, we see a shift in object handling: Craig moves his cursor on his toolbar, which previews the documents. Frames 23–24 demonstrate how change in the print mode is utilised while DESCRIBING and READING THE CONTENT OF THE RESOURCE (similar to Extract 4.3, Frames 22–29 first iteration). The final confirmation for access comes in Frame 23, in the spoken language mode ("can you see the gift the spa package? yeah?"). The remediation of CONFIRMING ACCESS TO THE (CORRECT) RESOURCE is completed following a 12 second wait when Kuzey demonstrates comprehension using the spoken language mode ("o:::::h okay tamam huh uh, yeah," Frame 23), posture shifts by leaning backwards (Frame 25), and facial expression (smile, Frame 27).

To summarise, in this extract, we observe that Craig employs the following modal configurations to ensure access to the (correct) resource:

- Object handling combined with gaze shifts and descriptions in the spoken language mode (e.g. Frames 9–11, when Craig, shifting his gaze upwards, navigates his own mouse to the textchat icon and describes it as a "speech bubble");
- Hand gestures, both static (Frames 10, 12, 15) and dynamic gestures (Frame 13) with iconic and deictic properties, combined with spoken language ("at the top right of your screen, click");

- Accentuated facial expressions with raised eyebrows and wide-open eyes (e.g. Frames 10, 18, 22) combined with a deictic gesture and spoken language with enunciated pronunciation for key words ("can you *click*") and gaze directed towards the learner's webcam image;
- Silence in the spoken language mode combined with sideways head tilts (e.g. Frames 5, 8, 20) that communicate a listening posture and invite Kuzey to respond.

To conclude, in our comparison of the delivery of MANAGING RESOURCES with two learners and a single learner, we put forth three arguments. First, it appears that even when only a single learner is present, CONFIRMING ACCESS TO THE (CORRECT) RESOURCE and FACILITATING USE OF THE RESOURCE are essential for successful task delivery. It is important not to assume that the learner can receive, locate, open, access, and use the electronic resources without confirmation or guidance.

Second, another factor that leads to successful management of resources for the HLA SENDING THE RESOURCE appears to be the teacher's engagement with the learners by articulating their off-screen actions (which take place in the object handling and print modes) in the spoken language, gaze, and facial expression modes. This is likely to ensure that the learners are cognisant of what is foregrounded in the teacher's attention/awareness when there is *modal density misalignment* and can follow the task instructions.

Third, while CONFIRMING ACCESS TO THE (CORRECT) RESOURCE, a modal configuration of a short question followed by silence in the spoken language mode and a listening posture such as direct gaze and tilted head appears to provide sufficient opportunities for learners to declare (lack of) access. We observed in Extract 4.5 that when access to the resource had to be remedied, a series of LLAs in the modes of gesture, gaze, object handling, and facial expression was required to support the learner in locating and accessing the resource.

4.4 Modal configuration and modal density misalignment: *managing resources*

This section explores similarities and differences in the modal configuration and modal density (intensity and complexity) of Craig's instruction-giving LLAs for the HLA MANAGING RESOURCES, particularly when he sends task resources on textchat either in the form of a message, an offline word processor document, or an online collaborative document.

In relation to modal configuration, we observed little variety in Craig's multimodal organisation of LLAs in both iterations when the videoconferencing window was visible in his site of engagement. Figure 4.2 demonstrates representative frames for the HLAs SUGGESTING WAYS INTO TASK in iteration

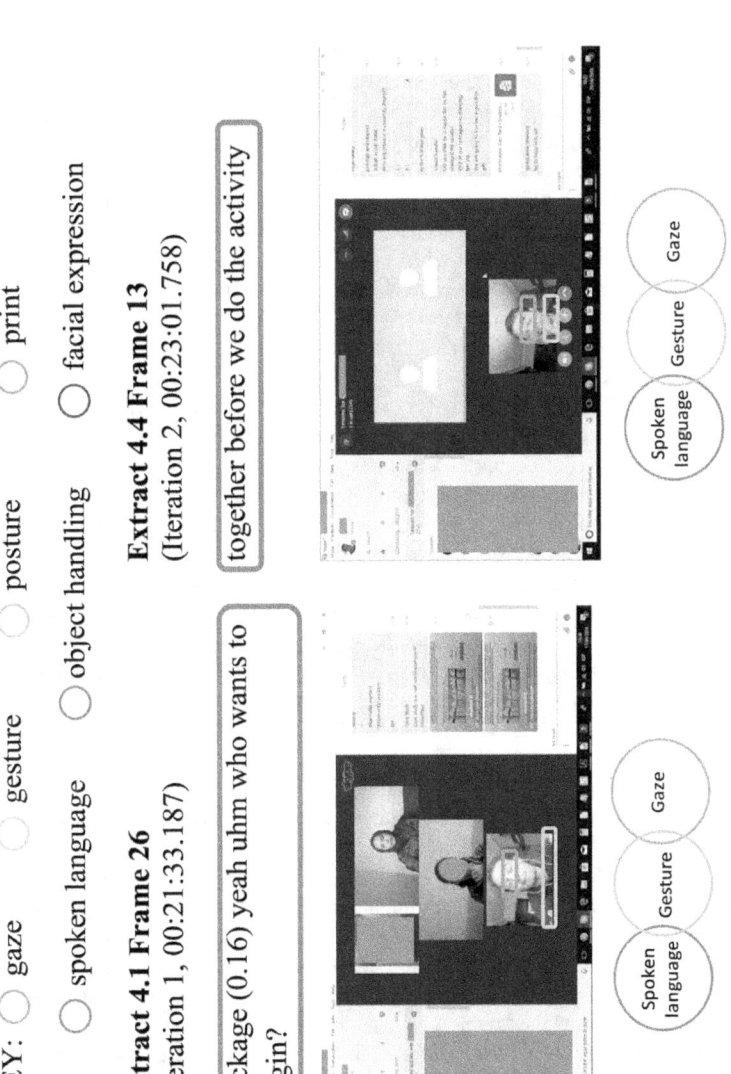

Figure 4.2 Craig's predominant modal configuration in the videoconferencing window

90 *Number of learners*

one, and FOCUSING ON TASK ACCOMPLISHMENT in iteration two. We see that in this screen layout, LLAs that compose the HLAs are performed in the spoken language, gesture, and gaze modes.

However, when the teacher interacted with electronic resources, during the HLA MANAGING RESOURCES, social actors' modal configuration differed during SENDING THE RESOURCE and READING THE CONTENT OF THE RESOURCE. Although it is difficult to claim with certainty whether variance was due to the number of learners, our data suggests this could well be the case.

We now explore how different modal configurations result in *semiotic* and *modal density (mis)alignment* through the presentation of three further modal configurations (Figures 4.3, 4.4, and 4.5).

Figure 4.3 focuses on SENDING THE RESOURCE. It illustrates how the social actors' videoconferencing layouts led to *semiotic misalignment* when a message was shared on textchat, whereas, when a document was shared via textchat both *semiotic* and *modal density misalignment* occurred. We expect that Kuzey's modal configurations were similar to the researcher's (and refer to this as the learner view, henceforth) because he did not experience trouble when messages on textchat were sent, but only when a document was shared through textchat.

Figure 4.3, Frame 7 (top) shows modal configurations when Craig sent a texchat message to Kuzey. Here, the print mode took on high modal density for both participants. For Craig (left), this was achieved through modal complexity: his directed gaze followed his typing and, once sent, the action of *sending a message* became accessible throughout the lesson as a frozen action in the print mode. For Kuzey (right), however, this was achieved through modal intensity: when a message was sent, the moving image of the social actor became darker and the messages sent on textchat were transposed on the actor's image, which likely created higher salience for Kuzey. Thus, print mode and the action of *sending a message* was foregrounded in both actors' attention/awareness continuum. Unfortunately, this *modal density alignment* lasted for a short period because textchat remained visible to the learner only for a few seconds before disappearing from Kuzey's site of engagement. Therefore, due to potentially different configurations of the site of engagement, in relation to the layout and temporality of modes, the print mode (textchat) did not carry the same intensity for the participants.

In contrast, Figure 4.3, Frame 6 (bottom) demonstrates *semiotic misalignment* when a document was sent through textchat. We observe that the modes that were foregrounded for Craig (left) were the same as those foregrounded when a message was sent on textchat. When he sent the document on textchat, SENDING THE RESOURCE became a frozen action, which Craig was able to later refer to later to remedy the trouble, as shown in Extract 4.5. However, for Kuzey (right), there was no indication of a document being sent: Kuzey only had access to the gaze mode (*semiotic misalignment*) and SENDING THE RESOURCE was not foregrounded for him (*modal density misalignment*). As explained in

KEY: ◯ gaze   ◯ gesture   ◯ posture   ◯ print
     ◯ spoken language   ◯ object handling   ◯ facial expression

Extract 4.4 Frames 7 and 6 Teacher and Researcher views
(Iteration 2, 00:22:14.850 and 00:22:05.070)

((Further conversation as regards Kuzey's response))

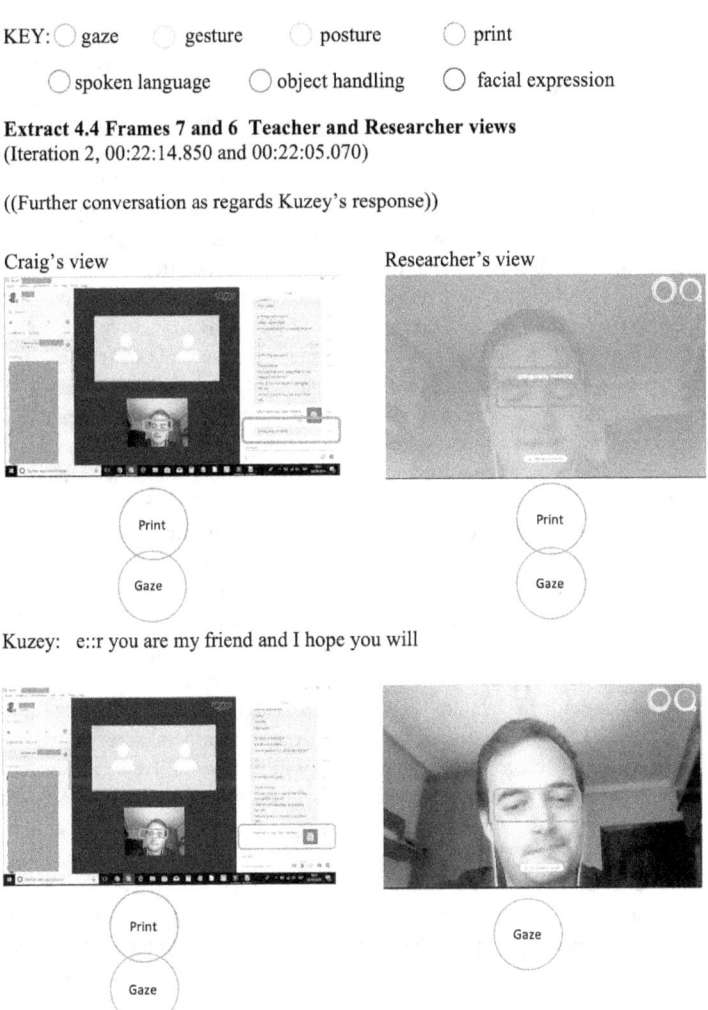

Kuzey: e::r you are my friend and I hope you will

Figure 4.3 Craig's and the researcher's modal configuration for the higher-level action MANAGING RESOURCES (SENDING THE RESOURCE) (semiotic and modal density misalignment) with one learner

Section 4.3.2, lack of foregrounding of the print mode in the learner's attention/awareness had major implications for access to electronic resources and understanding of task instructions.

Pedagogically, this indexes the need to, firstly, ensure *semiotic alignment* between the teacher and learners' interactional spaces whenever possible and, secondly, to not assume that these will correspond, or that the learner will have access to resources sent on textchat just because there is only one learner present. Unfortunately, we do not have data for the interactional space of the learners in the first iteration. However, given they did not experience any trouble accessing the resource, we fairly confidently assume three scenarios: (1) that there was *semiotic alignment*, that is, they had access to textchat at all times similar to Craig's videoconferencing window layout, or (2) that they were able to access textchat when required perhaps because Craig employed a different order of HLAs by first ANNOUNCING NEXT TASK STAGE (i.e. that he will send a resource – Extract 4.3) instead of SUMMARISING PREVIOUS TASK STAGE (i.e. that he has sent a resource – Extract 4.4), or (3) that the affordances of the videoconferencing environment meant that shared resources were made salient when adding a URL to an online document in the textchat, but not when an offline document was sent in the textchat through file share.

In Figure 4.4, we compare modal configurations during SENDING THE RESOURCE. In the first iteration, the same secondary-level HLAs of MANAGING RESOURCES was foregrounded in both Craig and the learners' attention/awareness. In the second, the teacher engaged in two HLAs simultaneously: SENDING THE RESOURCE and ACTIVATING SCHEMATA. Only ACTIVATING SCHEMATA, however, was foregrounded in the learner's attention awareness.

To consider what actions are foregrounded in the learners' attention/awareness, although we do not have data from the learners' screens, we use the researcher's screen recording as a proxy in Figure 4.4. Here, we see that none of the learners had access to the object handling and print modes when Craig engaged in SENDING THE RESOURCE. These modes are only available in Craig's site of engagement, which in both cases led to *semiotic misalignment* between the teacher and the learner(s) interactional spaces. In the first iteration, modal shifts produced by the teacher in the modes of spoken language, gesture, facial expression, and gaze are available to the learners and, thus, RECEIVING THE RESOURCE appears to be foregrounded in their attention/awareness. However, in the second iteration, the teacher's only noticeable modal shifts occur in the mode of gaze. As spoken language, gesture, and facial expression modes no longer form part of Craig's modal configuration, his facial expressions appear to carry less modal intensity. Although the HLA SENDING THE RESOURCE goes unannounced in the spoken language mode, Craig's gaze shifts away from the learner's webcam image (central position) (firstly directed to the lower right of the screen shown in Figure 4.4, top

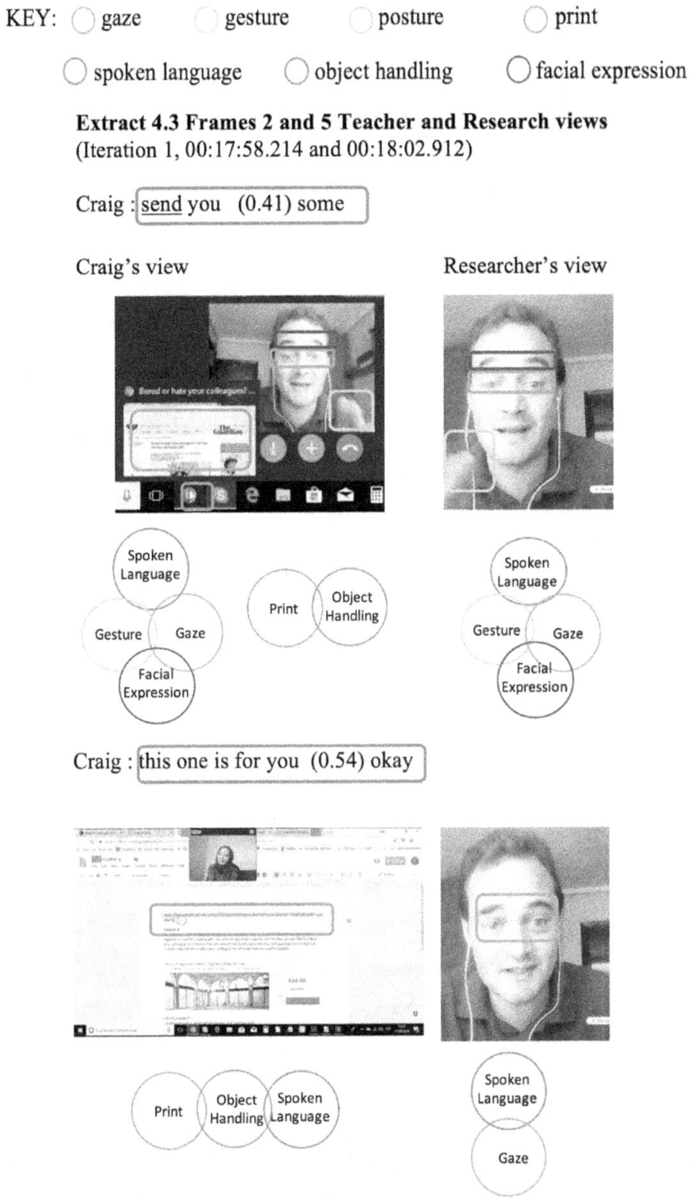

Number of learners 93

KEY: ◯ gaze ◯ gesture ◯ posture ◯ print
◯ spoken language ◯ object handling ◯ facial expression

Extract 4.3 Frames 2 and 5 Teacher and Research views
(Iteration 1, 00:17:58.214 and 00:18:02.912)

Craig : send you (0.41) some

Craig's view						Researcher's view

Craig : this one is for you (0.54) okay

Figure 4.4 Craig's modal configurations for the higher-level action SENDING THE RESOURCE in both iterations

94 *Number of learners*

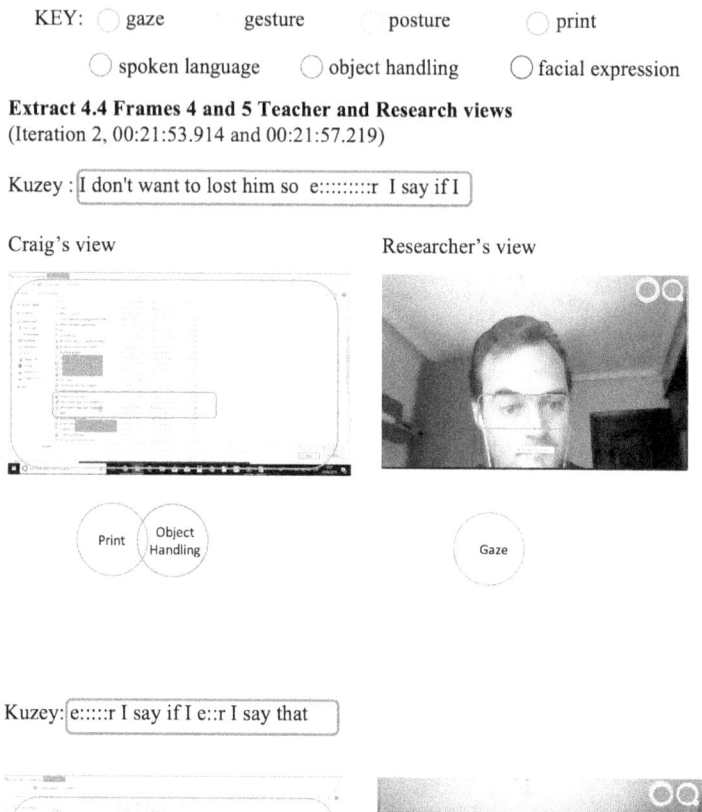

Figure 4.4 (Continued)

right, then to a mid-point on the left-hand side as in Figure 4.4, bottom right) could communicate a change in the teacher's modal configuration and, thus, attention/awareness. Accordingly, Craig's multitasking is potentially communicated by fewer gestures, less accentuated facial expressions, and gaze shifts. Yet, this does not seem to be the case as the learner does not recognise the resource sent on textchat. As we observe *modal density misalignment*, for the learner, Kuzey, ACTIVATING SCHEMATA appears to be the HLA foregrounded in his attention/awareness.

Finally, Figure 4.5 depicts modal configurations for READING THE CONTENT OF THE RESOURCE. We illustrate, despite seemingly similar modal configurations in both iterations, how the print mode – available through an online collaborative document in the first iteration – assists in achieving shared attention/awareness. In comparison, *semiotic misalignment* in the site of engagement between the teacher and the individual learner brings about *modal density misalignment* when an offline document is shared, in the second iteration.

Concerning the modal configurations of both iterations, there does not appear to be any salient differences either for the teacher or for the learners (again using the researcher's view as a proxy). When READING THE CONTENT OF THE RESOURCE, the print mode carries high intensity for Craig, along with spoken language and object handling as he highlights (Figure 4.5, top right) the sections of the resource he reads aloud and scrolls up and down (Figure 4.5, bottom right) the document. In both iterations, he can monitor one learner's moving image while focusing on the print mode. In contrast, for the learners, Craig's modal shifts in spoken language, gaze, and facial expression modes appear to be identical in both iterations. They again have access to neither Craig's modal shifts in the print nor object handling modes (highlighting and scrolling) since Craig does not screen share. All actors access the document, if they can, within their own site of engagement. Consequences of this *semiotic misalignment* include the learner's inability to access information that is foregrounded in Craig's attention/awareness continuum, thus, leading to *modal density misalignment* and an inability to follow the HLAs foregrounded in (inter)action.

Yet, this changes in the first iteration (bottom left) when, in Extract 4.3, Frame 29, we see evidence that one learner has joined the same resource sheet that Craig is utilising. Indeed, Eda now has access to the resource and the sections Craig highlights while READING THE CONTENT OF THE RESOURCE. Modal density for both Craig and the learner is now almost aligned as READING THE CONTENT OF THE RESOURCE becomes foregrounded in both their attention/awareness through modal intensity (modal aggregate: print and spoken language). Pedagogically, however, we do not observe Craig demonstrate any orientation towards acknowledging when learners sign in to the online document (beyond indicating that the document takes some time to load).

In summary, observation of task repetition with variance in number of leaners and in reference to modal configuration and density allows us to highlight a need for both modal configuration and density to be aligned between teacher and learner(s), with regards to foregrounding the print mode, in order for instructions and task launch to be successful.

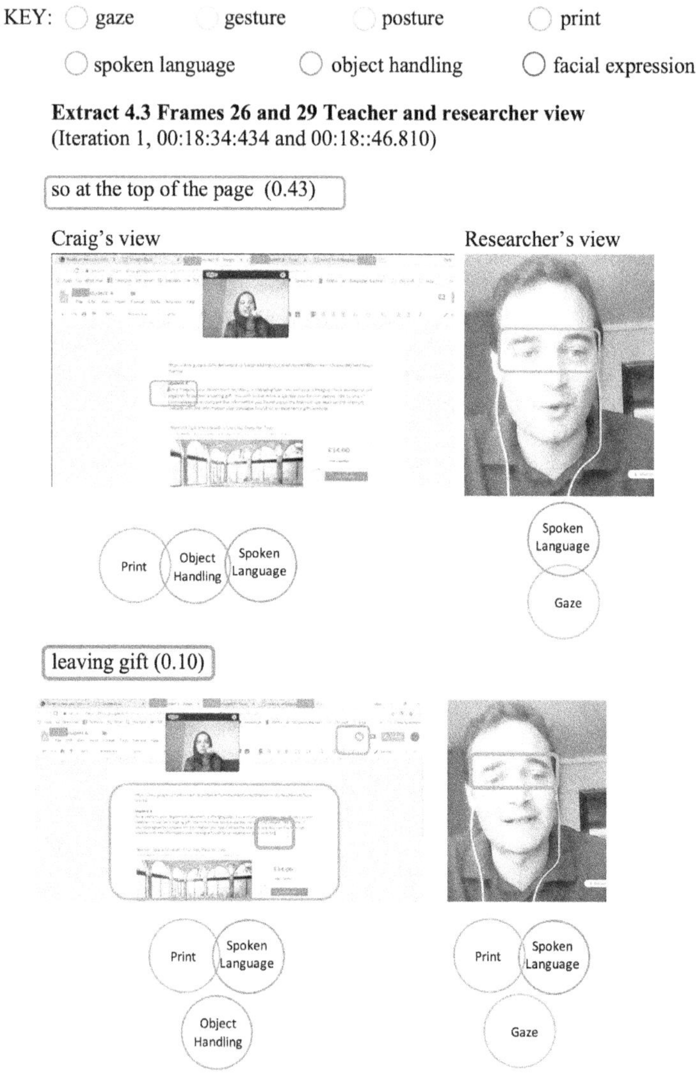

96 *Number of learners*

KEY: ○ gaze   ○ gesture   ○ posture   ○ print
○ spoken language   ○ object handling   ○ facial expression

Extract 4.3 Frames 26 and 29 Teacher and researcher view
(Iteration 1, 00:18:34:434 and 00:18::46.810)

so at the top of the page (0.43)

Craig's view   Researcher's view

leaving gift (0.10)

Figure 4.5 Craig's and the researcher's modal configuration during the higher-level action READING THE CONTENT OF THE RESOURCE: modal density (mis)alignment

Number of learners 97

KEY: ◯ gaze ◯ gesture ◯ posture ◯ print
◯ spoken language ◯ object handling ◯ facial expression

Extract 4.4 Frames 16 and 19 Teacher and researcher view
(Iteration 2, 00:23:23.304 and 00:24:01.679)

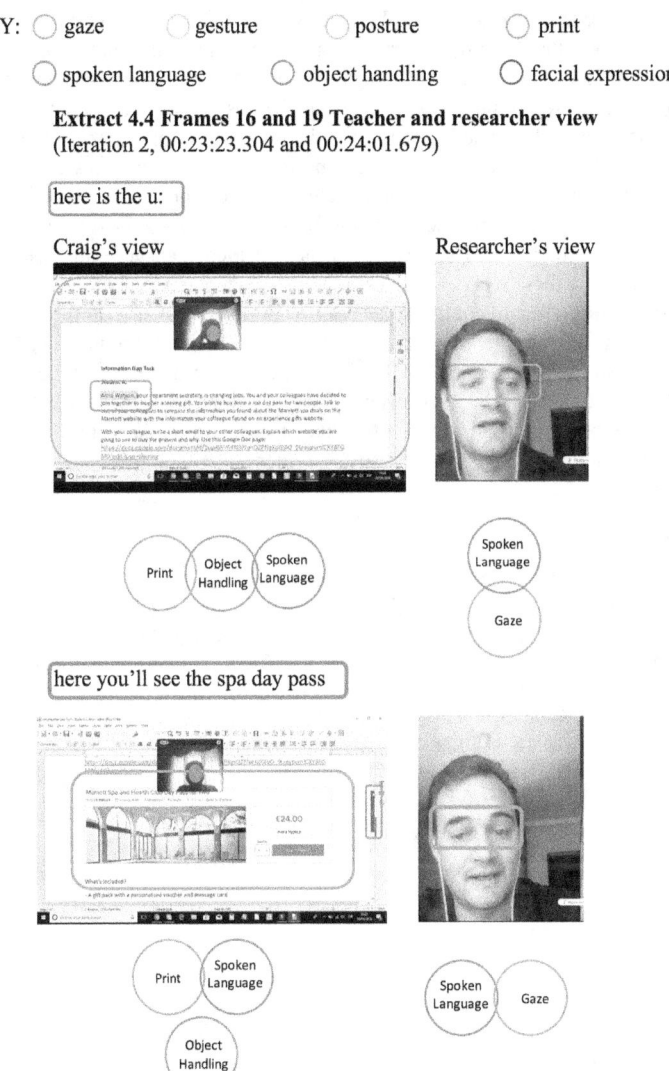

Figure 4.5 (Continued)

4.5 Chapter summary

This chapter examined whether instruction-giving HLAs and LLAs are dependent on the number of learners: do instruction-giving HLAs and their multimodal composition differ when the same teacher repeats the same task with one rather than two learners? We first examined Craig's site of engagement and showed that the only difference was in the number of social actors. Next, we compared the HLAs in the first and second iterations and demonstrated that there were two failed task attempts in the lesson with one learner. We then explored the HLAs and LLAs to shed light on the reasons for these failed attempts. We showed that LLAs for and prior to LAUNCHING THE TASK were similar in both iterations. However, there were differences on CONFIRMING ACCESS TO THE (CORRECT) RESOURCE, SENDING THE RESOURCE, and READING THE CONTENT OF THE RESOURCE. We identified two reasons, which resulted in unsuccessful task initiation during these HLAs in the lesson with one learner: (1) *semiotic misalignment* due to a lack of confirming access to the resource as soon as the resource was sent, and (2) *modal density misalignment* which foregrounded different HLAs in the teacher and the learner's attention/awareness continuum. We then illustrated how instruction giving was remedied at a micro-level. Finally, we explored similarities and differences in Craig's modal configuration in both iterations, which provided further evidence to our arguments.

References

Guichon, N. (2013). Une approche sémio-didactique de l'activité de l'enseignant de langue en ligne: Réflexions méthodologiques. *Education & Didactique*, *7*(1), 101–115. Retrieved from https://educationdidactique.revues.org/1679

Norris, S. (2020). *Multimodal theory and methodology: For the analysis of (inter)action and identity*. Abingdon: Routledge.

Wigham, C. R., & Satar, M. (2021). Multimodal (inter)action analysis of task instructions in language teaching via videoconferencing: A case study. *ReCALL*, *33*(3), 195–213.

5 Task type

Do teachers' instructions change when they give instructions for a different type of task?

Are instruction-giving higher- and lower-level actions task dependent? In other words, do instruction-giving higher-level actions (HLAs) and their multimodal composition differ when the same teacher gives instructions for a different type of task?

To answer this question, we compare the three teacher participants' HLAs in task instructions-as-process for the convergent role-play task (Lesson 2) with those for the divergent opinion-exchange task (Lesson 3). In Chapter 2, we introduced the details of the convergent and divergent tasks. The former included two micro-tasks, and the information-gap activity analysed in Chapters 3 and 4 was embedded in the first micro-task. For the divergent task, opinion-exchange was embedded in the second micro-task (Table 5.1).

The main arguments we will make in this chapter, are:

1 The convergent task required a greater number of HLAs to be relayed before learners embarked on task accomplishment.
2 The divergent task did not necessitate detailed instructions prior to task onset, but the process of task accomplishment resembled *instructional conversations* (Meskill & Anthony, 2015, 2018). Teachers were part of the conversations throughout the lesson orchestrating and corralling by asking questions to the learners, modelling, and saturating target language.
3 While modes and modal configurations for both tasks were similar, teachers' lower-level actions (LLAs) had higher multimodal density in the convergent task. This was due to a greater number of modal shifts performed in a shorter time. Here, in addition to Norris's (2009, 2019) identification of modal density (achieved through modal intensity or complexity), we propose that modal density can also be achieved through brisk modal shifts.
4 Teachers' own perspectives, as represented in the interviews, corroborated the observations above.
5 For the divergent task, teachers were asked to use a new resource: an interactive online whiteboard. In relation to this resource, we observed three

new HLAs under MANAGING RESOURCES: EDITING THE CONTENT OF THE RESOURCE, FACILITATING USE OF THE RESOURCE, and IDENTIFYING THE RESOURCE TYPE.

We begin by offering a comparison of task-as-workplan (resource sheet) and task-as-process (teachers' adaptations) for the opinion-exchange task because, unlike the convergent task, we observed differences in how the teachers adapted and presented the micro-tasks of the divergent task (Section 5.1). In Section 5.2, we then present the teachers' perspectives regarding the impact of task type on their behaviour. Section 5.3 explores how the HLAs for the convergent and divergent tasks compare: we investigate the existence of HLAs in all three teachers' lessons then compare the sequential employment of HLAs before learners start the task. In Section 5.4, we illustrate how HLAs in task instructions-as-process were multimodally presented with reference to the analyses we presented in Satar and Wigham (2020). In Section 5.5, we compare the two task types with respect to the teachers' multimodal configuration (on a single frame) and modal density (achieved through number of modal shifts). Finally, before providing a chapter summary, we present the new HLAs we observed for MANAGING RESOURCES (Section 5.6). A discussion of our key findings is offered in Chapter 6. All full-size Figures, Extracts and Tables that accompany this chapter are available in colour at https://doi.org/10.25405/data.ncl.20315142.

5.1 Divergent task micro-tasks: task-as-workplan versus task-as-process

As Chapter 2 describes, the task resource sheet (Appendix 2) for the divergent task was created by the researchers and shared with the teachers prior to the lessons. The teachers had flexibility to adapt the task according to teacher and learner needs. The resource sheet involved three micro-tasks designed as pre-, main-, and post-task stages (Micro-tasks 1, 2, and 3 respectively). Table 5.1 presents a description of each task stage (task-as-workplan) and each teacher's adaptation (task-as-process).

All teachers adopted a similar approach for Micro-task 1 (pre-task) and covered the suggested pre-task topics designed to activate schemata. Karen introduced the new resource – an interactive online whiteboard – at this stage, requesting learners to create a table of the food vegetarians do and do not eat. We examine this activity more closely in Section 5.6 to describe the new HLAs we observed.

We note that Micro-task 3 (post-task) was adapted differently by each teacher: Karen asked the learners to write an essay as homework; Craig created a convergent oral role-play task; and Sarah elicited verbal summaries and wrote these on the online whiteboard herself.

Task type 101

Table 5.1 Micro-tasks for the divergent task: task-as-workplan versus task-as-process

Micro-tasks	Resource sheet	Karen (G&E) – 60 minutes	Craig (D&E) – 60 minutes	Sarah (D & S) – 30 minutes
1	a) Describing vegetarianism b) Discussing what vegetarians do and do not eat c) Talking about familiarity with vegetarians	**00:00** Greeting learners; Giving feedback on writing homework; Introducing the lesson topic/task **21:21** a) Describing vegetarianism **24:44** c) Talking about familiarity with vegetarians **31:15** b) Discussing what vegetarians do and do not eat (online whiteboard)	**00:00** Greeting learners; Introducing the lesson topic/task **03:37** a) Describing vegetarianism **03:58** b) Discussing what vegetarians do and do not eat (based on the reading assigned at the end of Lesson 2) **04:47** c) Talking about familiarity with vegetarians	**00:00** Greeting learners; Confirming access to the task resource sheet **00:53** a) Describing vegetarianism **04:01** c) Talking about familiarity with vegetarians **06:54** b) Discussing what vegetarians do and do not eat
2	Sharing personal opinions for and against vegetarianism (ideas are provided, no requirement to defend or persuade)	**42:52** Eliciting learner opinions while taking notes in the textchat (ideas in the resource sheet are not shared with the learners)	**05:42** Eliciting learner opinions for and against vegetarianism (based on personal experience and choice) **16:31** Eliciting specific opinions in favour of vegetarianism (based on teacher-prepared arguments) **34:45** Eliciting specific opinions against vegetarianism (preparing the whiteboard)	**08:57** Eliciting learner opinions for and against vegetarianism **12:59** Eliciting further learner opinions for and against vegetarianism based on the ideas presented in the task resource sheet

(Continued)

102 Task type

Table 5.1 Continued

Micro-tasks	Resource sheet	Karen (G&E) – 60 minutes	Craig (D&E) – 60 minutes	Sarah (D & S) – 30 minutes
3	Summarising ideas shared on an online whiteboard	54:45 Assigning homework: requesting learners to write an opinion essay on the topic based on the ideas from the task resource sheet.	36:21 Requesting learners to role-play a debate to try and persuade one another and to identify the winner. (Learners could not access the whiteboard or a Google doc to write their summary.) 46:59 Offering feedback and recommendations	20:52 Summarising ideas elicited from the learners on a whiteboard (Learners dictate, teacher types.)
4			48:01 Using fillers to elicit further open-ended conversations related to the topic; Offering feedback and recommendations	

Our focus, in this chapter, is on Micro-task 2 (main-task) which is where the teachers requested learners to share their opinions for and against vegetarianism. See Satar and Wigham (2020) for a description of the micro-tasks used in the convergent task (Lesson 2), which forms the basis of the comparisons in this chapter.

5.2 Teacher perspectives on the impact of task type on their instruction-giving behaviour

In post-lesson interviews, each teacher reflected on their instructions for both tasks. All expressed that the divergent opinion-exchange task was easier to teach, more conversational, and flowed to the next topic naturally.

> Craig (interview, 27:29): "three was an easier lesson to teach because it was broadly conversational . . . that's the kind of class I teach most of the time"
>
> Karen (interview, 40:55): "so, the vegetarianism one, things just kind of flowed quite naturally"
>
> Sarah (interview, 26:05): "I always, at certain points, when I think they've said enough about each topic, I get them to move on to the next part."

The discussion questions from the resource sheet were also seen as enabling a clearer task plan that learners could follow and, potentially, when combined with the conversational nature of the task, reduced the importance teachers placed on instructions.

> Sarah (interview, 29:28): "Lesson 3 was easier because you had a picture and you had specific questions so they could follow those questions and they could see what were the pictures, the vegetables and everything, it was just a lot clearer."
>
> Sarah (interview, 25:06): "Because lesson three was a discussion activity and give their opinions about things so it wasn't so much that I had to give them instructions because it was a conversation."

One strategy adopted by this teacher, who appeared conscientious of capitalising on the online lesson time for learner interaction, was to send the lesson material prior to the lesson, which she did for both Lessons 2 and 3.

> Sarah (interview, 13:12): "I nearly always send the lesson plan before so that they have an idea of what we are going to talk about and sometimes to write something or check the vocabulary so they know what we're going to talk about"

104 *Task type*

For all three teachers, the use of the online whiteboard resource appeared challenging. During this micro-task, two teachers (Karen, Sarah) adopted the role of scribe. Sarah potentially took on this role to encourage learner-learner interaction and maintain the conversational nature of the task as one learner had difficulties using the resource. Craig suggested that the learners may have been more familiar with the collaborative writing tool used in the convergent task and that its affordances would have allowed for the same pedagogical outcome.

> Karen (interview, 31:18): "I'm not a big fan of the whiteboard . . . the students get a bit overwhelmed with it, it takes a lot of time. Maybe in the future if I would continue with the same students, I would go back to it, but because it's their first time, they get overwhelmed, they are a bit nervous about using it, doing it wrong, so they don't tend to do it, which is why I can encourage to do it but if (it's) taking too long, then I would actually do the (actual) writing."

> Sarah (interview, 25:20): "it was a conversation. Until we got to the part when they were supposed to summarize on the whiteboard and then I just wrote for them but that was quite difficult. Sevil could do it but Demet couldn't really summarize she got really confused with that."

> Craig (interview, 08:29): "we'll talk about the whiteboard in a minute of course but Google documents is normally sufficient if we need something extra erm like that."

Teacher perspectives indicate that in the divergent opinion-exchange task the HLAs in task instructions-as-process become more conversational. Potentially because the need to explain who will do what, when, and how becomes less important since the teacher is able to coordinate topic shifts and activity changes as the conversation flows naturally towards task completion: an open-ended discussion. Thus, we observe that the HLAs are predominantly presented in the form of individual orders or questions, such as 'tell me x', 'describe x', 'what do you think of x?', 'what is x?', etc. This is similar to observations in Chapter 4 when the convergent task instructions were presented to one learner.

5.3 Comparison of higher-level actions used in convergent and divergent tasks

We introduce four comparative tables in this section to demonstrate the differences between the HLAs employed by all three teachers for the convergent and divergent tasks. To examine whether HLAs differ depending on task type, we focus on the similarities and differences between the information gap activity (Micro-task 1, Lesson 2) that was convergent in nature and the divergent opinion-exchange activity (Micro-task 2, Lesson 3). There is, however, one key difference in the way we present the HLAs in task instructions-as-process for each task type.

- For the convergent task, we only focus on the HLAs prior to the learners' initiation of the task, ignoring further instructions teachers provide to facilitate task completion;
- For the divergent task, after initially examining only the HLAs prior to task initiation (Table 5.2), we then focus on HLAs throughout the micro-task (Tables 5.3, 5.4, and 5.5) to demonstrate a fundamental difference in the nature of delivery of the HLAs in task instructions-as-process: they are not offered all at once before task start but are introduced in a stepwise fashion, largely in the form of orchestrating the conversation through questions

(Meskill & Anthony, 2015, 2018).

Table 5.2 summarises the HLAs employed by the three teachers for both micro-tasks before task start. As can be seen, several HLAs were common to both task types: MANAGING RESOURCES, FOCUSING ON TASK ACCOMPLISHMENT, FORMULATING TASK STAGES, FOCUSING ON STUDY SKILLS, SUGGESTING WAYS INTO TASK, and LAUNCHING THE TASK.

In the information-gap task, in which there was a mismatch between the information possessed by the different learners in the paired role-play task, unsurprisingly, the HLA COMMUNICATING KEY TASK INFORMATION: IDENTIFYING LEARNERS HAVE DIFFERENT INFORMATION was important; whereas in the opinion-exchange task, it was not employed at all.

STATING TASK OUTCOME also appears to be task type dependent: in the convergent task, only one outcome was possible (the choice of gift package), and a decision was necessary to accomplish the second micro-task (writing an email collaboratively). In the divergent task, the outcome(s) were multiple and dependent on the opinions shared during the interactions and, thus, could not be foreseen. As such, they were not announced prior to the task in the instruction-giving phase.

In the divergent micro-task, DEFINING ROLES, such as learner and teacher roles in carrying out the tasks, as well as the social and interpersonal roles between the participants, was not drawn upon. Two other HLAs were also not used across the three teachers: CHECKING UNDERSTANDING (OF TASK) and ALLOCATING TIME. One potential explanation may relate to the role adopted by the teachers in which they orchestrated task accomplishment (see Section 5.4). This afforded them the possibility to (1) offer authentic responses in the spoken language mode whilst also (2) being available to introduce checkpoints during task accomplishment should they perceive task misunderstanding, and (3) manage the task rhythm and progress with regards time organisation. Whilst the information gap activity required learners

106 *Task type*

Table 5.2 Higher-level actions employed in the convergent (information-gap) and divergent (opinion-exchange) micro-tasks[1]

Higher-level actions		Convergent (Micro-task 1, Lesson 2: Micro-task 1, L2)			Divergent (Micro-task 2, Lesson 3: Micro-task 2, L3)		
		Craig	Karen	Sarah	Craig	Karen	Sarah
MANAGING RESOURCES	SENDING THE RESOURCE	x	x	x	x	x	x
	ALLOCATING THE RESOURCE	x	x	x			
	OPENING THE RESOURCE	x	x				
	CONFIRMING ACCESS TO THE (CORRECT) RESOURCE	x	x				x
	DESCRIBING THE CONTENT OF THE RESOURCE	x	x				x
	READING THE RESOURCE	x	x	x			x
FOCUSING ON TASK ACCOMPLISHMENT	DESCRIBING HOW TO ACCOMPLISH THE TASK	x	x	x	x		x
	CHECKING TASK COMPLETION	x	x				

Task type 107

DEFINING ROLES	EXPLAINING HOW STUDENTS WILL BE WORKING					x			
	ALLOCATING TASK ROLES					x			
ALLOCATING TIME		x				x			
STATING TASK OUTCOME			x			x	x		
FORMULATING TASK STAGES	ANNOUNCING NEXT TASK STAGE		x			x	x	x	x
COMMUNICATING KEY TASK INFORMATION	IDENTIFYING LEARNERS HAVE DIFFERENT INFORMATION		x			x	x		
	CLARIFYING KEY TASK VOCABULARY				x	x	x		
FOCUSING ON STUDY SKILLS	IDENTIFYING TASK TYPE/TOPIC		x					x	
	RELATING STUDY SKILLS TO PREVIOUS AND/OR FUTURE LEARNING					x	x		
	FORMULATING STUDY SKILLS					x			x

(Continued)

Table 5.2 (Continued)

Higher-level actions		Convergent (Micro-task 1, Lesson 2: Micro-task 1, L2)			Divergent (Micro-task 2, Lesson 3: Micro-task 2, L3)		
		Craig	Karen	Sarah	Craig	Karen	Sarah
ACTIVATING SCHEMATA	CONTEXTUALISING THE TASK	x					
	PERSONALISING THE TASK				x		
CHECKING UNDERSTANDING (OF TASK)			x	x			
SUGGESTING WAYS INTO TASK	SUGGESTING POTENTIAL INTERACTION PATTERNS	x	x	x		x	x
	SUGGESTING POTENTIAL ANSWERS	x	x			x	
LAUNCHING THE TASK		x	x		x	x	x

to reach a single outcome collectively, meaning that they both needed to understand the task information and instructions correctly before adopting the role of colleagues for task completion, the learning trajectory of the opinion-exchange activity appeared to be guided by the teacher during the task interactions, thus, affecting the nature of task instructions offered before the HLA LAUNCHING THE TASK.

Tables 5.3, 5.4, and 5.5 demonstrate a comparative view of the sequential employment of the HLAs in task instructions-as-process for the convergent and divergent tasks by each teacher. As mentioned previously, the convergent task HLAs only before learners' micro-task start are presented, and the divergent task tables include all HLAs until the end of the micro-task. Our aim here is to illustrate that initial instructions for the opinion-exchange took little time for the divergent task, but further instructions were provided throughout task completion as the teachers orchestrated the conversation through their questions and addressing the learners one by one.

Table 5.3 shows that, for the convergent task, Sarah used 13 HLAs before the learners started the task (in about 2 minutes, 27 seconds), whereas she used only 2 HLAs for the divergent task (in about 24 seconds). For the divergent task, after the initial task start, we observe Sarah's close corralling of the conversation through MANAGING RESOURCES (HLA numbers 8, 10, 12, 20) since the task resource sheet provided learners with linguistic input that can be used in their output. HLAs FOCUSING ON TASK ACCOMPLISHMENT (number 9) and FORMULATING TASK STAGES (number 11) support the orchestration of connected discourse (Meskill & Anthony, 2018): they offer links between different stages of the micro-task and inform learners about how to work towards task accomplishment. As such, they enable "successively building on prior utterances and pushing learners to new insights" (Meskill & Anthony, 2018, p. 161). We also observe several LAUNCHING THE TASK HLAs (numbers 4, 6, 13, 15, 17, 19, 22, 24), which predominantly take the form of conversation structuring questions (Meskill & Anthony, 2018).

In Table 5.4, Karen's Lesson 2, we see 65 HLAs before task start. This included three failed task initiation attempts and took 29 minutes 10 seconds. In contrast, HLAs in Lesson 3, took 12 seconds where learners embarked on the task following the HLAs FORMULATING TASK STAGES and LAUNCHING THE TASK. Karen then orchestrated the conversation by introducing two further HLAs during task accomplishment: SUGGESTING WAYS INTO TASK (numbers 4 and 9) and FOCUSING ON STUDY SKILLS (numbers 7 and 11). We observe further implementations of LAUNCHING THE TASK (numbers 5, 10, 12, 14, 16) but, overall, these four types of instructing-giving HLAs were sufficient for successful task completion.

So far, two HLAs are common to Sarah and Karen's divergent lessons: FORMULATING TASK STAGES and LAUNCHING THE TASK. While Sarah also used FOCUSING ON TASK ACCOMPLISHMENT and MANAGING RESOURCES, Karen employed FOCUSING ON STUDY SKILLS and SUGGESTING WAYS INTO TASK.

110 *Task type*

Table 5.3 Sarah's higher-level actions in task instructions-as-process for Lesson 2 until task start, and Lesson 3 throughout the task

No.	Time	Convergent: Micro-task 1, L2 (Sarah, D&S)	Time	Divergent: Micro-task 2, L3 (Sarah, D&S)
1	00:00:00.000	Checking understanding (of task)	00:08:57.130	Formulating task stages
2	00:00:15.813	Technical problem	00:09:01.899	Managing resources
3	00:00:28.625	Managing resources	00:09:21.074	Task
4	00:00:37.543	Focusing on task accomplishment	00:11:00.883	Launching the task
5	00:00:41.759	Communicating key task information	00:11:08.388	Task
6	00:01:42.111	Stating task outcome	00:12:03.584	Launching the task
7	00:01:53.786	Focusing on task accomplishment	00:12:03.976	Task
8	00:01:55.826	Stating task outcome	00:12:59.445	Managing resources
9	00:01:58.110	Communicating key task information	00:13:19.224	Focusing on task accomplishment
10	00:02:04.489	Focusing on task accomplishment	00:13:22.183	Managing resources
11	00:02:11.057	Stating task outcome	00:13:26.265	Formulating task stages
12	00:02:14.354	Checking understanding (of task)	00:13:27.418	Managing resources
13	00:02:16.327	Suggesting ways into task	00:13:31.432	Launching the task
14	00:02:26.949	Task	00:13:33.511	Task
15			00:14:09.897	Launching the task
16			00:14:16.469	Task
17			00:15:02.123	Launching the task
18			00:15:03.784	Task

19	00:16:20.851	Launching the task
20	00:16:21.384	Managing resources
21	00:16:25.963	Task
22	00:17:57.372	Launching the task
23	00:17:57.775	Task
24	00:19:20.342	Launching the task
25	00:19:21.533	Task

112 Task type

Table 5.4 Karen's higher-level actions in task instructions-as-process for Lesson 2 until task start and Lesson 3 throughout the task

No.	Time	Convergent: Micro-task 1, L2 (Karen, G&E)	Time	Divergent: Micro-task 2, L3 (Karen, G&E)
1	00:00:00.000	Checking understanding (of task)	00:42:52.884	Formulating task stages
2	00:07:26.930	Managing resources	00:42:57.260	Launching the task
3	00:07:31.710	Formulating task stages	00:43:04.534	Task
4	00:07:35.250	Defining roles	00:45:23.860	Suggesting ways into task
5	00:07:45.950	Managing resources	00:45:28.004	Launching the task
6	00:08:43.895	Defining roles	00:46:14.859	Task
7	00:08:49.208	Formulating task stages	00:46:36.956	Focusing on study skills
8	00:09:34.380	Checking understanding (of task)	00:46:44.824	Task
9	00:09:44.194	Defining roles	00:48:15.185	Suggesting ways into task
10	00:09:48.552	Focusing on study skills	00:48:20.638	Launching the task
11	00:10:54.849	Stating task outcome	00:48:21.963	Focusing on study skills
12	00:11:08.746	Communicating key task information	00:48:34.317	Launching the task
13	00:11:12.081	Stating task outcome	00:48:36.591	Task
14	00:11:55.059	Checking understanding (of task)	00:50:44.627	Launching the task
15	00:12:21.507	Communicating key task information	00:50:48.743	Task
16	00:12:44.835	Checking understanding (of task)	00:50:52.960	Launching the task
17	00:12:58.650	Stating task outcome	00:50:59.227	Task
18	00:13:22.910	Communicating key task information		

Task type 113

19	00:13:51.430	Focusing on task accomplishment
20	00:14:35.880	Managing resources
21	00:14:58.150	Focusing on task accomplishment
22	00:15:15.955	Focusing on study skills
23	00:15:47.432	Focusing on task accomplishment
24	00:16:40.280	Checking understanding (of task)
25	00:16:42.552	Focusing on task accomplishment
26	00:17:10.388	Managing resources
27	00:17:16.134	Stating task outcome
28	00:17:33.298	Communicating key task information
29	00:17:39.029	Focusing on task accomplishment
30	00:17:54.297	Managing resources
31	00:18:02.835	Focusing on task accomplishment
32	00:18:26.440	Checking understanding (of task)
33	00:18:30.610	Focusing on task accomplishment
34	00:18:39.387	Focusing on study skills
35	00:19:05.300	Focusing on task accomplishment

(*Continued*)

114 *Task type*

Table 5.4 (Continued)

No.	Time	Convergent: Micro-task 1, L2 (Karen, G&E)	Time	Divergent: Micro-task 2, L3 (Karen, G&E)
36	00:21:52.780	Checking understanding (of task)		
37	00:21:54.447	Focusing on study skills		
38	00:21:59.984	Checking understanding (of task)		
39	00:22:02.715	Focusing on study skills		
40	00:23:34.537	Focusing on task accomplishment		
41	00:23:43.447	Checking understanding (of task)		
42	00:23:45.830	Managing resources		
43	00:23:50.253	Defining roles		
44	00:23:57.551	Managing resources		
45	00:24:06.014	Focusing on task accomplishment		
46	00:24:09.283	Checking understanding (of task)		
47	00:24:11.149	Launching the task		
48	00:24:12.528	Learners' attempt at initiating the task		
49	00:25:32.950	Allocating time		
50	00:25:39.764	Learners' attempt at initiating the task		
51	00:25:46.984	Checking understanding (of task)		
52	00:26:37.919	Learners' attempt at initiating the task		

53	00:26:55.530	Checking understanding (of task)
54	00:27:21.764	Focusing on task accomplishment
55	00:27:43.787	Defining roles
56	00:27:50.663	Focusing on task accomplishment
57	00:27:53.574	Communicating key task information
58	00:27:57.441	Focusing on task accomplishment
59	00:28:12.326	Checking understanding (of task)
60	00:28:13.681	Suggesting ways into task
61	00:28:28.523	Focusing on task accomplishment
62	00:28:37.245	Suggesting ways into task
63	00:28:47.016	Communicating key task information
64	00:28:56.097	Suggesting ways into task
65	00:29:09.081	Launching the task
66	00:29:15.706	TASK

116 *Task type*

Craig's number and type of HLAs and the allocated time for HLAs before task start differs from those of Sarah and Karen. His delivery of the convergent task instructions involved 26 HLAs and took about 6 minutes 25 seconds (Table 5.5); whereas those of the divergent task included 11 HLAs and took 12 minutes 13 seconds. While divergent task HLAs were fewer in number (less than half), the time allocated to instructions was twice as long. Compared to Sarah and Karen, Craig used a higher variety of HLA types before task start in the divergent task. Similarly, he employed FORMULATING TASK STAGES and LAUNCHING THE TASK, but he also used FOCUSING ON STUDY SKILLS (like Karen), FOCUSING ON TASK ACCOMPLISHMENT and MANAGING RESOURCES (like Sarah), as well as ACTIVATING SCHEMATA and COMMUNICATING KEY TASK INFORMATION.

Following the first task initiation, Craig's HLAs for the divergent Micro-task 2 were largely in the form of structuring conversations through questions, saturating and modelling new vocabulary, as well as corralling by asking questions and introducing new topics (Meskill & Anthony, 2015, 2018). We elaborate on how these were accomplished multimodally in Section 5.4.3.

5.4 Multimodal configuration of higher-level actions and lower-level actions in different task types

In Section 5.3, we have shown that teachers used only a few HLAs in task instructions-as-process before the learners' first task start for the divergent task compared to the multiple HLAs used for the convergent task. We now investigate how all three teachers launched the divergent task and present how they then orchestrated task completion multimodally with further step-by-step instructions. We presented micro-level analyses for these three teachers' instructions prior to launching the convergent task in an earlier paper. To avoid repetition, we do not re-analyse these extracts here, but refer the reader to our open-access publication: Satar and Wigham (2020).

5.4.1 *Sarah's multimodal composition of higher-level actions and lower-level actions*

Sarah's lessons were 30 minutes long, which was half the lesson length compared to Karen and Craig, whose lessons were 60 minutes each. For both tasks, Sarah sent the task resource sheet to the learners via email asking them to read the information beforehand. Table 5.6 shows textchat records from both lessons. In Lesson 2 (convergent task) when one learner declared she had not checked her emails, Sarah also sent both resource sheets using the Skype text-chat function. Likewise, in Lesson 3, Sarah sent the link to the online whiteboard using textchat about three hours before lesson start time. This prompted an explanation request by one of the learners. In response, Sarah briefly explained Micro-task 3 and sent the task resource sheet. In both instances, task

Task type 117

Table 5.5 Craig's higher-level actions in task instructions-as-process for Lesson 2 until task start and Lesson 3 throughout the task

No.	Time	Convergent: Micro-task 1, L2 (Craig, E&D)	Time	Divergent: Micro-task 2, L3 (Craig, E&D)
1	00:15:53.500	Activating schemata	00:05:42.336	Formulating task stages
2	00:16:57.742	Formulating task stages	00:05:48.030	Activating schemata
3	00:17:15.700	Focusing on study skills	00:08:19.496	Focusing on study skills
4	00:17:57.210	Managing resources	00:10:17.755	Activating schemata
5	00:18:20.435	Formulating task stages	00:15:02.437	Communicating key task information
6	00:18:24.424	Managing resources	00:15:07.988	Activating schemata
7	00:18:47.431	Identifying task rationale	00:16:31.684	Formulating task stages
8	00:18:50.136	Stating task outcome	00:16:41.917	Focusing on task accomplishment
9	00:18:56.333	Communicating key task information	00:16:51.637	Managing resources
10	00:19:11.978	Activating schemata	00:16:56.469	Communicating key task information
11	00:19:22.872	Communicating key task information	00:17:47.393	Launching the task
12	00:19:33.331	Formulating task stages	00:17:55.935	Task
13	00:19:34.892	Focusing on task accomplishment	00:18:19.532	Activating schemata
14	00:19:36.790	Stating task outcome	00:19:12.477	Launching the task
15	00:19:42.676	Suggesting ways into task	00:19:19.708	Task
16	00:19:54.078	Focusing on task accomplishment	00:22:18.076	Formulating task stages
17	00:19:55.608	Managing resources	00:22:27.977	Communicating key task information

(Continued)

118 *Task type*

Table 5.5 (Continued)

No.	Time	Convergent: Micro-task 1, L2 (Craig, E&D)	Time	Divergent: Micro-task 2, L3 (Craig, E&D)
18	00:20:07.924	Suggesting ways into task	00:22:57.896	Formulating task stages
19	00:20:11.100	Managing resources	00:22:59.112	Formulating task stages
20	00:20:44.659	Allocating time	00:23:02.416	Suggesting ways into task
21	00:20:47.750	Managing resources	00:23:14.402	Launching the task
22	00:20:58.600	Formulating task stages	00:23:18.206	Task
23	00:21:01.825	Communicating key task information	00:32:09.658	Formulating task stages
24	00:21:15.979	Focusing on task accomplishment	00:32:15.422	Activating schemata
25	00:21:20.666	Suggesting ways into task	00:32:23.679	Task
26	00:22:14.722	Launching the task	00:32:51.567	Launching the task
27	00:22:18.276	Task	00:32:55.324	Task
28			00:34:45.029	Formulating task stages
29			00:34:48.471	Launching the task
30			00:35:06.689	Task
31			00:35:50.854	Launching the task
32			00:35:52.815	Task

Table 5.6 Sending the task resource sheet on textchat prior to lesson start

Lesson 2 (convergent task)	Lesson 3 (divergent task)
15 April 2018	20 April 2018
Sarah at 09:59	**Sarah at 07:37**
Demet, did you check your email? I've sent you a document	https://awwapp.com/b/u8wgt1f4c/
Demet at 09:59	**Demet at 07:45**
no I did not check :(	Why should we use this application
Sarah at 10:00	**Sarah at 08:00**
Can you have a look now before we start?	Have you seen the Lesson 3 document I sent to you?
Demet at 10:00	After your discussion you have to work together and summarise your discussion visually on the whiteboard. Opinion-exchange Task_Sarah.docx
ok I will look	
Sarah at 10:01	
We're just waiting for Sevil . . .	
Sarah at 10:05	
Information-Gap Task_Student A.docx	
Sarah at 10:06	
Information-Gap Task_Student B.docx	
((Call starts at 10:07 but due to connection issues and because Demet has not read the document, Sarah reschedules the lesson).	Here's the file . . .
	Demet at 08:27
Sarah at 10:34	Thanks:)
Sevil and Demet, read through your role plays and prepare for tomorrow	
Call starts at 10:29 on 16 April 2018	Call starts at 10:57 on 20 April 2018

resource sheets were shared for learners to read prior to the lesson and to follow during the lesson. We can confidently conclude that Sarah's practice of textchat use to share task resources (and, thus, instructions) before the lesson was similar for both the convergent and divergent tasks.

In Satar and Wigham (2020), Extract 5.2, we presented the LLAs that constituted Sarah's instructions prior to launching Micro-task 1 in Lesson 2 (convergent task). These included COMMUNICATING KEY TASK INFORMATION, FOCUSING ON TASK ACCOMPLISHMENT, DEFINING ROLES (EXPLAINING HOW STUDENTS WILL BE WORKING), and LAUNCHING THE TASK. The extract also demonstrated how Sarah invited one learner to read the resource sheet (MANAGING RESOURCES) to elicit the instructions, which Sarah then summarised before learners began the task. This extract showed how some of these HLAs were repeated.

Sarah was unable to screen-record her lessons, but provided some screenshots during her lessons to exemplify her screen layout and site of engagement. Figure 5.1 shows representative screen layouts at minutes 07:16 and 16:10 during Lesson 3. The former illustrates the moments when Sarah referred to the task resource sheet. She did this by moving the cursor onto the

120 Task type

Time: 07:16   Time: 16:10

Figure 5.1 Sarah's screen layout and site of engagement in Lesson 3

office document symbol on the task bar to preview the document while still having access to the learners' webcam images (Sevil on the left, and Demet on the right). The latter demonstrates a representative moment when Sarah did not refer to any documents. Sarah's own image was small at the bottom right, next to the researcher's Skype avatar. Neither the textchat nor participant window were visible during the call. This layout is almost identical to the one presented for Sarah's convergent task instructions in Satar and Wigham (2020), Extract 5.2, line 22.

The screenshots in Extract 5.1 come from the researcher recording. Here, we analyse the first three HLAs in Sarah's instructions for Micro-task 2 in Lesson 3 (divergent task). Sarah employs the first two HLAs (FORMULATING TASK STAGES and MANAGING RESOURCES) just before Sevil embarks on the task. During the task, Sarah encourages continuation through head nods, and we then observe Sarah asking a question to Demet, thus, initiating the learners' progress to another task step (LAUNCHING THE TASK). These are shown in Table 5.3, HLAs 1–5 and in Extract 5.1.

Extract 5.1 Frame 1 demonstrates how Sarah engages with the HLA FORMULATING TASK STAGES. This is achieved by announcing that they are going to move to the next micro-task. Sarah's facial expressions are not animated and her head movements are stable. In Frame 2, Sarah engages in the HLA MANAGING RESOURCES: READING THE TASK RESOURCE as she requests one of the learners, Sevil, to read the resource. During this HLA, we observe that Sarah's gaze moves briskly from right to left. During this time, she might be monitoring the task resource sheet, which tends to be placed at the bottom left of the screen (see Figure 5.1), yet it is difficult to know for certain without her screen-recording. The same HLA continues in Frame 3. This time, after Sevil reads the task instructions (question for the opinion-exchange), she then immediately embarks on task accomplishment. In the mode of gaze, we observe shifts in Sarah's direction of gaze from left to right. Towards the end of Sevil's response (Frame 4) and in Frame 5, in the mode of head movement, Sarah employs brisk and small head-nods.

Task type 121

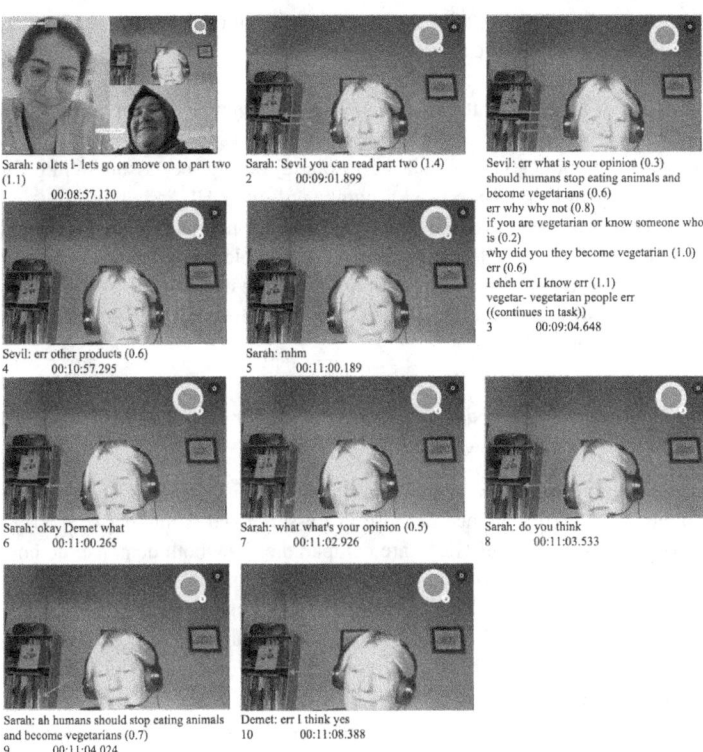

Extract 5.1 Sarah's divergent task instructions: FORMULATING TASK STAGES, MANAGING RESOURCES, LAUNCHING THE TASK

In Frames 6–9, Sarah engages with the HLA *LAUNCHING THE TASK* as she orchestrates connected discourse by structuring the conversation. She does this by addressing an initial question (Meskill & Anthony, 2018) to the other learner (Demet) to elicit her opinion. This allows the teacher to maintain task rhythm. We observe Sarah's gaze shifts between looking to the left and downwards. As her gaze shifts, she repeats the question word three times in the spoken language mode (Frames 6–7) and addresses questions to elicit learner opinion (Frames 7–8). By reference to Figure 5.1, her hesitations (Frames 7 and 9) and her use of the same wording of the question as presented in the resource sheet, we predict that the print mode, the task resource sheet preview, is foregrounded in her attention/awareness in Frames 7 and 9. In Frame 10, Demet provides her own response to the question while Sarah adopts a listening posture with a modal aggregate combining her gaze directed towards the learner's webcam image, a head-tilt with her face turned towards the learner, and a smile in the facial expression mode.

Compared to Extract 5.2 in Satar and Wigham (2020), we observe that Sarah's first HLA for both tasks is MANAGING RESOURCES. This involves SENDING THE RESOURCE before the lesson and READING THE RESOURCE (or more specifically asking one learner to read the resource) during the lesson. While for the convergent task, Sarah used a number of other HLAs before allowing learners to start the task, the divergent task did not require such detailed level of guidance. Sevil embarked on task completion as soon as she had completed reading the instructions. Sarah's action of instruction giving then became one of orchestrating conversations by addressing relevant questions to each learner.

5.4.2 Karen's multimodal composition of higher-level actions and lower-level actions

In this section, we focus on the HLA numbers 1–5 in Karen's Lesson 3 (divergent task) with reference to those in Lesson 2 (HLA numbers 63–66) in Table 5.4. These lines of HLAs are comparable: they both demonstrate how Karen offered learners potential directions to embark on the task and launched the task. For Lesson 3, we present a multimodal transcript in Extract 5.2. For Lesson 2, the multimodal micro-analysis is available in Satar and Wigham (2020), Extract 5.1. We have also provided more detailed multimodal transcripts in Chapter 3, Extracts 3.1, 3.4, 3.5, and 3.6.

In Lesson 3, Micro-task 2, Karen starts with the HLA: FORMULATING TASK STAGES (ANNOUNCING NEXT TASK STAGE) by telling learners, in the spoken language mode, that they will move to the next micro-task that involves sharing opinions. As soon as she has announced the task type, Karen launches the task with an open question (LAUNCHING THE TASK, Table 5.4 HLA2). During these two HLAs, Karen's screen displays the print mode (task resource sheet) which is foregrounded in her attention/awareness. Extract 5.2, Frame 1 illustrates ANNOUNCING NEXT TASK STAGE: she scrolls down to Micro-task 2 in the resource sheet accompanied by a transition in the spoken language mode: "the next thing is." She then moves her mouse cursor from the resource sheet to the videoconferencing window as she formulates the open question (Frames 3–4).

The teacher then shifts her attention to the videoconferencing window, foregrounding interaction with the learners. We observe a gaze shift (Frames 4 and 5) before the adoption of a listening posture (Frame 6) with proxemic shift away from the webcam and a gesture: chin propped on hand. The learner, Erol, then begins the task.

Once Erol's turn is completed, Karen orchestrates the interaction by offering the next turn in the spoken language mode to the second learner, Gonca. Karen engages in SUGGESTING WAYS INTO TASK (Table 5.4, HLA4) by employing a slight smile in the mode of facial expression (Frame 8) and a vocative in the spoken language mode. This vocative is accompanied by lateral shifts in the modes of gaze and head movement directed towards the learner's webcam image.

We presented the multimodal composition of Karen's HLAs and LLAs in Lesson 2 (convergent task) in Extract 3.1 in Chapter 3. For the first iteration of the lesson with Gonca and Erol, we portrayed the HLA *SUGGESTING WAYS INTO TASK* for the convergent task (Table 5.4 Micro-task 1, HLA64) and underlined the teacher's quick successions of hand gestures and posture shifts that were held in the frame for half a second at most and were neither foregrounded nor centralised within the webcam frame (Extract 3.1, Frames 2, 4, 6, 7, 9, 10, 12). For the same HLA in the divergent task, we observe that the gesture previously adopted at the end of the HLA *LAUNCHING THE TASK* (Table 5.4, Micro-task 2 HLA2) is sustained throughout the task interaction but is low in modal density: it does not add anything to the HLA *SUGGESTING WAYS INTO TASK* (Table 5.4, HLA 4). As Karen engages with the HLA *SUGGESTING WAYS INTO TASK: SUGGESTING POTENTIAL INTERACTION PATTERNS*, in the spoken language mode, the HLA structures the subsequent learner interaction by being directed towards one specific learner with the use of a vocative (Extract 5.2, Frame 8), rather than suggesting general interaction patterns for both learners: "one of you . . . the other person can say . . ." as seen in the convergent task (Extract 3.1, Frames 2, 6–8).

In both lessons, Karen then proceeds with the HLA *SUGGESTING WAYS INTO TASK: SUGGESTING POTENTIAL ANSWERS* (Table 5.4 Micro-task 1 HLA65 and Micro-task 2 HLA5). She achieves this in the divergent task by asking the learner to offer an argument for or against vegetarianism (Extract 5.3, Frames 9–13). This HLA is initially achieved through modal aggregates combining the spoken language mode and hand gestures. The latter portray both deictic and metaphoric properties to refer to points for and against vegetarianism (Extract 5.3, Fames 9–11) by lateral hand gesture shifts to foreground contrast (for or against). This is achieved in a similar manner for the convergent task as we observe lateral posture and hand gesture shifts in Extract 3.1, Frames 15 and 19 (same or different).

In Extract 5.2, Frames 12–13, as Karen refers to the task resource sheet on her screen in the print mode and scrolls upwards, it is foregrounded in her attention/awareness. Embodying the print mode, she reads the information aloud to formulate the discussion topic. In this lesson (divergent task), the conversation flows naturally as Karen orchestrates turns and topic changes using questions to structure the conversation (Meskill & Anthony, 2018). Following the question, the learner, Gonca, embarks on task accomplishment, thus the question also acts as the HLA *LAUNCHING THE TASK* (Table 5.4, Micro-task 2, HLA5). In contrast, for the convergent task, Karen clearly signalled to the learners the completion of the instructions and that they should begin the task (Extract 2.6) in the modes of spoken language, hand gesture, gaze, facial expressions, posture, and proxemics.

124 *Task type*

Extract 5.2 Karen's divergent task instructions: FORMULATING TASK STAGES, LAUNCHING THE TASK, SUGGESTING WAYS INTO TASK

5.4.3 Craig's multimodal composition of higher-level actions and lower-level actions

We now investigate Craig's multimodal delivery of instruction-giving HLAs and LLAs in Lessons 2 and 3. For comparative purposes, we draw on our earlier analyses of Craig's delivery of the convergent task in Lesson 2, presented in Satar and Wigham (2020), Extract 5.3. We also illustrate how the number of Craig's HLAs for the divergent task was greater and took significantly longer to deliver, compared to those of Sarah and Karen. We explore

Task type 125

how Craig's HLAs were closer to instructional conversations described by Meskill and Anthony (2015, 2018). Here, we specifically focus on and provide a multimodal micro-analysis for HLA numbers 7–21 for Lesson 3 (see Table 5.5). These were FORMULATING TASK STAGES, FOCUSING ON TASK ACCOMPLISHMENT, MANAGING RESOURCES: SENDING THE RESOURCE, COMMUNICATING KEY TASK INFORMATION, FORMULATING TASK STAGES, SUGGESTING WAYS INTO TASK, and LAUNCHING THE TASK.

In Extract 5.3, we observe Craig's HLAs for the divergent opinion-exchange task. Craig initiates the instructions by FORMULATING TASK STAGES(Frames 1–4). In this sequence, as he introduces the new topic and task stage, he also signals the transition in the textchat. He types three dashes (Frame 4), which visually depicts a separation between the micro-tasks, foregrounding the new HLA in the learners' attention/awareness. Craig's facial expressions, with raised eyebrows and pronounced lip movements (Frames 3–4), instil higher modal density and, thus, further foreground the new micro-task introduction.

Next, Craig turns to how learners will accomplish the task (Frames 5–12: FOCUSING ON TASK ACCOMPLISHMENT). First, he identifies the resource type, that is, that they will need to use an online whiteboard. The introduction of the new resource is accompanied by an iconic hand gesture, wide open eyes with gaze directed towards the screen, and enunciated lip movements (Frames 6–7). Craig then explains that they will use the whiteboard to take notes and what they need to do before they can begin this (Frames 7–12). We observe a pattern in Craig's use of multimodality as the modal density of his instructions increases for emphasis. Similar to Frames 3–4 which carry the core content, Frames 8–9 include iconic and beat gestures and facial expressions to foreground what to do in the next step ("make some notes") and what they need to do first ("but before"). In Satar and Wigham (2020), Extract 5.3, we evidenced how Craig foregrounds the core content for COMMUNICATING KEY TASK INFORMATION ("two similar but slightly different") in similar ways using his hand and facial gestures. Further evidence to this pattern – long periods with fewer modal shifts followed by higher modal density to emphasise meanings of significance – are Frames 24, 25–27, 30, 40, and 45–46.

In frames 11–12, Craig's attention/awareness shifts away from the learners towards his lesson plan. Following this, Frames 13–14 evidence identification of the resource type (Skype window) as we observe Craig's gaze being directed towards the bottom left corner of his screen. This LLA achieves the HLA MANAGING RESOURCES since the Skype textchat window becomes the vehicle for COMMUNICATING KEY TASK INFORMATION. In Frames 13–14, Craig embodies the print mode by copying information from his lesson plan, pasting it in textchat, and sending it to the learners. Thus, his LLAs in the spoken language mode ("I'm gonna be using the Skype speaking box here") and his embodied actions (in gaze, print, and object handling modes) show how he simultaneously completes both HLAs.

Frames 16–23 show Craig's further engagement with the HLA COMMUNI-CATING KEY TASK INFORMATION (in this extract relating to "moral reasons"). The print mode again becomes foregrounded in his attention/awareness as Craig copies, pastes, and sends the key task information in textchat: the first reason, that is, moral. During these frames his hand and facial gestures, as well as his posture and head movements, are fairly stable, thus, increasing modal intensity in the spoken and written language modes.

In the next 30 seconds, the learners respond to Craig's checkpoint by offering their understanding of the meaning of moral. Craig summarises the ideas before he embarks on LAUNCHING THE TASK (Frames 22–27). In terms of his LLAs, the modes of hand and facial gesture, proximity, and head movement foreground the core content: "moral reasons they're not going to eat meat" (Frames 24–27). What follows is learners' task accomplishment as they provide their answers and a conversation on a tangent topic of morality and cruelty towards animals. Craig interacts with the learners with authentic responses and introduces "bullfighting", "running of the bulls", and "fox hunting" as examples of "blood sports" to explore the concept of morality further. During this episode, he also requests examples of blood sports from the learners (:dog fighting", "chicken fighting") and elicits their perspectives on morality versus culture. Craig capitalises on these *teachable moments* and offers the phrases "illegal dog fighting" and "cockfighting". He uses textchat (print mode) (Frame 28) which further supports modelling and saturating (Meskill & Anthony, 2015) these new vocabulary items.

Craig then re-launches the task by, first, FORMULATING TASK STAGES: SUM-MARISING PREVIOUS TASK STAGE (Frames 29–31) followed by an introduction of further key vocabulary (COMMUNICATING KEY TASK INFORMATION): omnivore and carnivore. The LLAs that compose this HLA are similar to the ways in which the new vocabulary item 'moral' was introduced: written language and the print mode, gaze shifts, head movements, and enunciated facial gestures with raised eyebrows and expressive lip movements.

Once this is complete, Craig engages in SUMMARISING THE PREVIOUS TASK STAGE and ANNOUNCING NEXT TASK STAGE (Frames 34–36). He then introduces the next argument (SUGGESTING WAYS INTO TASK: SUGGESTING POTENTIAL ANSWERS): religious reasons (Frames 37–38). To introduce this new potential reason, his LLAs demonstrate shifts in the written language and print modes (Frame 38) as he embodies his lesson plan to copy the next argument, and pastes and sends it in the textchat. In Frame 39, Craig returns his attention/awareness towards the learners. This is visible in Frames 40–43, 44–46. These moments are again salient points in his instructions, which foreground meanings of significance: 'not eating meat', as well as example responses: "Islam" and "pork".

Frames 49–54 demonstrate the HLA LAUNCHING THE TASK which is carried out in the form of a question. Craig's modal composition becomes slightly more dynamic towards the end of the question ("that have this kind of restriction") with raised eyebrows (Frames 51–54), vertical backwards head tilts

(Frames 50, 54), and beat hand gestures (Frames 52, 54). Frame 55 shows a static modal configuration: Craig pauses (no modal shifts in any of the modes) with gaze directed towards the learners, and a titled head accompanied by a forward-facing posture. It is again the learners' turn to speak and complete the task.

In Extract 5.3, compared with Lesson 2 instructions (Satar & Wigham, 2020, Extract 5.3), we have demonstrated a similar pattern in increasing modal density (through complexity) for parts of the instruction that carry meanings of significance: key content words. However, as presented in Table 5.5, and similar to Karen's and Sarah's instructions, the discourse organisation of the divergent task instructions was different with multiple task re-starts as instructions were not delivered all at once for learners to carry out the task but introduced in stages. This enabled Craig to orchestrate the interaction through corralling by asking questions and introducing new topics. We observe evidence of this in the following frames whereby Craig makes conversations instructional (Meskill & Anthony, 2015, 2018):

- Frames 16–27: Number one is *moral*. What do I mean by *moral*? What do you think I mean? How does this affect vegetarianism? Why might some people say for *moral* reasons they're not going to eat meat?
- Frames 29–31: Very good. This was the *moral* argument against eating meat.
- Frames 34–36: This was the *moral* argument. What other arguments are there against eating meat?
- Frames 49–54: Can you think of any other religions that have this kind of restriction?

These frames also provide evidence in relation to how Craig models and saturates new vocabulary (key task information: moral) by "inundating instructional discourse throughout the online instructional venue with the targeted vocabulary and accompanying conceptualizations" (Meskill & Anthony, 2018, p. 9). Craig achieves this multimodally in the modes of spoken language, print, hand and facial gestures, head movement, and posture. As he repeats and models the use of the word *moral*, he is able to corral, that is, direct learner attention to specific content and language where learners and the teacher scaffold the construction of the joint discourse and orchestrate the smooth flow of conversation calling attention to lexis during meaning-focused interaction.

5.4.4 Modes, modal configurations, and modal density

In this section, we compare the modal configuration and density of the teachers' LLAs for both the convergent (Lesson 2) and the divergent task (Lesson 3). The HLAs we focus upon are LAUNCHING THE TASK for Sarah, COMMUNICATING

128 Task type

Extract 5.3 Craig's divergent task instructions

19	do I mean by 00:17:06.824	20	moral yeah this is one reason 00:17:07.740		
21	that people might be vegetarian what do you think I mean 00:17:09.963	22	so how does this affect vegetarianism do we think why might some people say for 00:17:45.437	23	00:17:47.393
24	moral reasons 00:17:51.722				

Between 00:17:12.303 and 00:17:45.437, Didem and Eda give their opinions on the meaning of 'moral'. and Craig establishes that: "It's um morality is kind of how we treat each other and the world around us exactly". Craig, then, initiates the HLA Launching the task.

25	they're 00:17:53.021	26	not going to 00:17:53.228	27	eat meat 00:17:53.914	28	00:22:18.024

TASK Learners' task imitation start at 00:17:55.935 as Didem takes the turn and provides her response. Craig then seeks Eda's perspective. Between 00:18:19.532 and 00:22:18.076, we observe a tangent conversation on the topic of morality and cruelty towards animals. Craig introduces 'bullfighting ', ' running of the bulls', and 'fox hunting' as examples of 'bloodsports' to explore the concept of morality further. During this episode, he also requests examples of bloodsports from the learners ('dog fighting', 'chicken fighting') and elicits their perspectives on morality versus culture. During this time, Craig capitalises on these 'teachable moments' and offers the phrases 'illegal dog fighting' and 'cockfighting'. Craig uses the text chat in the written language mode to corrall (Meskill & Anthony, 2015) these new words. Craig then re-launches the task as follows.

29	very good well this was the 00:22:18.076	30	moral 00:22:19.452	31	argument against erm eating meat yeah uhh if you're eating meat the 00:22:20.056	32	argument 00:22:24.731

33	of course is you're hurting an animal so very good yeah 0:22:25.283		

((Next Craig explains 'omnivore' and 'carnivore'))

Extract 5.3 (Continued)

130 *Task type*

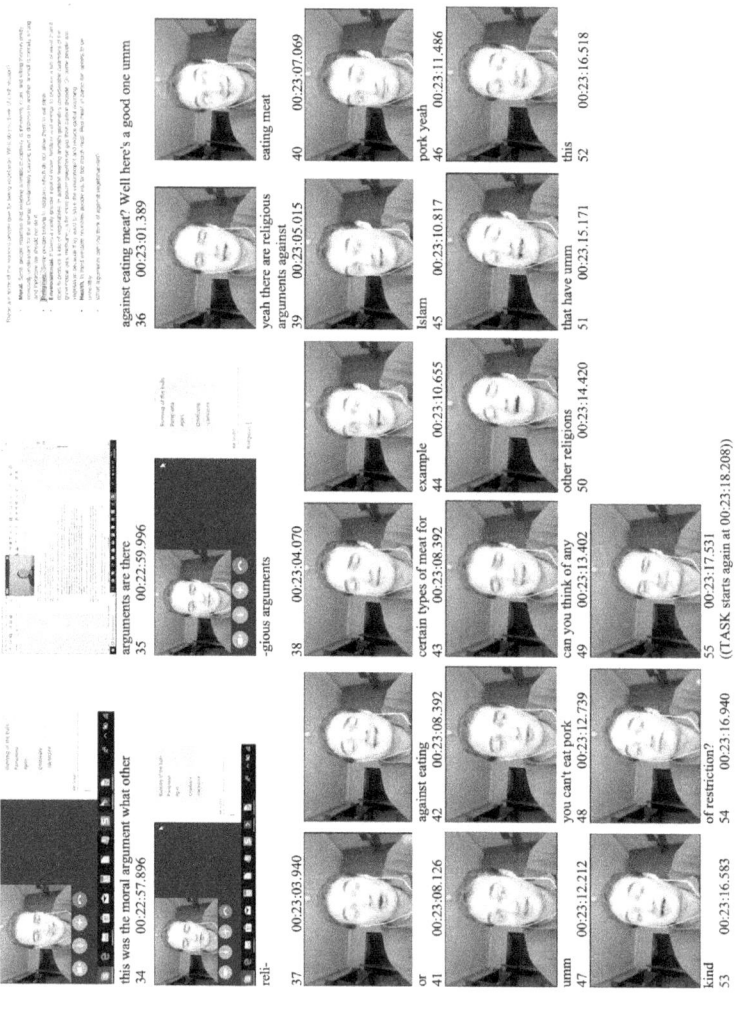

Extract 5.3 (Continued)

Task type 131

KEY TASK INFORMATION for Craig, and SUGGESTING WAYS INTO TASK for Karen. Figure 5.2 illustrates the configurations observed in a single frame. These frames are taken from the extracts presented later in this section which offer a contextualised perspective.

Figure 5.2 shows that, for both tasks, Sarah's modal configuration was exactly the same: spoken language was always foregrounded in her attention/awareness and carried high modal density because without the spoken language the HLA could not be achieved. Her webcam framing choices for both lessons were also the same (close-up shot) which did not afford her hand gestures to be visible. Sarah, however, was able to draw on gaze shifts, posture shifts, and head movement to deliver the instructions.

Craig's modal configuration was also similar for both lessons. While the spoken language mode was again foregrounded, this was enhanced by other modes to emphasise core content (as we argued in Section 5.4.3). In Figure 5.2, we see how Craig employed his gaze, hand gestures, and facial

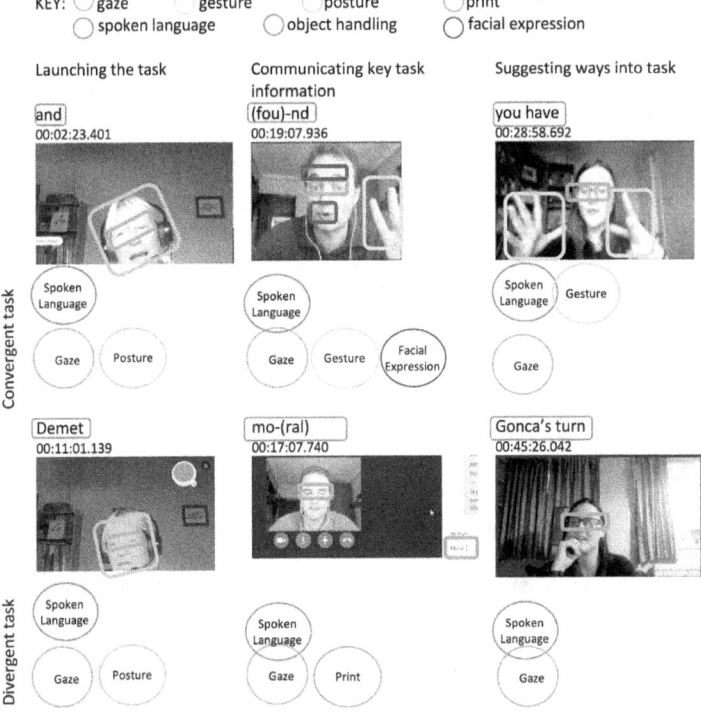

Figure 5.2 Modal configurations of Sarah, Craig, and Karen for the convergent and divergent task higher-level actions

132 *Task type*

expressions for the convergent task, while the other modes in action were gaze and print for the divergent task. However, we note that these differences are specific to these frames to demonstrate the variety of modes in his lessons, and that Craig also employed the modes of hand and facial gestures in Lesson 3, and the print mode in Lesson 2 (as we have discussed in Section 5.4.3).

Like the other teachers, Karen's webcam framing was consistent across the lessons. Both frames in Figure 5.2 demonstrate the importance of the spoken language mode (similar to the other teachers) as well as gaze and posture shifts and head movements. The frame we use as representative of Karen's modal configuration also foregrounds hand gestures which were directed towards the learner (i.e. their moving image on the teacher's screen) while the teacher was SUGGESTING WAYS INTO TASK. Neither frame includes Karen's use of the print mode, which was similar for both lessons (Extract 5.2 in this chapter, and Satar & Wigham, 2020, Extract 5.1).

Exploring modal configurations on a single frame does not fully represent what we were able to observe in the screen recordings. We, therefore, present a comparison of these specific HLAs on a timeline. Extract 5.4 shows a comparison of the HLA LAUNCHING THE TASK from Sarah first for the convergent task (Lesson 2, Satar & Wigham, 2020, line 36), followed by the divergent task (Lesson 3). For both tasks, we note direction shifts in the mode of gaze between the learners' webcam images, and potentially between the print mode (the task resource preview). These are observed in Frames 1–2 and 7–8 for the convergent and Frames 2–3 and 7–8 for the divergent task. While head tilts accompanied by gaze shifts were more frequent for LAUNCHING THE TASK for the convergent task (Frames 1–8, taking place in 1.3 seconds), Sarah's head tilts were more relaxed during the divergent task and were particularly used for turn allocation when addressing an initial question to one of the learners (Frames 1–11, taking place in 7 seconds). Extract 5.4, Lesson 3, Frame 1 shows Sarah's lateral tilt in the mode of head movement when addressing Demet in the spoken language mode. Her head direction stays the same throughout until Frame 10 with a concomitant shift in the facial expression mode (smile). This appears to signal a shift in turn: Demet takes the floor and responds. Overall, it is clear in Extract 5.4 that, although the multimodal configuration of the HLAs were similar in both lessons, there was less modal density for the divergent task with fewer shifts in head movement and gaze modes, which were the predominant modes comprising the LLAs.

We now investigate differences in speed and frequency of modal shifts in Karen and Craig's HLAs for both tasks.

Extract 5.5 demonstrates that the pattern was more observable in Karen's lessons than in Sarah's. We observe that the multimodal composition of the HLA SUGGESTING WAYS INTO TASK for the divergent task (Lesson 3) involved one sustained gesture (chin propped on hand) and a single co-modal gaze and head movement shift which took place in two frames in three seconds. In the

Task type 133

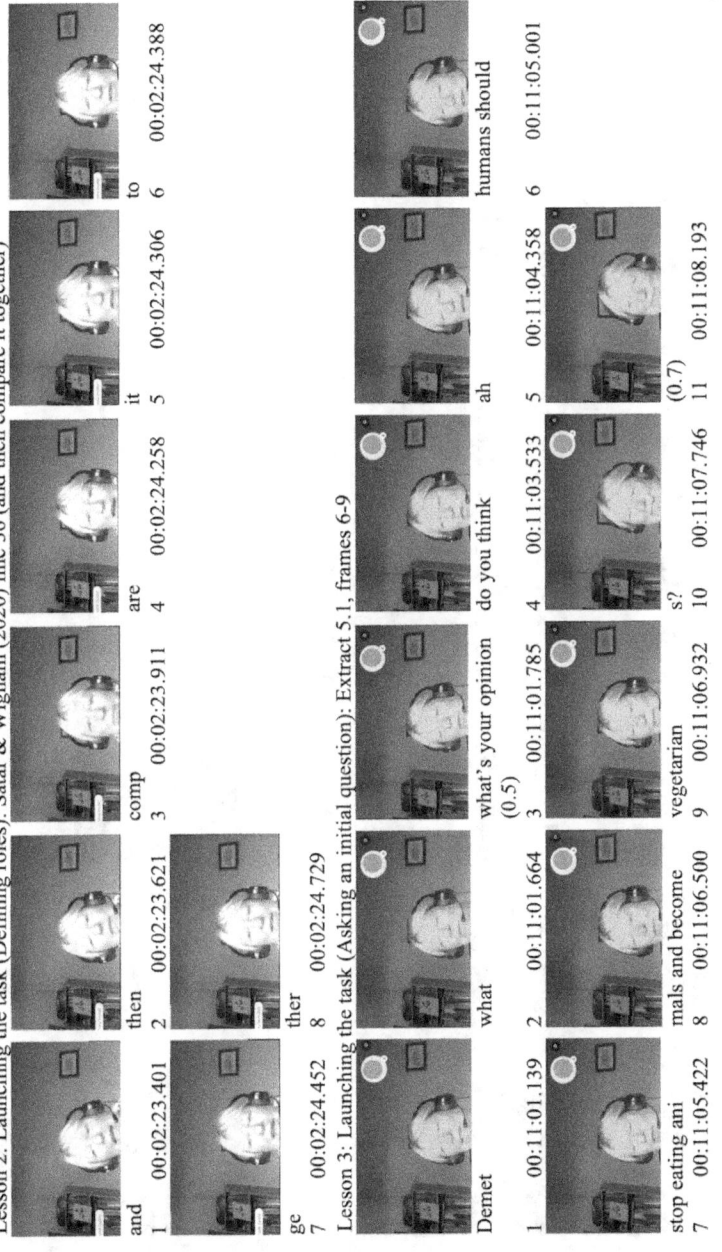

Extract 5.4 Sarah: LAUNCHING THE TASK (Lesson 2 and 3 compared)

134 *Task type*

Lesson 2: Suggesting ways into task (first time)

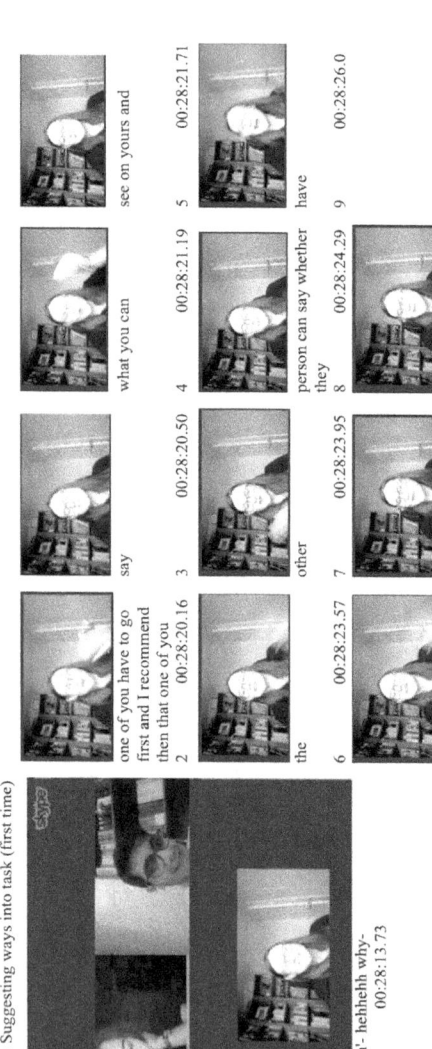

so why don'- hehhehh why-
1   00:28:13.73

one of you have to go   say   other   see on yours and
first and I recommend
then that one of you   what you can
2   00:28:20.16   3   00:28:20.50   4   00:28:21.19   5   00:28:21.71

the   same   person can say whether   have
                                                          they
6   00:28:23.57   7   00:28:23.95   8   00:28:24.29   9   00:28:26.0

the   thing or something different
10   00:28:26.26   11   00:28:26.60   12   00:28:26.64

Lesson 3 Suggesting ways into task

okay therefore it is (1.1)   Gonca's turn
7   00:45:23.860   8   00:45:26.042

Extract 5.5 Karen: SUGGESTING WAYS INTO TASK (Lesson 2 and 3 compared)

Task type   135

spoken language mode, the instruction was short comprising six words. For the convergent task (Lesson 2), however, we observe multiple hand gesture, facial expression, posture, head movement, and proximity shifts (12 frames delivered in 13 seconds) in quick succession. The spoken language mode involves a much longer instruction as well. The speed and frequency of modal shifts suggests that our claim holds: that is, divergent task LLAs had a lower modal density compared to those for the convergent task.

Extract 5.5 Karen: SUGGESTING WAYS INTO TASK (Lesson 2 and 3 compared)Finally, we investigate modal density of Craig's LLAs for the HLA COMMUNICATING KEY TASK INFORMATION in the convergent and divergent tasks (Extract 5.6). For the convergent task we observe modal shifts in 12 frames taking place in 4 seconds. For the divergent task, we observe modal shifts in 8 frames within 5 seconds. While modal shifts in hand gesture, facial expression, and proximity are observed throughout the HLA in Lesson 2, modal shifts in Lesson 3 centre around the target vocabulary item 'moral' in the print mode as Craig delivers the lexical item bimodally (spoken and written language). We believe that this adds further evidence to our argument that:

- The divergent task HLAs are more conversational in style;
- They do not require teachers to be as animated as they are for the convergent task HLAs displaying multiple modal shifts;
- While modal configurations (intensity and complexity) of the teachers' LLAs are similar in both task types, modal density is higher in the convergent task through a higher number of and more frequent modal shifts.

5.5   New higher-level actions observed in the divergent task for *managing resources*

Within the opinion-exchange task, three new HLAs in task instructions-as-process emerged from our data as secondary-level HLAs of MANAGING RESOURCES. These related specifically to how the teachers introduced and guided learners in using the online whiteboard: IDENTIFYING THE RESOURCE TYPE, FACILITATING USE OF THE RESOURCE and EDITING THE CONTENT OF THE RESOURCE. To illustrate these, we present a micro-analysis from Karen's Lesson 3 data (Extract 5.7). It is extracted from Micro-task 1b (see Table 5.1) in which the social actors are discussing what vegetarians do and do not eat.

In the print mode (textchat), Karen sends the learners a URL to an online whiteboard. This action is announced in the spoken language mode "so try clicking on this" (Extract 5.7, Frame 1) before Karen invites both learners to identify themselves within the collaborative whiteboard by changing their username in the print mode. This functions as FACILITATING USE OF THE RESOURCE: Karen guides learners in rendering their actions recognisable by the other participants (Frame 2). Karen reads aloud system notifications in

136 *Task type*

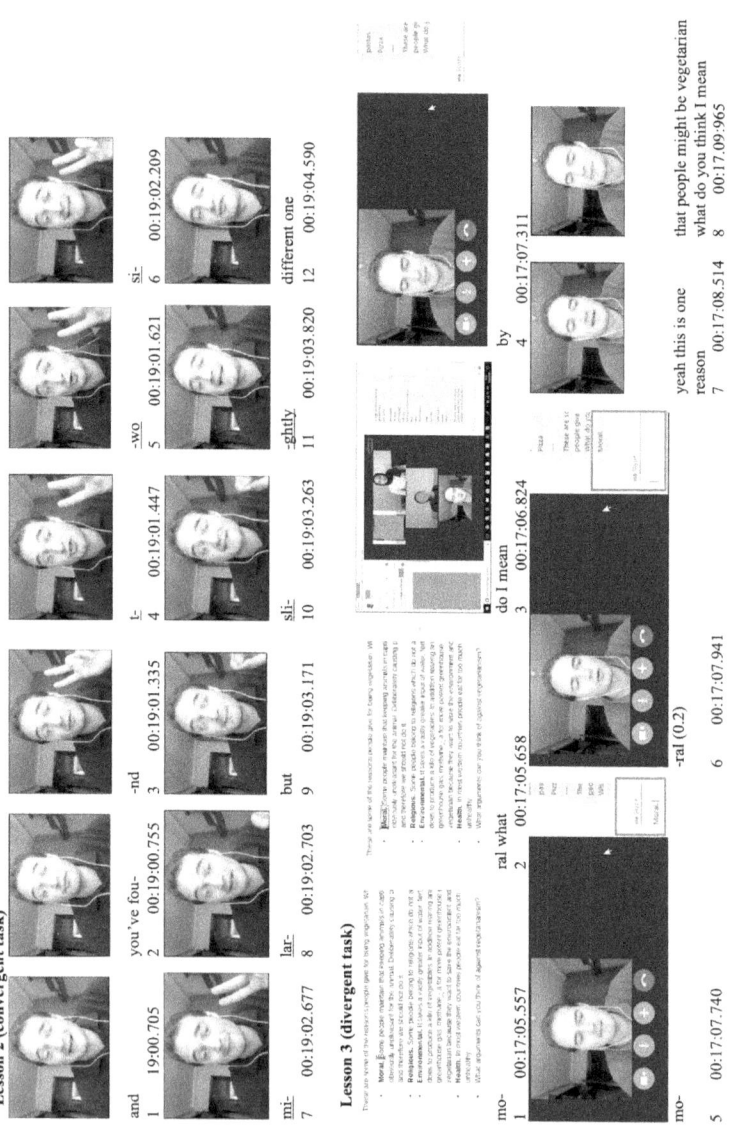

Extract 5.6 Craig: communicating key task information (Lesson 2 and 3 compared)

the print mode (Frame 3), which allow her to confirm that learners have successfully accessed the tool. The participants proceed by EDITING THE CONTENT OF THE RESOURCE, selecting either the pen or line drawing functions (e.g. Frames 3, 18) before annotating the whiteboard space (e.g. Frames 4, 7) or selecting the typing function and adding text in the print mode (Frames 14, 15). Once Karen realises that her initial actions (Fames 12,13) to type in the print mode were successful (but hidden by the pop-up menu, see Frame 12), she again uses the HLA FACILITATING USE OF THE RESOURCE by guiding learners towards the text function (Frame 16). The HLA FOCUSING ON TASK ACCOMPLISHMENT then occurs with Karen describing that the learners should write and directing them to the area in which to do so (Frame 17) before LAUNCHING THE TASK in the spoken language mode (Frame 18).

In Craig's third lesson, Craig explicitly informs the learners of the resource type they will be using in the spoken language mode as he simultaneously sends the URL link in the print mode: "Here is the whiteboard," thereby IDENTIFYING THE RESOURCE TYPE. Craig also employs the HLA EDITING THE CONTENT OF THE RESOURCE. Different modalities are employed in the print mode, however: rather than annotating the whiteboard space using the drawing and typing tools as Karen does, Craig directly adds text in the print mode by copying and pasting from the resource sheet as he announces his action "I'm going to try to do some copying and pasting and see if that works."

Examples of new secondary-level HLAs under
MANAGING RESOURCES

EDITING THE CONTENT OF THE RESOURCE
I'm going to try to do some copying and pasting and see if that works. (Craig)
Could you undo that or I'll delete it. (Karen)
So if I put a line in the middle. (Karen)

FACILITATING USE OF THE RESOURCE
Type your name in. (Karen)
So if you click on the text button here you can write underneath. (Karen)

IDENTIFYING THE RESOURCE TYPE
Here is the whiteboard. (Craig)

These observations of how Karen and Craig introduce and guide learners in using a new digital tool allow us to introduce three new HLAs into our revised framework of HLAs in task instructions-as-process (see Figure 6.1), further underlining the extent to which the HLA MANAGING RESOURCES takes on importance in online language teaching (Wigham & Satar, 2021).

138 *Task type*

Extract 5.7 Karen Micro-task 1b – MANAGING RESOURCES

Task type 139

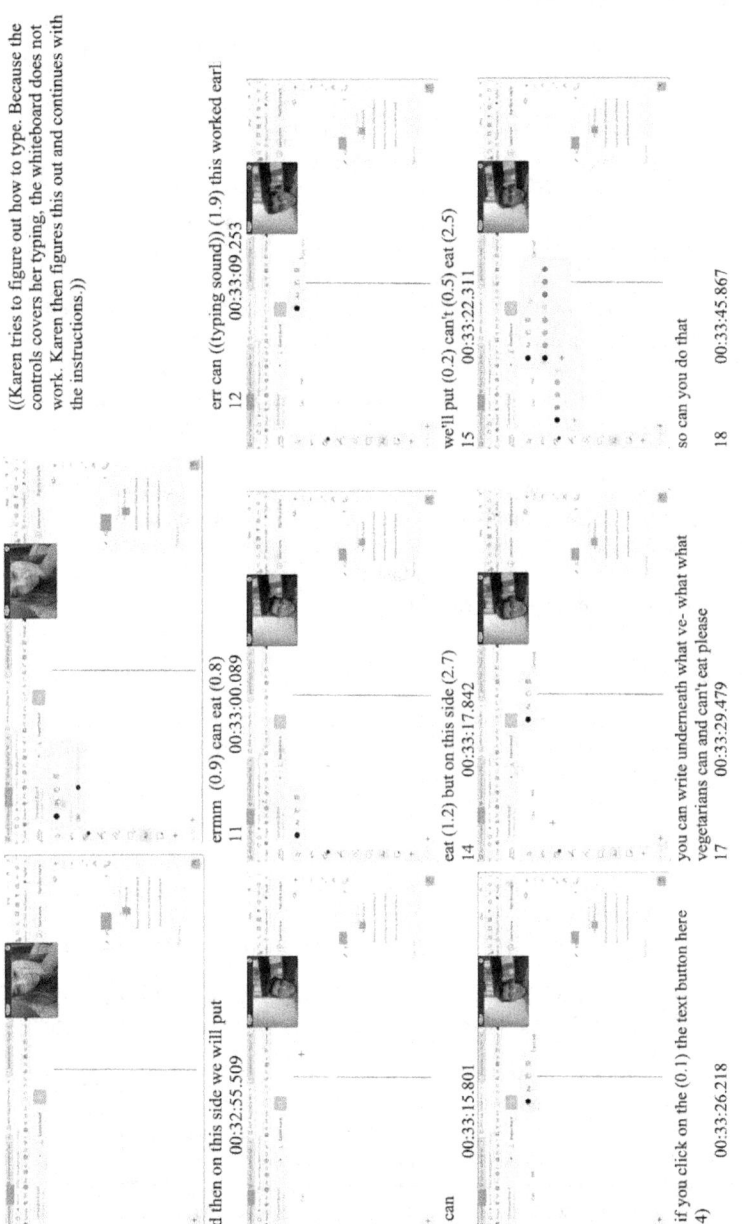

((Karen tries to figure out how to type. Because the controls covers her typing, the whiteboard does not work. Karen then figures this out and continues with the instructions.))

10 and then on this side we will put
    00:32:55.509

11 ermm (0.9) can eat (0.8)
    00:33:00.089

12 err can ((typing sound)) (1.9) this worked earl
    00:33:09.253

13 oh can
    00:33:15.801

14 eat (1.2) but on this side (2.7)
    00:33:17.842

15 we'll put (0.2) can't (0.5) eat (2.5)
    00:33:22.311

16 so if you click on the (0.1) the text button here (0.4)
    00:33:26.218

17 you can write underneath what ve- what what vegetarians can and can't eat please
    00:33:29.479

18 so can you do that
    00:33:45.867

Extract 5.7 (Continued)

5.6 Chapter summary

This chapter examined whether instruction-giving higher- and lower-level actions are task dependent: do instruction-giving HLAs and their multimodal composition differ when the same teacher give instructions for convergent (information-gap) and divergent (opinion-exchange) tasks?

Data analysis revealed that with regards HLAs COMMUNICATING KEY TASK INFORMATION (IDENTIFYING LEARNERS HAVE DIFFERENT INFORMATION), DEFINING ROLES, STATING TASK OUTCOME, and ALLOCATING TIME were specific to the convergent task. The HLAs of MANAGING RESOURCES, FOCUSING ON TASK ACCOMPLISHMENT, FORMULATING TASK STAGES (ANNOUNCING NEXT TASK STAGE), FOCUSING ON STUDY SKILLS, SUGGESTING WAYS INTO TASK, and LAUNCHING THE TASK were present in both the convergent and divergent tasks. With respect to MANAGING RESOURCES, the HLAs of IDENTIFYING THE RESOURCE TYPE, FACILITATING USE OF THE RESOURCE, and EDITING THE CONTENT OF THE RESOURCE were identified in the divergent task although these would appear to be specific to the divergent task's design, with use of an online whiteboard, rather than the task type per se.

While modes and modal configurations of the LLAs were similar in both task types, in the convergent task, the teachers' LLAs took on higher multimodal density. This was due to a higher number of modal shifts performed in a shorter time period. The divergent tasks being more conversational in style did not require teachers to be as animated.

Note

1 The grey crosses in Sarah's lessons for SENDING THE RESOURCE, ALLOCATING THE RESOURCE, and CONFIRMING ACCESS TO THE (CORRECT) RESOURCE were achieved prior to the beginning of the synchronous lesson.

References

Meskill, C., & Anthony, N. (2015). *Teaching languages online* (2nd ed.). Bristol: Multilingual Matters.

Meskill, C., & Anthony, N. (2018). *Teaching children online*. Bristol: Multilingual Matters.

Norris, S. (2009). Modal density and modal configurations: Multimodal actions. In C. Jewitt (Ed.), *The Routledge handbook of multimodal analysis* (pp. 78–90). London: Routledge.

Norris, S. (2019). *Systematically working with multimodal data: Research methods in multimodal discourse analysis*. Hoboken, NJ: John Wiley and Sons.

Satar, M., & Wigham, C. R. (2020). Delivering task instructions in multimodal synchronous online language teaching. *ALSIC, 23*.

Wigham, C. R., & Satar, M. (2021). Multimodal (inter)action analysis of task instructions in language teaching via videoconferencing: A case study. *ReCALL, 33*(3), 195–213.

6 Contributions, pedagogical reflections, and future perspectives

Synchronous online language learning and teaching settings are highly multimodal environments, just like in-person face-to-face classrooms. However, delivered through (mobile or desktop) computer screens, multimodality in online learning and teaching is limited to a two-dimensional on-screen frame. Whilst all actions are mediated through the body and language during in-person interaction, electronic transfer and transformation of participant embodied and on-screen actions introduces a second layer of mediation. As a result, mediated actions of learning and teaching lose certain multimodal qualities, including atmosphere, touch, proximity, free access to embodied actions (e.g., gaze, gestures, facial expressions), and perception of materiality of actors and objects presented on-screen. However, mediated learning and teaching settings also introduce novel affordances, such as a readily-accessible collaborative whiteboard, omnipresent textchat, direct access to other electronic resources, and moving images of participants (when available). Teaching skills developed for the face-to-face classroom are, therefore, not directly transferable to online contexts. Indeed, multimodal synchronous online teaching requires unique competencies, including the ability to offer effective task instructions-as-process. To enact such instructions, teachers need to capitalise on the affordances of a range of semiotic modes: spoken language, proxemics, posture, gesture, head movement, gaze, layout, music, and print (Norris, 2004).

This book offered robust, in-depth, and systematic multimodal analyses of experienced online language teachers' instruction-giving practices in synchronous online teaching (videoconferencing) within a task-based language teaching perspective. We addressed two research gaps in the field: a lack of research into online synchronous language teaching settings regarding instruction giving and instruction-giving practices of *experienced* teachers.

We defined task instructions as followable directives with procedural information for task completion (St. John & Cromdal, 2016) and focused on how they are delivered in interaction with the learners (instructions-as-process). We explored the impact of the contextual factors of task repetition (instructions delivered by the same teacher for a second time to a different group

DOI: 10.4324/9781003274216-6

of learners), number of learners (instructions delivered by the same teacher for a second time to a single learner) and task type (convergent compared to divergent tasks) on task instructions-as-process. We utilised Multimodal (Inter)action Analysis, which brings together the strengths of discourse and conversation analysis, and explored both macro- and micro-level perspectives focusing on higher- and lower-level (inter)actions. For each contextual factor, we presented robust analyses of the similarities and variance in three experienced online language teachers' instruction-giving practices and investigated hierarchical organisation of actions achieved through modal shifts, and their multimodal composition (complexity and density).

Our overarching argument in this book is that effective instruction giving in online language lessons is a multimodally complex process, understanding the nature of which fully requires attendance to both higher- and lower-level mediated actions. In this final chapter, we first summarise our contributions to methodology and knowledge (Section 6.1) and discuss our findings in light of previous literature (Sections 6.2, 6.3, and 6.4). In Section 6.5, we present a heuristic framework of task instruction-as-process in synchronous online language lessons elaborating on the changes introduced to the initial version of our framework (Satar & Wigham, 2020). We then discuss research-informed pedagogical perspectives that our analysis offers (Section 6.6). We conclude the chapter with a discussion of study limitations, future research perspectives (Section 6.7), and final thoughts (Section 6.8).

6.1 Contributions to methodology and knowledge

Our work is innovative and makes contributions to the field in several ways. Firstly, our choice of qualitative analysis method to study online multimodal interactions, Multimodal (Inter)action Analysis (MIA) (Norris, 2004, 2019, 2020), is novel particularly in Applied Linguistics. More specifically, in online language learning and teaching literature, several researchers (e.g., Balaman & Sert, 2017; Cappellini & Azaoui, 2017) have utilised Multimodal Conversation Analysis for a micro-analysis of the sequential organisation of talk-in-interaction in multimodal computer-mediated pedagogical interactions. However, adopting MIA and mediated action as our fundamental theoretical unit of analysis allowed us to focus on both macro- and micro-mediated actions and, particularly, on the hierarchy, rather than sequentiality, of actions and modes since higher-level actions (HLAs) and discernable chains of lower-level actions (LLAs) mutually produce each other.

Secondly, Norris (2019) positions MIA as a coherent framework to analyse video-based qualitative research of human action, interaction, and identity, which stemmed from and is applied to the analysis of actions mediated through the body and language during in-person interactions. However, few studies apply MIA to video-conferencing data (e.g., Norris, 2016; Norris & Pirini, 2017) and with a focus on how social actors interact with their physical environment while interacting with others online or on mobile devices in various settings. To the best of our knowledge, except our initial publications from this dataset (Satar & Wigham, 2020; Wigham & Satar, 2021), MIA has not been utilised for the study of language learning pedagogical interactions where social actors only interact via the online space. By employing MIA within this specific context, we responded to the need for "researching online language learning . . . from new and innovative approaches, . . . [which] requires a conscious effort and redirection of research energies to deal with the material differences that make online language learning unique" (Stickler & Hampel, 2019, p. 24).

Third, we build on MIA by employing Grounded Theory to systematically identify HLAs. Indeed, Norris (2019) describes the process of demarcating higher-level mediated actions in a table then bundling the latter to avoid overemphasising something that is rare or de-emphasising HLAs that frequently occur in the dataset. She does not, however, detail the method by which to do so. Grounded Theory enabled us to ensure that all HLAs are mutually exclusive by grouping and refining HLA categories until theoretical saturation. This allowed us to more systematically recognise the pertinence or the rarity of the HLAs. We suggest this approach offered more rigour to HLA bundling in our dataset.

Concerning MIA's transcription conventions, using LLAs as the analytical unit to guide our frame selection choices in transcript production is novel within CALL research. Most research to date delineates modes and, in particular, the spoken language mode, to guide multimodal transcript choices. With MIA, we used the construct of a mode to examine interaction in its multimodal complexity and, in transcript production, we were guided by modal shifts in the LLAs performed. As Norris (2019) argues, this enables greater replicability in the practice of transcript production: should one researcher place a particular movement (e.g. a head movement) in one mode during transcription (head movement) but another researcher place the same movement in another mode (posture), the movement will be produced in both researchers' final transcripts in the same manner because the movement (LLA) guides the transcript, with mode providing a theoretically-founded way to describe the action. The transcription of multimodal CALL data is time-consuming and often requires dividing annotation, transcription, and transcript production practices across several researchers (Guichon, 2017). Guiding transcript production by LLAs would thus allow for greater consistency across the researchers involved. This could, in turn, encourage both data/corpora access and dissemination, and data repurposing (Wigham & Aranha, 2020).

Another contribution we make is to extend theoretical constructs of Norris' MIA framework. In our previous work, we used frozen actions which are entailed in material objects in the interactional setting (Norris, 2004) to describe those entailed in electronic objects, and the print mode to encompass electronic print (Wigham & Satar, 2020). These extensions of the analytical framework are operationalised within this book. In Wigham and Satar (2020), we introduced notions that are specific to the mediation of actions via the computer screen. We proposed the notion of *semiotic lag* relating to the desynchronisation of mode transmission that can affect communication, the relative timing of actions, and the way in which participants orient to the latter. We also advanced that *semiotic (mis)alignment* can result from this screen mediation when differences in semiotic meaning-making resources available to social actors occur either due to variations in hardware and/or software specifications which impact the layout mode or when one participant uses or has access to a resource in their online or physical environment that is not seen by the other. Here, we have been able to apply these notions and illustrate their pertinence through additional examples.

In this work, we also put forward and illustrated the notion of *modal density misalignment* which we define as different modes or modal aggregates – and through which different LLAs or HLAs – being foregrounded in different social actors' attention/awareness continua. In comparison to *semiotic misalignment* which refers to social actors' *access* to different modes in their site of engagement, *modal density misalignment* refers to the differences in the HLAs being *foregrounded* in social actors' attention/awareness, regardless of the modes which are available to them in their site of engagement. We, thus, extended Norris' notion of *modal density* to encompass that of *modal density (mis)alignment*. Another extension is proposed in Chapter 5 where we suggested that, in addition to modal intensity and complexity, modal density can be achieved by brisk modal shifts.

Regarding previous work in instruction giving, this book contributes to the nascent but growing body of literature on the topic of instruction giving in present-in-person classroom settings (e.g. Badem-Korkmaz & Balaman, 2020, Kunitz, 2021; Markee, 2015; Somuncu & Sert, 2019), and in online language teaching (Cappellini & Combe, 2017; Codreanu & Combe Celik, 2012; Satar & Wigham, 2017, 2020; Wigham & Satar, 2021). Regarding our dataset, as we reported in Chapter 1, few CALL studies concentrate on experienced online teachers. Indeed, research is often conducted within higher education institutions examining trainee teachers' practices (including our earlier work in Satar & Wigham, 2017). We hope our findings based on data collected from experienced freelance teachers contribute to bridging this gap whilst potentially offering insights for teacher training.

In addition, we investigated a semi-controlled corpus (Chapter 2) which enabled generation of data that allowed for comparisons in relation to task repetition, learner numbers, and task type in teachers' instructions. The measures implemented only related to the provision of lesson materials and learners and, thus, did not impede collection of naturally-occurring data with respect to freedom teachers had to adapt the material to suit their everyday teaching practices. No further interventions were imposed and participants were not guided to (inter)act in any specific way (Norris, 2019). This book, thus, demonstrates the potential to examine variety in teacher practices in an exploratory fashion, while preserving an interest in naturally-occurring data. The next three sections discuss our contributions to knowledge further with regards to our findings on teachers' instruction-giving practices when they re-use the same task or activity with different learners and give instructions for different task types.

6.2 Instruction giving and task repetition

Regarding task repetition (Chapter 3), data analysis demonstrated that the second iteration appeared to be more efficient: fewer HLAs were performed, and the time spent on instruction-giving sequences was shorter. Interaction and interview data suggest this may be linked to contextualising before turning to the HLA of MANAGING RESOURCES. The HLAs of ACTIVATING SCHEMATA, giving an overview of the task by FORMULATING TASK STAGES and DEFINING ROLES, FOCUSING ON STUDY SKILLS and COMMUNICATING KEY TASK INFORMATION allow preparation for "work-to-come" (Heyman, 1986) and assist resource management. In an in-person classroom-based study, Kunitz (2021) also observed a teacher's instructions and found that while the teacher's first iteration of instructions was lengthy and required repair and rephrasing, instructions in subsequent iterations were shorter and did not trigger learner clarification requests. While Kunitz (2021) attributes the efficiency in instructions to learners having heard prior instructions given to other learners in the same lesson, our findings show that teachers are responsive to learner reactions and able to set expectations of potentially repairable sections of the instructions when using the same task or activity in subsequent lessons with different learners. By reflecting on these sections following the first iteration, the instructions are modified pre-emptively in future iterations making them more succinct, as Tomlinson and Masuhara (2017) recommend.

With respect to LLAs, we observed many similarities in both instruction-giving iterations. Analysis revealed that the teacher formed modal aggregates combining LLAs in the gesture and spoken language modes, particularly when repeating the instructions following learners' lack of alignment with the instructed activity and their signalling of trouble (Badem-Korkmaz & Balaman, 2020). During instruction repetition, the teacher ensured that LLAs in the gesture mode were within the webcam frame and sustained long enough to be perceived by learners, demonstrating *critical semiotic awareness* (Guichon & Wigham, 2016). It also enabled the teacher to achieve increased modal density and, thus, to present the instruction repetition as the focal point of attention by more explicitly foregrounding them in the social actors' awareness/ attention (Norris, 2004). Through the use of more visible modal aggregates, the teacher created a single pedagogical focus (Seedhouse, 2008).

For certain HLAs, for example, COMMUNICATING KEY TASK INFORMATION and SUGGESTING WAYS INTO TASK, in both iterations, the teacher relied on iconic, metaphoric, and deictic gestures combined with the spoken language mode. On some occasions these were the exact same gestures, whilst on others they were the same type of gestures in different forms. Deictic gestures that addressed each learner were aligned with the position of each social actor's webcam image on the teacher's screen and, thus, adapted to the layout mode of the teacher's site of engagement, regardless of the learners' screen layout.

Regarding the proxemics mode, during the HLA of LAUNCHING THE TASK, the LLA of proxemic withdrawal was salient in both iterations and accompanied by a slight shift in posture. The proxemic and postural shifts indicated that the teacher was withdrawing from the interaction space and would no longer engage in the spoken language mode despite still being present visually. This provided a clear visual cue to the division between the teacher's instruction-giving sequence and learners' task initiation. In Satar and Wigham (2017), we observed similar employment of these multimodal elements by trainee teachers to demonstrate withdrawal from interactional space when LAUNCHING THE TASK.

Our analyses also focused on the LLAs in the print mode, which were systematically employed to achieve the HLAs of MANAGING RESOURCES (SENDING THE RESOURCE, READING THE RESOURCE, DESCRIBING THE CONTENTS OF THE RESOURCE), FOCUSING ON TASK ACCOMPLISHMENT, FOCUSING ON STUDY SKILLS, and CLARIFYING KEY TASK VOCABULARY. The textchat affords the potential to enhance teaching by employing LLAs in the spoken language and print modes (Meskill & Anthony, 2015) and compensating for the lack of a blackboard (Hampel & Stickler, 2012). Regarding the print mode's function in CLARIFYING KEY TASK VOCABULARY, as Wigham and Chanier (2013) and Kozar (2016b) describe, the textchat was used in both iterations to serve pedagogical functions. As discussed in Wigham and Satar (2021), textchat messages sent during instruction-giving sequences functioned as frozen actions during task accomplishment to which all social actors could refer to and helped achieve task accomplishment. Likewise, Kozar (2016b) reported that learners were more likely to incorporate new vocabulary if produced bimodally.

Finally, the teacher's webcam framing, with a choice of head and torso shot, screen layout and use of predominantly free gaze patterns were consistent across the two iterations. The teacher's gaze choices seem compatible with other research (Develotte, Guichon, & Vincent, 2010) that describes the semio-pedagogical difficulty of maintaining fixed gaze in an attempt to sustain eye-contact (Satar, 2013). One of the teachers in our data showed *critical semiotic awareness* with regards to her gaze choices by stating that they monitor student faces to get feedback on their comprehension. Our analysis of webcam framing over the two iterations supports Sindoni's (2013) argument that the ways in which participants position themselves in front of a webcam involves an "intentional act on the part of each participant" and as such becomes an "integral part of the interaction" (p. 57). Indeed, the teacher's framing choice allowed particular configurations of modes (modal aggregates) to become possible (Jones, 2009).

Contributions, pedagogical reflections, and future perspectives 147

Our analysis of the two iterations showed little variety in Karen's hierarchical organisation of LLAs (modal configuration) and the intensity and complexity of the different modes (modal density). The mediated interaction space seemed to govern her modal density depending on whether the videoconferencing window or electronic resource was foregrounded in the layout mode. Her predominant configuration was the videoconferencing layout where HLAs were achieved through a combination of LLAs principally in the spoken language, gesture, and gaze modes. When delivering HLAs related to MANAGING RESOURCES, the teacher foregrounded the electronic resource in her attention/awareness. Modal density during these sequences varied per social actor due to *semiotic misalignment*. Learners did not have access to the teacher's LLAs in the non-shared electronic resource space and the teacher did not have access to her own LLAs communicated visually through her webcam image. Thus, differing sites of engagement caused a loss of common "site of display" (see Jones, 2009, p. 115) and provoked *modal density misalignment* with the print mode carrying high modal intensity for the teacher, while spoken language mode was of high intensity for the learners. Therefore, online teachers need to be cognisant of potential *semiotic misalignment* and *modal density misalignment*, and seek confirmation that their actions are visible by the other social actors. It is essential that teachers manage such complexity to organise the semio-pedagogical activity (Guichon, 2009) and plan ahead for the HLAs related to instruction giving.

6.3 Instruction giving and number of learners

In Chapter 4, we compared and contrasted Craig's HLAs and LLAs in instructions-as-process for the same task in his lessons with two learners (first iteration) and a single learner (second iteration). We observed differences largely in relation to the HLA MANAGING RESOURCES and its multimodal accomplishment at the micro-level (LLAs). We noted two failed task attempts by the learner in the second iteration and attributed this to two reasons: (1) teacher's failure to enact CONFIRMING ACCESS TO THE (CORRECT) RESOURCE as soon as the resource was sent, which caused *semiotic misalignment* between the teacher and the learner's site of engagement, and (2) foregrounding of different HLAs in the attention/awareness of the teacher (SENDING THE RESOURCE) and the learner (ACTIVATING SCHEMATA) due to *semiotic density misalignment* between their interactional spaces. Hampel (2019) describes the complexity of online language teaching and explores technological disruption. In Wigham and Satar (2021), we proposed that MANAGING RESOURCES is more complex than other instruction-giving HLAs in online teaching. Here, we reiterated this argument and suggested that MANAGING RESOURCES (particularly SENDING THE RESOURCE and CONFIRMING ACCESS TO THE (CORRECT) RESOURCE) is an essential and complex HLA for instruction giving, regardless of the number of learners in online lessons, even in one-to-one tutoring. It is important for teachers not to presume that the learner can receive, locate, open, access, and use the electronic resources without confirmation or guidance.

We drew several other conclusions in Chapter 4. First, the participating teacher suggested that it was easier to give task instructions when multiple learners were present because they lend each other support in interpreting task instructions. This is in line with socio-cultural approaches to language learning (Vygotsky, 1978) and indicates that instruction-giving sequences can create authentic interactions between the teacher and learners (Thornbury, 2000) but also among learners themselves. Second, regardless of the number of learners, we found that the second iteration of task instruction delivery was more efficient, which corroborated our argument in Chapter 3 and Kunitz's (2021) observation that teachers' instructions became more succinct as they repeated them within the same lesson.

Apart from the number of social actors, we did not observe any differences in the teacher's predominant site of engagement with respect to class size. Moreover, we observed little variety in Craig's hierarchical organisation of LLAs and his modal configuration when the videoconferencing window was visible in his site of engagement. In relation to gaze direction, Craig's gaze was predominantly directed downwards when engaged with the HLA *MANAGING RESOURCES*, but towards the screen when interacting with the learners. In our pedagogical recommendations (Section 6.6), we suggest that gaze direction can signal what is foregrounded in social actors' attention/awareness, especially if these are described at the onset of the lessons. Research in understanding joint attention between the online teacher and learners is gaining traction (Cappellini & Hsu, 2022; Shi, Stickler, & Lloyd, 2017) in CALL research using eye-tracking methodology. Potential synergies between the methods can be explored in future work (see Section 6.7).

In Chapter 4, we also demonstrated that many HLAs, such as *COMMUNICATING KEY TASK INFORMATION*, were achieved with high modal complexity, which foregrounded essential information for task completion in the teacher's attention/awareness continuum. We proposed that it is likely that the same HLAs were also foregrounded in the learners' attention/awareness since the teacher's expressive embodied modes were also available to the learners through the teacher's webcam image. This is in line with Norris (2020) in which she suggested the potential to explore the HLAs foregrounded in other interlocutors' attention/awareness through studying one social actor's HLAs and LLAs since the notion of attention/awareness is studied in (inter)action and participants' (inter)actions build on and are impacted by each other.

Likewise, when two learners were present, the teacher actively (inter)acted with the learners during *SENDING, ALLOCATING*, and *DESCRIBING THE CONTENT OF THE RESOURCE* in the modes of spoken language, gaze, gesture, and facial expressions while simultaneously being engaged in object handling and print modes. This appeared to ensure *modal density alignment* by foregrounding the HLAs in all social actors' attention/awareness continuum. In contrast, when teaching

Contributions, pedagogical reflections, and future perspectives 149

a single learner, the print mode was foregrounded in the teacher's attention/ awareness, and other modes lost intensity; his facial gestures were no longer as expressive; there were less frequent gaze shifts, as well as fewer hand gestures and head tilts. Combined with the learner's lack of access to the print mode, and the teacher's engagement with multiple HLAs simultaneously, this led to *modal density misalignment*. We found that the HLA SENDING THE RESOURCE was more effectively achieved and signalled to the learners when the teacher:

1 Engaged with a single HLA at a time;
2 Addressed the learners in spoken language, gaze, gesture, and facial expression modes;
3 Articulated, in the spoken language mode, any actions taking place only in their own site of engagement, , that is, on-screen actions which were not shared to the other interlocutors, and thereby not available to them;
4 Ensured there was *modal density alignment* between the teacher and the learners which meant that the same modes and HLAs were foregrounded in all actors' attention/awareness, regardless of *semiotic misalignment* (i.e. access to different resources or different screen layout). Relatedly, when access to the resource had to be remedied (e.g., Extract 4.5), a series of LLAs in the modes of gesture, gaze, object handling, and facial expression assisted the learner in locating and accessing the resource.

In present-in-person teaching, the HLA CONFIRMING ACCESS TO THE (CORRECT) RESOURCE is primarily accomplished in the modes of object handling and gaze. However, when online, these modes are not necessarily or accurately available to learners. Our analyses suggested that spoken language and print modes had high modal intensity to achieve this HLA in online teaching. Moreover, the teacher's modal configuration comprising a short question followed by silence in the spoken language mode, a listening posture such as gaze towards the screen, and tilted head appeared to provide sufficient opportunities for learners to declare (lack of) access to the resource. Finally, we reported that regardless of the number of learners, lack of shared access to the print and object handling modes (unless the teacher shares their screen) can be partially overcome when an electronic resource is shared as an online collaborative document rather than as an offline word processor.

6.4 Instruction giving and task type

Chapter 5 examined task instructions-as-process with relation to task type and compared a convergent information-gap task and a divergent opinion-exchange task. Our analysis revealed that several HLAs were common to both task types: MANAGING RESOURCES, FOCUSING ON TASK ACCOMPLISHMENT, FORMULATING TASK STAGES, FOCUSING ON STUDY SKILLS, SUGGESTING WAYS INTO TASK, and LAUNCHING THE TASK. Some HLAs were specific to task type: COMMUNICATING KEY TASK

INFORMATION: IDENTIFYING LEARNERS HAVE DIFFERENT INFORMATION, STATING TASK OUTCOME, DEFINING ROLES, CHECKING UNDERSTANDING (OF TASK), and ALLOCATING TIME were only used for the convergent task. In this chapter, we also identified three new HLAs under MANAGING RESOURCES related to the use of a new electronic resource (an interactive online whiteboard): EDITING THE CONTENT OF THE RESOURCE, FACILITATING USE OF THE RESOURCE, and IDENTIFYING THE RESOURCE TYPE.

Our main finding as regards task type variance, however, relates to the number and relative position of instruction-giving HLAs during the lesson. The convergent task required a higher number of HLAs before learners commenced the task because learners had to reach a single outcome collectively and needed to understand task information and instructions correctly before task completion. The opinion-exchange task, however, did not require as many initial HLAs. Indeed, our analyses revealed that during divergent task accomplishment, teachers introduced instruction-giving HLAs in a stepwise fashion guiding the learning trajectory during interactions. Thus, during the convergent task, teachers' HLAs were primarily in "setting up the language learning task" (Meskill & Anthony, 2007, p. 11) whereas in the divergent task these HLAs were minimal and rather HLAs took on an important role in "orchestrating instructional conversation around that task" (Meskill & Anthony, 2007). Teachers achieved this by offering links between different stages of the micro-task and informing learners about how to work within the HLAs FOCUSING ON TASK ACCOMPLISHMENT and FORMULATING TASK STAGES. Teachers also employed conversation structuring questions (Meskill & Anthony, 2018) to saturate and model new vocabulary, and corralling by asking questions and introducing new topics. Instructional conversations involve authentic socio-emotional and humorous interactions between the teacher and learners (Meskill & Anthony, 2015, 2018) and, thus, potentially increase social presence (Satar, 2015, 2020) projected by the teacher.

Teachers used similar mode and modal configurations for LLAs in both task types. Similar configurations included, for example, the use of textchat to share task resources prior to the lesson, modal aggregates comprising spoken language, lateral posture in the proxemics mode and hand gesture shifts within the HLA SUGGESTING WAYS INTO TASK, and increasing modal density (through complexity) for parts of the instructions that carry meanings of significance comprising spoken language, print, hand and facial gestures, head movement, and posture modes. Teachers' webcam framing choices (Guichon & Wigham, 2016) organised the multimodal pedagogical interaction and provided a certain number of affordances for the mode and modal configurations adopted by the teachers. These were similar for each teacher across the lessons despite differences in task type.

However, the teachers' LLAs had higher multimodal density in the convergent task compared to the divergent tasks. Norris (2004, 2020) considers a HLA to be multimodally dense when either (a) a mode plays a central role (modal intensity), or (b) an action can only be performed by multiple modes

Contributions, pedagogical reflections, and future perspectives 151

being inextricably linked (modal complexity). Our analysis suggests that modal density can also be achieved through brisk modal shifts that foreground the LLA in the teacher's attention/awareness. Multimodal density appears important in online synchronous language teaching as it demonstrates the teacher's engagement and may help to direct learners' attentional resources in effective ways to be cognitively engaged in the task – a condition that is necessary for task completion (Philp & Duchesene, 2016).

In the following sections, we present our revised heuristic framework of higher-level actions in task instructions-as-process, offer pedagogical suggestions, and discuss limitations and future research directions before concluding with some final thoughts.

6.5 A heuristic framework of higher-level actions in task instructions-as-process

One contribution of this volume is a revised heuristic framework of instruction-giving HLAs initially presented in Satar and Wigham (2020). We made some minor amendments to the original framework as we explored the HLAs for Lesson 3 (see Section 5.5 and Figure 6.1)).[1]

Given that in the divergent task, learners had access to the same resource as opposed to in the convergent task where they had different resources and the teachers needed to confirm that they had accessed the resource that was designated for them, we edited the HLA CONFIRMING ACCESS TO THE RESOURCE to CONFIRMING ACCESS TO THE (CORRECT) RESOURCE to encompass both ensuring the learners have access to a shared resource (divergent task) and ensuring learners have access to a resource that differs for each learner (convergent task).

We deleted the HLA IDENTIFYING TASK RATIONALE as in our dataset we only found one instance of this HLA in a single teacher's convergent task. Given the analysis proposed in Chapter 5, we now interpret this as an *instructional conversation*. However, this HLA would apply should, for example, a teacher explain the lesson objectives, for example, "we are going to do a role play to learn about how to ask for directions".

In Chapter 5, we identified that the teachers during the *HLA FOCUSING ON STUDY SKILLS* introduced, within the secondary level of HLAs, the task topic for the divergent task (vegetarianism) and, therefore, modified the HLA IDENTIFYING TASK TYPE to IDENTIFYING TASK TYPE/TOPIC. A final amendment was to the secondary level HLA action READING THE RESOURCE within MANAGING RESOURCES, which we modified to READING THE CONTENT OF THE RESOURCE in order to harmonise the naming with one of the new HLA actions introduced.

Indeed, in Wigham and Satar (2021), we argued that the HLA MANAGING RESOURCES was particularly distinct in synchronous online language teaching. This study further confirmed that postulate: our analysis of a divergent opinion-exchange task in which participants used an online whiteboard demonstrated three further HLAs under MANAGING RESOURCES as we observed how

Figure 6.1 A heuristic framework of higher-level actions in task instructions-as-process

teachers introduced and guided learners in using a new digital tool (online whiteboard): IDENTIFYING THE RESOURCE TYPE, EDITING THE CONTENT OF THE RESOURCE and FACILITATING THE USE OF THE RESOURCE.

We present the framework of task instructions-as-process as a guide for teachers in thinking explicitly about instruction preparation. Any single task instruction could contain all – or more likely, some – of these possible actions

Contributions, pedagogical reflections, and future perspectives   153

and, as our analysis of task variance in Chapter 5 underlined (see Section 5.3), teachers' choices will relate to task type.

6.6 Pedagogical reflections for language teachers

The Multimodal (Inter)action Analysis of instruction giving presented in three analysis chapters allow us to offer the following pedagogical reflections. Yet, as we underlined in our previous work (Satar & Wigham, 2020; Wigham & Satar, 2021), we must caution against overly simplistic pedagogical suggestions or best practices for instruction giving in synchronous online language teaching given little research on the relationship between different practices and outcomes in such environments (see Chapter 1). Indeed, for such research, the benchmark for success must be clearly defined based on cognitive, social, affective or task-based outcomes (Satar & Wigham, 2020). We, thus, avoid premature best practice recommendations and offer the following recommendations as a set of *reflections* for planning task instructions-as-workplan and engaging in task instructions-as-process. To enhance readability, in this section, we employ the second-person pronoun *you* to directly address practitioners.

6.6.1 *Managing electronic resources*

Related to the HLA of MANAGING RESOURCES, in Wigham and Satar (2021), we suggested that with new learners it appears useful to set up ways of how electronic resources in the print mode (resource sheets, textchat, URL) will be used at the onset of lessons, including sharing information about how they will be delivered and where they can be found. We examined the practice of sharing electronic resources during the lesson, using file-sharing or sending URLs via textchat in the print mode, and suggested using clear and simple file names for the electronic documents, compiling the materials in a single online folder or repository, and preparing a list of the resources' URLs ready to be shared. Should different learners need to access different information, as is the case in our convergent task, we further recommend including learners' names in file names.

In Chapter 4, when file-sharing or sending URLs via textchat, we highlighted the need to confirm learners' access to both the textchat and, once electronic resources are sent, to the resources themselves. This will help avoid misunderstanding of instructions and consequently unsuccessful task launches.

Chapters 4 and 5, however, highlighted one teacher's strategy of sending to learners the lesson plan and resources (URLs and/or resource sheets) prior to the lesson rather than during the lesson itself. This practice decreased the number of HLAs required prior to the learners' task initiation (see Table 5.3 and Section 5.4.1). When introducing a new resource type (e.g. the online whiteboard as discussed in section 5.6), we suggested ensuring access to it

154 *Contributions, pedagogical reflections, and future perspectives*

before the lesson and knowing how to manipulate its functions learners will be asked to use. When using an online whiteboard, it appears useful to prepare the contents ahead of the lesson, and organise them visually to create different areas for different task steps. This can be achieved by using line dividers and titles for each step to identify areas (Extract 5.7) or copying and pasting a list of different task steps (Extract 5.3).

When planning instructions, it is crucial to reflect on how to describe to learners the use of a new resource. Our analysis suggests this can include, in the spoken language mode, explicitly introducing a new resource type (e.g. Section 5.6, HLA *IDENTIFYING THE RESOURCE TYPE*) by identifying its type/name and making clear references, including to different areas in the visual presentation of the resource (Extract 5.7) instead of employing deictic pronouns (this/that). Screen sharing could help you to avoid accessing documents in your personal space (Extract 4.2) and forgetting learners do not have access to the latter. Screen sharing would also allow you to focus on specific elements within an electronic resource and ensure that highlighting and scrolling object handling actions are shared with the learners.

We also suggest considering strategies that can be introduced should learners have trouble manipulating the resource. In Chapter 5, these included moving to another resource type with which learners were more familiar (Craig) and the teacher writing down the learners' contributions when they were unable to or unsure how to do so themselves (Sarah, Karen).

Finally, relating to resources, it would appear preferable to use a large screen or two monitors that will allow you to access to your own resources and shift gaze between different windows more easily (cf. Extract 4.4). Indeed, we recommend everyone in the lesson explain their screen layout (site of engagement) to better understand gaze direction and attention/awareness. Alternatively, use software developed specifically for learning and teaching (e.g. Big Blue Button) which can enable you to force a specific layout for the learners, instead of general computer-mediated communication software (e.g. Skype or Zoom). Furthermore, when moving between windows, articulate in the spoken language mode your actions to help keep the HLA in your attention/awareness but also align the learners' attention/awareness with the same HLA.

6.6.2 Managing semiotic resources

The multimodal orchestration of instructions that we have evidenced throughout this study highlights the need to plan not only for instruction-delivery in the spoken language mode but also the importance of planning concurrent modes. To help your instructions create a pedagogical focus, we recommend using a head and torso shot in your webcam framing to allow your learners access to your gestures. Use your gestures effectively in this centralised position and sustain them long enough to be perceived by the learners. Speak

Contributions, pedagogical reflections, and future perspectives   155

slowly, articulate clearly and emphasise key words in your instructions whilst employing free gaze with a relaxed posture. You can present instructions bimodally using the print mode simultaneously with the spoken language mode and monitor learners' response by looking at their moving images on the screen. You can signal the end of instruction giving by moving back and shifting your gaze (Extract 3.6).

In planning complex instructions, it may be useful to consider where you need multimodal intensity and where you need multimodal complexity. For example, if the print mode in a resource sheet is of particular importance, it could be useful to turn off your webcam and focus explicitly on this mode with shared access to increase its intensity.

Should instructions be presented in the print mode (e.g. by sending a resource sheet prior to the lesson), an effective method of instruction delivery appears to be to invite one learner to read the resource sheet aloud to elicit instructions before summarising these (Section 5.4.1). LAUNCHING THE TASK can then be achieved by addressing an initial question to the learners from whom you did not elicit the instructions (Extract 5.4). You can then involve the other learner in the task interaction by redirecting questions. When referring to learners, use their names rather than the pronoun *you*.

6.6.3   Instructions-as-workplan in light of our findings

Regarding different task types, for information-exchange tasks, consider how you will organise your instructions multimodally to scaffold difficult instructions and their stages so as to include frequent gaze shifts, posture changes and gestures in order to punctuate the complex, and often longer, instructions these tasks require (Chapters 3 and 4). For opinion-exchange task, introduce instructions in a stepwise fashion by orchestrating and structuring the interaction through questions (Sections 5.3 and 5.4). Should you find instructions for a specific task to be challenging, do not give up and recycle the same task: our study demonstrates that instructions will improve with each iteration (Chapter 3).

Pedagogical reflections for instruction giving in synchronous online language lessons

Managing electronic resources

Prior to the lesson:

- Set up ways of how electronic resources in the print mode (resource sheets, text chat, URLs, online collaborative writing spaces) will be used at the onset of the lesson.
- Create online versions of the materials prior to the lesson.

- Use clear and simple file names for the electronic documents. For those to be sent to different learners, include learner names to the file name to indicate which learner should access which resource.
- Compile the materials in a single online folder or repository.
- Send the lesson plan and resources to learners prior to the lesson.
- Send the URL links to any online resources prior to the lesson or alternatively prepare a list of the URLs of the materials ready to be shared with the learners during the lesson.
- Ensure that you have accessed any new resource types before the lesson and know how to manipulate the functions you will be asking the learners to use. Prepare any contents ahead of the lesson and consider how you will describe how to use it to the learners.
- Organise the layout of online resources to visually create different areas for learners to complete different task steps. This can be achieved by using line dividers and titles for each step to identify areas or copying and pasting a list of different task steps.

During the lesson:

- Describe your screen layout to your learners so that they know what you are looking at and articulate your on-screen actions which are not visible to them. Ideally, also ask the learners to do the same so that all social actors have a better understanding of the interactional space and each other's site of engagement.
- Contextualise the task before interacting with task resources if they have not been sent prior to the lesson.
- Identify explicitly a new resource type when it is introduced.
- Check learners' access to the materials before giving the instructions.
- Confirm learner(s)' access to textchat in the print mode. When using this mode to send electronic resources, confirm their access to the resource(s) even if there is one learner.
- Engage the learners in the process of sending the resource by articulating your actions so that they are aware of what is foregrounded in your attention/awareness.
- Guide the learners in the use of the electronic resources and ask them to share their screens where relevant (e.g. in small groups or one-to-one lessons).
- Use clear references to the resources instead of deictic pronouns (this/that).
- Should learners find the use of the print mode in a new online resource challenging or if they are unable to or unsure how to do so themselves, write down learner contributions yourself.

Multimodal orchestration

- Plan your instructions not only in the spoken language mode but also in other concurrent modes, particularly gestures.
- Organise your screen layout: preferably use a large screen or two monitors that will allow you to access to your own resources without losing access to the videoconference window.
- Speak slowly, articulate clearly, and emphasise key words in your instructions.
- Adopt a head and torso shot in your webcam framing to allow your learners access to your gestures.
- Use your gestures effectively with centred position and sustain them long enough to be perceived by the learners. This will help your instructions create a pedagogical focus.
- Use the print mode and present your key instructions bimodally.
- Employ a free gaze with relaxed posture. Do not look directly in the webcam (unless for a specific purpose); look at the screen to monitor learner response.
- Consider, for complex instructions, where you need modal intensity and where you need modal complexity.
- Employ screen sharing if you want to focus on specific elements within an electronic resource so that highlighting and scrolling object handling actions can be shared with learners.

Eliciting instructions

- Invite one learner to read the resource sheet to elicit instructions then summarise these, emphasising key words, before learners begin the task.

Referring to learners

- Remember that learners may not have the same screen layout as yourself when referring to the learners with your hand gestures.
- Use vocatives instead of the pronoun *you*.

Launching the task

- Launch the task with an initial question addressed to the learners from whom you did not elicit the instructions.
- Signal to the learners that your turn is over with your body by moving back and shifting your gaze.
- Involve the second learner in the interaction by redirecting questions.

Instructions related to specific task types

- For opinion-exchange task, introduce instructions in a stepwise fashion by orchestrating and structuring the interaction through questions.
- For information-exchange tasks, consider how you will organise your instructions multimodally to include frequent gaze shifts, posture changes and gestures in order to punctuate the complex, and often longer, instructions these tasks require.
- Do not give up and recycle the same task should you find instructions for a specific task to be challenging: your instructions will improve with each iteration.
- Reflect on how you use your gestures, facial expressions, body movement, and textchat to scaffold difficult instructions.

6.7 Limitations and future research

Instruction giving in synchronous online language teaching is an area ripe for future research. In this section, we discuss some of the limitations of our work and the research perspectives that emerged.

When comparing task type, our analysis focused specifically on comparing the articulations and adaptions in the specific examples of convergent (information-gap) and divergent tasks (opinion-exchange) presented in Chapter 2. Further research should explore different convergent task types, for example, a reasoning gap activity in which learners must derive new information and use inference, deduction, practical reasoning, and logic to decide what information to convey and the resolution to make (Prabhu, 1987). Problem-solving activities in which learners must recognise the problem, analyse it, and suggest solutions together could also shed light on other HLA and LLA configurations involved in instruction giving for specific task types.

The convergent task examined in our study required a higher number of instruction-giving HLAs before the learners embarked on task accomplishment and higher multimodal density in teachers' LLAs. Teacher interviews corroborated our observations. Further research could explore modal density differences between two tasks which are of the same task type but which have different levels of complexity. Indeed, unlike the convergent task used here, some convergent tasks may not necessarily require complex instructions. This would help overcome one of the limitations of this study, that is, the small data set. Indeed, data from a larger set or an uncontrolled corpus could help generalise the results.

A natural progression of our work would be to conduct a similar study with lower-level proficiency learners to explore whether modal configuration of teachers' HLAs would differ in relation to learners' language proficiency. This will enable identification of multimodal density (intensity and complexity) indicating whether and how teachers foreground instructions in their and the learners' attention/awareness continuum, thus scaffolding learner engagement.

Additionally, other data collection methods, including eye-tracking could be useful to increase our understanding of gaze during instruction-giving. MIA is concerned with (inter)actional attention, that is, "overt multimodal display of attention by one interlocutor and the produced multimodal reaction by another interlocutor" (Norris, 2020, p. 13). Previous eye-tracking research in synchronous online teaching demonstrated how gaze direction can signal teachers' attention to different aspects of the on-screen teacher-learner interactions (Shi et al., 2017). An exploration of teachers' and learners' gaze direction during task instructions can thus inform and complement MIA by offering evidence as to which modes social actors' gaze is directed towards. This can potentially demonstrate which HLAs configured with those modes are foregrounded within their attention/awareness continuum.

Concerning the number of learner participants in our study, we initially organised lessons between two learners and one teacher to allow for comparisons with our previous research that focused on trainee-teachers (Satar & Wigham, 2017). We also collected and analysed data from one one-to-one teaching to analyse variance in learner numbers. While our findings did not reveal any major differences, participating teachers described one-to-one tutoring as their more common teaching set-up. Relatedly, future research can investigate task instructions in other one-to-one teaching contexts. Moreover, the Covid-19 pandemic increased reliance on large group synchronous language lessons. In the future, online lessons with larger groups may become more widespread, and a relevant context for future research to examine both task instructions-as-workplan and -as-process.

Another area of future research related to instruction-giving HLAs is task facilitation, that is, teachers' instructions to scaffold task completion once the learners are engaged in the task. Our analyses indicated that this was common especially for divergent tasks where task instructions resembled *instructional conversations* (Meskill & Anthony, 2007, 2015, 2018). This line of research would be particularly useful to inform initial teacher training and continued professional development as regards task facilitation strategies.

6.8 Final thoughts

The main theme of this book was experienced online language teachers' instruction-giving practices in multimodal synchronous online teaching (videoconferencing) within a task-based language teaching pedagogy. We employed Multimodal (Inter)action Analysis and drew on Grounded Theory in our analysis, which culminated in a heuristic framework of task instructions-as-process in synchronous online teaching. Specifically, we investigated variation in experienced teachers' instructions (1) when they repeat the same task with a different pair of learners, (2) when they repeat the same task with a different number of learners, and (3) when they give instructions for a different task type. For each variation, we unpacked the similarities and differences in higher-level, lower-level, and frozen actions and in the multimodal configuration and density (complexity and intensity) of the teachers' instructions. We underscored the relevance and challenges in MANAGING RESOURCES and proposed the notion of *modal density (mis)alignment* to be used alongside the notion of *semiotic (mis)alignment* to study the relative position of HLAs in social actors' attention/awareness continuum, thereby leading to joint or different focal points of attention on (inter)actions.

Our work has implications beyond the specific context of this research. First, our findings indicated that MANAGING RESOURCES presented multiple challenges to the teachers who achieved this HLA in high modal density through complexity or intensity. Thus, teachers of other subject areas can benefit from our depiction of the macro- and micro-processes in giving task instructions. Second, our MIA approach informed by Grounded Theory and the ways in which we adapted the tools to the study of online interaction can be implemented for the investigation of other aspect of online teaching, such as computer-supported collaborative writing and feedback provision. Finally, we have shown that MIA is a powerful tool to examine the multimodal construction of online mediated actions within scales of higher- and lower-level actions that comprise social practices. Thus, it can be utilised for the analysis of computer-mediated communication and social interaction in settings beyond learning and teaching.

Online language teaching is a flourishing area of research, which has gained traction particularly since the Covid-19 pandemic. In the post-pandemic world, with increased attention and upskilling of teachers, online learning and teaching has the potential to continue to cater for wider access to education for a wide range of individuals, including people with accessibility needs, adult learners in full-time work, learners with various learning styles, and those who live in remote areas. We hope our work can inspire other researchers in Applied Linguistics who need a rigorous tool for robust, in-depth investigation of online (computer-mediated) social interaction.

Note

1 A full-size version of Figure 6.1 and all figures, tables, and extracts in this book are available at https://doi.org/10.25405/data.ncl.20315142.

References

Aranha, S. & Wigham, C.R. (2020). Virtual exchanges as complex research environments: facing the data management challenge. A case study of Teletandem Brasil. *Journal of Virtual Exchange, 3.* pp. 13-38.

Badem-Korkmaz, F., & Balaman, U. (2020). Third position repair for resolving troubles in understanding teacher instructions. *Linguistics and Education, 60,* 100859.

Balaman, U., & Sert, O. (2017). Development of L2 interactional resources for online collaborative task accomplishment. *Computer Assisted Language Learning, 30*(7), 601–630.

Cappellini, M., & Azaoui, B. (2017). Sequences of normative evaluation in two telecollaboration projects: A comparative study of multimodal feedback through desktop videoconference. *Language Learning in Higher Education, 7*(1), 55–80.

Cappellini, M., & Combe, C. (2017). Analyser des compétences techno-sémio-pédagogiques d'apprentis tuteurs dans différents environnements numériques: résultats d'une étude exploratoire. *ALSIC, 20*(3). Retrieved from http://journals.openedition.org/alsic/3186

Cappellini, M., & Hsu, Y. (2022). Multimodality in webconference-based language tutoring: An ecological approach integrating eye-tracking. *ReCALL, 34*(3), 1–19.

Codreanu, T., & Combe Celik, C. (2012). La médiation de l'interaction pédagogique sur une plateforme de visioconférence poste à poste. *ALSIC, 15*(3). Retrieved from https://journals.openedition.org/alsic/2572

Develotte, C., Guichon, N., & Vincent, C. (2010). The use of the webcam for teaching a foreign language in a desktop videoconferencing environment. *ReCALL, 23*(3), 293–312.

Guichon, N. (2009). Training future language teachers to develop online tutors' competence through reflective analysis. *ReCALL, 21*(2), 166–185.

Guichon, N. (2017). Sharing a multimodal corpus to study webcam-mediated language teaching. *Language Learning and Technology, 21*(1), 55–74.

Guichon, N., & Wigham, C. R. (2016). A semiotic perspective on webconferencing-supported language teaching. *ReCALL, 28*(1), 62–82.

Hampel, R., & Stickler, U. (2012). The use of videoconferencing to support multimodal interaction in an online language classroom. *ReCALL, 24* (2), 116–137.

Hampel, R. (2019). *Disruptive technologies and the language classroom: A complex systems theory approach.* Palgrave.

Heyman, R. D. (1986). Formulating topic in the classroom. *Discourse Processes, 9*(1), 37–55.

Jones, R. H. (2009). Technology and sites of display. In C. Jewitt (Ed.), *The Routledge handbook of multimodal analysis* (pp. 114–126). London: Routledge.

Kozar, O. (2016b). Text chat during video/audio conferencing lessons: Scaffolding or getting in the way? *CALICO Journal, 33*(2), 231–259.

Kunitz, S. (2021). Instruction-giving sequences in Italian as a foreign language classes: An ethnomethodological conversation analytic perspective. In S. Kunitz, O. Markee, & O. Sert (Eds.), *Classroom-based conversation analytic research: Theoretical and applied perspectives on pedagogy* (pp. 133–161). Switzerland: Springer International Publishing.

Markee, N. (2015). Giving and following pedagogical instructions in task-based instruction: An ethnomethodological perspective. In P. Seedhouse & C. Jenks (Dir.), *International perspectives on the ELT classroom* (pp. 110–128). Basingstoke: Palgrave MacMillan.

Meskill, C., & Anthony, N. (2007). Learning to orchestrate online instructional conversations: A case of faculty development for foreign languages. *Computer Assisted Language Learning, 20*(1), 5–19.

Meskill, C., & Anthony, N. (2015). *Teaching languages online* (2nd ed.). Bristol: Multilingual Matters.

Meskill, C., & Anthony, N. (2018). *Teaching children online*. Bristol: Multilingual Matters.

Norris, S. (2004). *Analyzing multimodal interaction: A methodological framework*. London: Routledge.

Norris, S. (2016). Concepts in multimodal discourse analysis with examples from video conferencing. *Yearbook of the Poznan Linguistic Meeting, 2*(1), 141–165. Retrieved from https://pressto.amu.edu.pl/index.php/yplm/article/view/21618

Norris, S. (2019). *Systematically working with multimodal data: Research methods in multimodal discourse analysis*. Hoboken, NJ: John Wiley and Sons.

Norris, S. (2020). *Multimodal theory and methodology: For the analysis of (inter)action and identity*. Abingdon: Routledge.

Norris, S., & Pirini, J. (2016). Communicating knowledge, getting attention, and negotiating disagreement via video conferencing technology: A multimodal analysis. *Journal of Organizational Knowledge Communication, 3*(1), 23–48.

Prabhu, N. S. (1987). *Second language pedagogy*. Oxford: Oxford University Press.

Philp, J., & Duchesne, S. (2016). Exploring engagement in tasks in the language classroom. *Annual Review of Applied Linguistics, 36*, 50–72.

Satar, H. M. (2013). Multimodal language learner interactions via desktop videoconferencing within a framework of social presence: Gaze. *ReCALL, 25*(1), 122–142.

Satar, H. M. (2015). Sustaining multimodal language learner interactions online. *CALICO Journal, 32*(2), 480–507.

Satar, H. M. (2020). L1 for social presence in videoconferencing: A social semiotic account. *Language Learning & Technology, 24*(1), 129–153.

Satar, H. M., & Wigham, C. R. (2017). Multimodal instruction-giving practices in webconferencing-supported language teaching. *System, 70*, 63–80.

Satar, H. M., & Wigham, C. R. (2020). Delivering task instructions in multimodal synchronous online language teaching. *ALSIC, 23*.

Satar, H. M., & Wigham, C. R. (2020). Delivering task instructions in multimodal synchronous online language teaching. *ALSIC* (Rubrique Recherche), *23* (1).

Seedhouse, P. (2008). Learning to talk the talk: Conversation analysis as a tool for induction of trainee teachers. In S. Garton & K. Richards (Eds.), *Professional encounters in TESOL: Discourses of teachers in training* (pp. 42–57). Basingstoke: Palgrave Macmillan.

Shi, L., Stickler, U., & Lloyd, M. E. (2017). The interplay between attention, experience and skills in online language teaching. *CercleS, 7*(1), 205–238.

Sindoni, M. G. (2013). *Spoken and written discourse in online interactions*. New York: Routledge.

Somuncu, D., & Sert, O. (2019). EFL trainee teachers' orientations to students' nonunderstanding: A focus on task instructions. In H. T. Nguyen & T. Malabarba (Eds.), *Conversation analytic perspectives on English language learning, teaching, and esting in global contexts* (pp. 110–131). Bristol: Multilingual Matters.

St. John, O., & Cromdal, J. (2016). Crafting instructions collaboratively: Student questions and dual addressivity in classroom task instructions. *Discourse Processes, 53* (4), 252–279.

Stickler, U. & Hampel, R. (2019) Qualitative research in online language learning: What can it do? International Journal of Computer-Assisted Language Learning and Teaching, 9(3): 14–28.

Thornbury, S. (2000). A dogma for EFL. *IATEFL Issues, 153*, 2. Retrieved from www.scottthornbury.com/articles.html

Tomlinson, B., & Masuhara, H. (2017). *The complete guide to the theory and practice of materials development for language learning.* Oxford: Wiley-Blackwell.

Vygotsky, L. S. (1978). *Mind in society: The development of higher psychological processes.* Cambridge, MA: Harvard University Press.

Wigham, C. R., & Chanier, T. (2013). A study of verbal and non-verbal communication in Second Life – The ARCHI21 experience. *ReCALL, 25*(1), 63–84.

Wigham, C. R., & Satar, M. (2021). Multimodal (inter)action analysis of task instructions in language teaching via videoconferencing: A case study. *ReCALL, 33*(3), 195–213.

Appendices

Appendix 1
Information-gap task

Student A

Anne Watson, your department secretary, is changing jobs. You and your colleagues have decided to join together to buy her a leaving gift. You wish to buy Anne a spa day pass for two people. Talk to one of your colleagues to compare the information you found about the Marriott spa deals on the Marriott website with the information your colleague found on an experience gifts website.

With your colleague, write a short email to your other colleagues. Explain which website you are going to use to buy the present and why. Use this Google Doc page: <URL>

(Image of a Spa and Health Club Day Pass for Two for £24.00)

What's included?

- A gift pack with a personalised voucher and message card.
- Full use of the leisure facilities for two people.
- A complimentary tea or coffee.
- The possibility to join the Mariott spa Leisure Club and pay no membership-joining fee.

On arrival at the leisure club you are both free to make full use of the extensive facilities on offer for one day. Facilities include gym, pool, sauna, steam room and jacuzzi. You will also receive complimentary use of towels.
Access to our restaurant and a 5% discount on the lunchtime special.
NB. The minimum age is 18 and the voucher cannot be used at weekends.

Student B

Anne Watson, your department secretary, is changing jobs. You and your colleagues have decided to join together to buy her a leaving gift. You wish to buy Anne a day pass for two people. Talk to one of your colleagues to compare the information you found about the Marriott spa deals on an experience gifts website with the information your colleague found directly on the Marriott spa's website.

With your colleague, write a short email to your other colleagues. Explain which website you are going to use to buy the present and why. Use this Google Doc page: <URL>

(Image of a Spa and Health Club Day Pass for Two for £22.00)

What's included?

- A gift pack with a personalised voucher for two people and a message card.
- On arrival at the leisure club you are both free to make full use of the extensive facilities on offer for one day.
- The possibility to join the Mariott spa Leisure Club and receive 10% discount on the membership fee.
- Facilities include gym, indoor and outdoor swimming pools, sauna, steam room and a relaxation lounge. You will receive complimentary use of dressing gowns. Clients, however, must provide their own towels.

NB. Please note that lunch is not included. The minimum age is 18 and the voucher can be used any day except bank holidays.

Appendix 2
Opinion-exchange task

1. What is vegetarianism? Are you vegetarian? Or do you know anyone who is vegetarian? What foods do vegetarians eat? What foods do they NOT eat?
   (Image: https://propagandaprofessordotnet2.files.wordpress.com/2015/06/cow.jpg)
2. What is your opinion? Should humans stop eating animals and become vegetarians? Why? Why not? If you are vegetarian, or know someone who is, why did you/they become vegetarian? (PS. This is a discussion, and not an argumentation, so you do not need to defend one point of view.)
3. Go to <custom URL from https://awwapp.com > and working together summarise your discussion visually on the whiteboard.

Please arrange your screen so that you can see both your video call window and the whiteboard window.
Here are some ideas for your discussion:

Humans should stop eating animals.	*Humans should continue to eat animals.*
Animals have emotions like humans. Animal life is as valuable as human life and they should have rights, too. The meat industry is mistreating animals.	Humans need the nutrients from meat; otherwise they will suffer from malnutrition. Human life is more valuable than animal life. The meat industry can be monitored better.

Further reading: http://debatepedia.idebate.org/en/index.php/Debate:_Vegetarianism#Background_and_context

Appendix 3
Semi-structured interview guide

For the teachers:

1. Do you plan for how you will give task instructions before your lessons? How?
2. What do you do to ensure that your learners understand the task instructions correctly? Can you give an example?
3. How long do your instructions usually take?
4. Are there any types of tasks/activities that you find difficult to explain to your learners? Can you give an example?
5. Ask the teacher short stimulated reflections on certain segments of their lesson recording (e.g. You use your hands here. Can you explain what you aim to achieve with this?)

For the learners:

1. When your teacher gives instructions for a task during the lesson, do you understand what to do easily? Can you give me an example?
2. Do you remember a time when you found it difficult to understand your teacher's explanations in relation to what to do as part of the task?

Index

Note: Numbers in *italics* indicate figures and numbers in **bold** indicate tables on the corresponding page.

activating schemata 26, 31
alignment of teacher's spoken language, gesture, gaze, and posture 44–48, *45*, *47*
allocating learner roles 48
allocating the resource 57; multimodal composition of, with different number of learners 74–88, *75–76*, *79–80*, *82–83*, *85–86*
Applied Linguistics 142
attention/awareness continuum 18–20

bimodal instruction-giving in modes of spoken language and print 49–51
Breen, M. P. 6

Cappellini, M. 9
checking understanding 31; multimodal composition of similar higher-level actions prior to launching the task with different number of learners and 73
clarifying key task vocabulary 51
Codreanu, T. 9
Cohen, C. 3
Combe, C. 9
Combe Celik, C. 9
communicating key task information 26, 31–33; bimodal instruction-giving in the modes of spoken language and print and 49–51; gestures and 40–44; multimodal composition of similar higher-level actions prior to launching the task with different number of learners and 69–74, *71–72*; task type and 105–116, **106–108**, **110–115**
communicative language teaching (CLT) 4
completing a language-learning task 64
confirming access to the (correct) resource 68, 74; multimodal composition of similar higher-level actions prior to launching the task with different number of learners and 73
context, research 13–17, **14**, **16**
convergent tasks, higher-level actions used in 104–116, **106–108**, **110–115**
conversation analysis (CA) 8
Covid-19 pandemic and online language teaching 1–2
critical semiotic awareness 3, 51, 146

decision-making tasks 15
defining learner roles 26, 31; modal configuration and modal density 54–57, *55–56*; task type and 105–116, **106–108**, **110–115**
describing how to accomplish the task 50
divergent tasks: higher-level actions used in 104–116, **106–108**, **110–115**; for managing resources, new higher-level actions observed in 135–137, *136*, *138–139*; micro-tasks 100–103, **101–102**

electronic resources 153–154
exchanging information 44

facial expressions 21, 33–34
Falodun, J. 14–15
focusing on study skills 26, 31, 33; bimodal instruction-giving in the modes of spoken language and print and 49–51; modal configuration and modal density 54–57, *55–56*; task type and 105–116, **106–108**, **110–115**
focusing on task accomplishment 31, 33; bimodal instruction-giving in the modes of spoken language and print and 49–51; modal configuration and modal density misalignment 90; multimodal composition of similar higher-level actions prior to launching the task with different number of learners and 69–74, *71–72*; number of learners and 67; task type and 105–116, **106–108**, **110–115**
formulating task stages 26; task type and 105–116, **106–108**, **110–115**
frozen actions (FA) 17; raising children as 18; sites of engagement of 18

gaze 3, 18, 20–21; alignment of teacher's spoken language, gesture, posture, and 44–48, *45*, *47*; site of engagement and semiotic misalignment 51–54, *53*
gestures 18, 20, 33–34; alignment of teacher's spoken language, gaze, posture, and 44–48, *45*, *47*; culturally-specific 20; same or same type of 40–44, *41*, *43*; sustained and central hand, following learners' lack of understanding 34–40, *35–36*, *38*
giving instructions for a convergent task 64
Greiffenhagen, C. 5
Grounded Theory analysis 6, 143; methodological framework 17; research context 13–17, **14**, **16**
Guichon, N. 3, 21

Ha, C. B. 5–6
Hampel, R. 3

head movement 18, 20, 21
Hellermann, J. 8
higher-level actions (HLAs) 6, 17; activating schemata 26, 31; allocating the resource 57, 77; announcing the next task stage 74; baking a cake 19; bimodal instruction-giving in the modes of spoken language and print 49–51; checking understanding 31, 73; clarifying key task vocabulary 51; communicating key task information 26, 31–33, 40–44, 69; completing a language-learning task 64; confirming access to the (correct) resource 68, 73, 74; in convergent and divergent tasks 104–116, **106–108**, **110–115**; defining learner roles 26, 31, 54–57, *55–56*; describing how to accomplish the task 50; engaging in conversation 18; exchanging information 44; focusing on study skills 26, 31, 33, 54–57, *55–56*, 105–116, **106–108**, **110–115**; focusing on task accomplishment 31, 33, 67, 69, 90, 105–116, **106–108**, **110–115**; formulating task stages 26, 105–116, **106–108**, **110–115**; giving instructions for a convergent task 64; Grounded Theory analysis on 6; heuristic framework of, in task instructions-as-process 151–153, *152*; launching the task 31, 32, 37, 48–49, *49*, 64, 69, 105–116, **106–108**, **110–115**; limitations and future research 158–159; managing resources 26, 31, 33, 54–57, *55–56*, 67–68, 74–88, *75–76*, *79–80*, *82–83*, *85–86*, 88–95, *89*, *91*, *93–94*, *96–97*, 105–116, **106–108**, **110–115**, 135–137, *136*, *138–139*; modal density in 19–20; Multimodal (Inter)action Analysis (MIA) of 6–8, 20–22; multimodal composition of similar higher-level actions prior to launching the task with different number of

Index 173

learners 69–74, *71–72*; multimodal configuration in different task types 116–135, **117–119**, *120–121*, *124*, *128–131*, *133–134*; number of learners and 64–68, **65–66**; observed in divergent task for managing resources 135–137, *136*, *138–139*; reading the content of the resource 90; sending the resource 57, 74–77, 90; sites of engagement of 18, 22; stating task outcome 67, 73, 105–116, **106–108**, **110–115**; suggesting ways into task 26, 31, 32, 34, 37, 44, 46, 105–116, **106–108**, **110–115**; used in convergent and divergent tasks 104–116, **106–108**, **110–115**; vacationing together 18; walking 18; work-to-come 26; writing collaboratively 44

high modal intensity 19

information gap tasks 15, 167–168
instruction-giving 141–142; contributions to methodology and knowledge 142–145; higher level actions (*see* higher-level actions (HLAs)); limitation and future research on 158–159; lower-level actions (*see* lower-level actions (LLAs)); number of learners and (*see* number of learners); previous studies on 6–8; procedural 5–6; research gap on 8–9; in task-based language teaching 4–6; task repetition and (*see* task repetition); task type and (*see* task type); written versus spoken 5; *see also* online language teaching
instructions-as-process 20; heuristic framework of higher-level actions in task 151–153, *152*; higher-level actions number of learners and 64–68, **65–66**; higher-level actions task repetition and 26–32, **27–30**; lower-level actions number of learners and 68–88, *71–72*, *75–76*, *79–80*, *82–83*,

85–86; lower-level actions task repetition and 32–54, *35–36*, *38*, *41*, *43*, *45*, *47*, *49*, *53*
instructions-as-workplan 155–158
iTalki 13

jigsaw tasks 15

Kanagy, R. 14–15
Kentnor, H. 1
Kozar, O. 3–4
Kunitz, S. 145, 148

launching the task 31, 32, 37; multimodal composition of similar higher-level actions prior to launching the task with different number of learners and 69–74, *71–72*; number of learners and 64; signalling removal from interaction in proxemics/posture mode and 48–49, *49*; task type and 105–116, **106–108**, **110–115** layout mode 18, 20, 21; alignment of teacher's spoken language, gesture, gaze, and posture with 44–48, *45*, *47*; site of engagement and semiotic misalignment 51–54, *53*
Lindwall, O. 5
Lloyd, M. E. 3
lower-level actions (LLAs) 7, 17; alignment of teacher's spoken language, gesture, gaze, and posture 44–48, *45*, *47*; bimodal instruction-giving in the modes of spoken language and print 49–51; modal configuration and modal density 18–19, 54–57, *55–56*; Multimodal (Inter)action Analysis (MIA) of 20–22; multimodal configuration in different task types 116–135, **117–119**, *120–121*, *124*, *128–131*, *133–134*; number of learners and 68–88, *71–72*, *75–76*, *79–80*, *82–83*, *85–86*; same gestures or same type of gestures in both iterations 40–44, *41*, *43*; signalling removal from interaction in proxemics/posture mode 48–49, *49*; site of engagement and

semiotic misalignment 51–54, 53; sites of engagement of 18; sustained and central hand gestures following learners' lack of understanding 34–40, 35–36, 38; in task instructions-as-process 32–54, 35–36, 38, 41, 43, 45, 47, 49, 53
low modal intensity 19
Lymer, G. 5

Makboon, B. 18
managing resources 26, 31, 33; bimodal instruction-giving in the modes of spoken language and print and 49–51; electronic resources 153–154; modal configuration and modal density 54–57, 55–56; modal configuration and modal density misalignment 88–95, 89, 91, 93–94, 96–97; multimodal composition of, with different number of learners 74–88, 75–76, 79–80, 82–83, 85–86; new higher-level actions observed in divergent task for 135–137, 136, 138–139; number of learners and 67–68; semiotic misalignment and modal density misalignment 57–58; semiotic resources 154–155; task type and 105–116, 106–108, 110–115
Markee, N. 5, 6, 8, 9
Masuhara, H. 5
McNeill, D. 20
mediated actions and communication modes 18
medium modal intensity 19
methods: context 13–17, 14, 16; data collection procedures 15–17, 16; methodological framework 17–22; participants 13–14, 14; pedagogical organisation 14–15
micro-tasks 100–103, 101–102
modal complexity 19
modal configuration 18–20, 54–57, 55–56; managing resources 88–95, 89, 91, 93–94, 96–97
modal density 19–20, 54–57, 55–56
modal density misalignment 25; managing resources 88–95, 89, 91, 93–94, 96–97; semiotic misalignment and 57–58

Multimodal (Inter)action Analysis (MIA) 6–8, 142–144, 159–160; mediated actions and communication modes in 18; methodological framework 17–22; modal configuration, modal density, and attention/awareness continuum in 18–20; operationalising 20–22; research context 13–17, 14, 16; research gaps and 8–9; sites of engagement 18
multimodal composition: of managing resources with different number of learners 74–88, 75–76, 79–80, 82–83, 85–86; of similar higher-level actions prior to launching the task with different number of learners 69–74, 71–72
music 18

Norris, S. 18, 21, 142–144
number of learners 61–98, 147–149; higher-level actions in task instructions-as-process and 64–68, 65–66; lower-level actions in task instructions-as-process and 68–88, 71–72, 75–76, 79–80, 82–83, 85–86; modal configuration and modal density misalignment 88–95, 89, 91, 93–94, 96–97; multimodal composition of similar higher-level actions prior to launching the task with different 69–74, 71–72; site of engagement and 62–64, 63

online language teaching 141–142; Covid-19 pandemic and 1–2; growth of 1–2; high levels of attrition in 2; importance of instructions in task-based language teaching 4–6; as semio-pedagogical activity 1–4; use of text-chat in 3–4; see also instruction-giving
opinion exchange tasks 15, 169

Pekarek Doehler, S. 8
Pica, T. 14–15
posture 18, 20; alignment of teacher's spoken language, gesture, gaze,

and 44–48, *45*, *47*; signalling
  removal from interaction in
  proxemics/posture mode
  48–49, *49*
print mode 18, 20, 21; bimodal
  instruction-giving in modes of
  spoken language and 49–51
problem-solving tasks 15
procedural instructions 5–6, 141–142
proxemics 18, 20; signalling removal
  from interaction in proxemics/
  posture mode 48–49, *49*

reading the content of the resource 90

Satar, H. M. 3, 6, 7, 9, 20, 146, 147, 151;
  on five types of gaze 21; on
  managing electronic resources
  153; on spoken language 20
Seedhouse, P. 5
semio-pedagogical activity, online
  language teaching as 1–4
semiotic density misalignment 74
semiotic lag 2
semiotic misalignment 2, 25; modal
  density misalignment and
  57–58; multimodal composition
  of similar higher-level actions
  prior to launching the task with
  different number of learners
  and 73; site of engagement and
  51–54, *53*
semiotic resources, managing 154–155
semi-structured interview guide 170
sending the resource 57; modal
  configuration and modal density
  misalignment 90; multimodal
  composition of, with different
  number of learners 74–88,
  75–76, *79–80*, *82–83*, *85–86*;
  multimodal composition of
  similar higher-level actions
  prior to launching the task with
  different 74–88, *75–76*, *79–80*,
  82–83, *85–86*
Sert, O. 9
Shi, L. 3
sites of engagement 18, 22; number of
  learners and 62–64, *63*; semiotic
  misalignment and 51–54, *53*
Somuncu, D. 9
SpeakPlus 13
spoken language 18, 20, 21–22, 33–34;
  alignment of teacher's gesture,
  gaze, posture, and 44–48, *45*,
  47; bimodal instruction-giving
  in modes of print and 49–51
stating task outcome 67, 73; task
  type and 105–116, **106–108**,
  110–115
Stickler, U. 3
suggesting ways into task 26, 31, 32;
  alignment of teacher's spoken
  language, gesture, gaze, and
  posture and 44, 46; gestures
  and 34, 37; modal configuration
  and modal density misalignment
  88; multimodal composition
  of similar higher-level actions
  prior to launching the task with
  different number of learners
  and 70; task type and 105–116,
  106–108, **110–115**

task-as-workplan versus task-as-process
  100–103, **101–102**
task-based language teaching (TBLT)
  4–6; higher-level actions in
  26–32, **27–30**; task types in
  14–15
task repetition 25–60, 141–142,
  145–147; higher-level actions
  in task instructions-as-process
  26–32, **27–30**; lower-level
  actions in task instructions-
  as-process 32–54, *35–36*,
  38, *41*, *43*, *45*, *47*, *49*, *53*;
  modal configuration and
  modal density 54–57, *55–56*;
  semiotic misalignment and
  modal density misalignment
  57–58
task type 99–140, 149–151;
  comparison of higher-level actions
  used in convergent and divergent
  tasks 104–116, **106–108**,
  110–115; divergent task micro-
  tasks 100–103, **101–102**;
  instructions-as-workplan
  and 155–158; multimodal
  configuration of higher-level
  actions and lower-level
  actions in different 116–135,
  117–119, *120–121*, *124*,
  128–131, *133–134*; teacher
  perspectives on impact of, on
  instruction-giving behaviour
  103–104

text-chat 3–4
Tomlinson, B. 5

visual framing 3

Wanphet, P. 5–6
webcam framing 51–54, *53*

Wigham, C. R. 3, 6, 7, 9, 146, 147, 151; on managing electronic resources 153; on spoken language 20
work-to-come 26
writing collaboratively 44
written versus spoken instructions 5

For Product Safety Concerns and Information please contact our EU
representative GPSR@taylorandfrancis.com
Taylor & Francis Verlag GmbH, Kaufingerstraße 24, 80331 München, Germany

www.ingramcontent.com/pod-product-compliance
Lightning Source LLC
Chambersburg PA
CBHW051743230426
43670CB00012B/2142